The Bhagavad Gita

in the Light of Kriya Yoga

Book Three

PARAMAHAMSA HARIHARANANDA

Based on Babaji, Lahiri Mahasaya and Shriyukteshwarji's original and authentic teachings of Kriya Yoga

Edited by
Paramahamsa Prajñanananda

THAT IS THE PATH WHICH IS DIRECTED BY THE REALIZED

क्षणमिह सज्जन सङ्गतिरेका भवति भवार्णव तरणे नौका

Acknowledgments

We would like to offer our deepest love and thanks for the many volunteers who have participated in the production of this book. Their love and service to God and gurus has been exemplary.

Typing and correcting: Jan Teegardin, Deja Mitchell, Ron MacLennan
Editing: Peter Bumpus and Little Ma
Cover design: Chip Weston
Original art: Karen Johnson
Introduction for Book One: Michael Winn

The cover illustration is a classical style of hand painting from Orissa, India. The scene from the Mahabharata depicts Lord Krishna addressing Arjuna regarding the entire realm of the manifestation of the human spirit. The dialogue between Arjuna and the Lord on the battle field is the Bhagavad Gita.

Edited, designed, and produced by
Kriya Yoga Institute
P.O. Box 924615
Homestead, FL 33092-4615
U.S.A.

Dedication

I dedicate this book to all true seekers

Paramahamsa Hariharananda

Library of Congress Catalog Card Number: 93-61393
ISBN 0-9639107-1-X
Printed in the United States of America

Introduction

The Bhagavad Gita's eighteen chapters each describe a special type of yoga—starting from the "Yoga of Dejection" to the "Yoga of Liberation through Renunciation." These eighteen chapters are broadly divided into three books, which are called *sataka* in Sanskrit, meaning a book of six chapters. The three books explain different spiritual practices in detail: *karma* (action), *jñana* (knowledge), and *bhakti* (devotion or supreme love). In reality, *karma, jñana,* and *bhakti* are not different paths. People may think or say that they are practicing *karma yoga* or *bhakti yoga* or *jñana yoga,* but this is not correct. Through work (*karma*), knowledge (*jñana*) is achieved, and through knowledge, one attains divine love (*bhakti*). *Karma, jñana,* and *bhakti* are correlated and causally connected. *Karma yoga* is the foundation, and *bhakti yoga* is the ultimate achievement of spiritual life.

The last six chapters (Chapters 13 to 18) explain practical spiritual life. In Chapter 13, there is a description of *prakriti* and *purusha.* Chapter 14 highlights the three qualities of nature—the *gunatraya.* According to these *gunatraya* (three qualities of nature), there are three *purushas,* described in Chapter 15. Following this, Chapter 16 elaborates the divine and demonic qualities of man. Chapter 17 discusses three types of faith in spiritual life, and in conclusion, Chapter 18 explains the yoga of liberation through the path of cosmic consciousness and complete surrender.

Kriya Yoga is the essence of all spiritual practices and the essential teaching of the Gita. It is the synthesis of the three aspects of yoga—*karma, jñana,* and *bhakti.* Kriya is the sum total of these three. It is integrated yoga. Through the practice of Kriya, one can achieve the ultimate realization in this life very easily.

In the Yoga Sutras of Patañjali (*Sadhana Pada*, Verse 1), the clearest and most precise definition of Kriya Yoga is given: *tapaḥ svādhyāya īśvara-praṇidhānāni kriyā yogaḥ*. These three aspects—*tapas* (meditation on fire), *svadhyaya* (self-study, soul culture), and *ishvara-pranidhana* (surrender and love for God)—are Kriya Yoga. These three aspects of the spiritual life are explained in detail in these three books of the Bhagavad Gita. The first book is devoted to *tapas*, which is *karma* (action).

Tapas is not penance or austerity in the ordinary sense; it is the breath by which body heat is maintained. *Tapas* means temperature. Through every breath, body temperature is preserved. The breath is inhaled and exhaled by God's living presence. This is *karma*. Through this *karma* (action), specifically *pranakarma*, divine knowledge comes, which is *jñana*. *Svadhyaya* is *sva*, self, and *adhyaya*, study—self-study. People read spiritual books, but in fact spiritual study is not this; it is the study of one's own self. To do this, one must sit silently and perceive the presence of God in the crown of the head. This practice is described is the second *sataka* of the Bhagavad Gita.

From this knowledge, the flow of divine love comes to life—this is *bhakti*, supreme love. This love brings liberation. This is *ishvara-pranidhana* as declared by the great sage Patañjali and beautifully explained by Maharshi Vyasa in the last six chapters of the Bhagavad Gita.

In these six last chapters, the Bhagavad Gita presents clear and complete knowledge of the divine self, which is achieved by avoiding all negative aspects of human life. As long as one is attracted and attached to nature, one is cannot overcome the three qualities, the three *gunas*, which create the demonic and worldly habits, and one cannot be crowned with the glory of *moksha*—liberation.

Real love is the manifestation of divine knowledge in every step of life. This will become clear with a simple example. Suppose that you see a man walking by the way and wonder who he might be. You ask someone, who tells you that he is a doctor living in this area. This is *karma* (action). Then you develop some health problems and go see this doctor. He treats you nicely, which leads you to a clear knowledge of this person. So, through *karma* comes *jñana*. When you have benefited from his treatment, you develop deep love and gratitude for him. This is *bhakti* or devotion. Action breeds knowledge, and knowledge generates *bhakti*. Divine love is essentially liberation.

There are two beautiful aphorisms on *bhakti*, divine love. The one is the Bhakti Sutra of Narada and the other is the Bhakti Sutra of Shandilya. In the Bhakti Sutra (2:3) of Narada, it says

sā tu parama prama rupā
amṛta svarupā ca:

"The love divine is the form of absolute and the supreme devotion that brings immortality." The taste of immortality and the state of supreme bliss can be achieved by perceiving and realizing the self through deep meditation. Shandilya defined devotion as *paranu raktih ishvare*, which means, "Complete and absolute attachment to the Lord is divine love."

Shri Shankara in his famous book on Vedanta—the Viveka Chudamani—discussed *bhakti* or divine love as well, saying,

mokṣakāraṇasāmagryām bhaktireva garīyasī
sva svarūpa anusandhānam bhaktiḥ iti abhidhīyate:

"Among all the things that bestow liberation, devotion alone holds the supreme place. Self-knowledge is the manifestation of devotion."

After the study and practice of the 12 chapters of the Bhagavad Gita, when one is really ready to enjoy the taste of divine love, and through this love gets complete transformation of one's nature into one's own real state—this is emancipation or liberation.

Chapter 13

Kṣetra kṣetrajña vibhāga yoga

The Yoga of the Body Field and its Knower

Introduction

To create anything tangible or material, both raw material (material cause, *upadana karana*) and know-how (instrumental cause, *nivitta karana*) are needed. In ordinary manmade creation, there is a complete distinction between the two. For example, to manufacture an ornament of gold, we need gold, tools, and a goldsmith. Each is distinct from each other. But for the creation of the cosmos, God is the cause of both. God is the material as well as the instrumental cause, and therefore, creation is nothing but the manifestation of God. Through meditation, one perceives the state of awareness of continuous unity of individual with the almighty.

Achieving the state of complete realization and perfect happiness is the birthright of every human being. But for complete realization, one must know what the body is. The body is the microcosm of the cosmos. The individual Self in each living being is also the universal cosmic form of God in the complete creation. God is the creator. Having created, the formless God permeated His entire creation. Even though creation has form, it is still the formless form of God.

Every individual considers his body to be the nearest and the dearest object in all creation. Although this body is constantly being modified from birth to death, it is always the temple of God. The body is beautiful, as long as the soul stays in its bodily residence. Without the play of the soul, without the breath of life, the body is not only useless, but is also ugly, dirty, and filthy.

Love your body as the temple of God. Keep it clean, pure, and divine. Love your body as the gateway of realization, because without the body, you cannot realize the Self. Keep the body in perfect condition, otherwise your life's journey will be delayed and incomplete. But do not be too attached to the body temple. Although you must come to the body temple to get the vision of God through prayer, do not become so busy watching the beautiful play in and around the temple that you forget the reason for being in the body temple in the first place.

Instead of being attached to the temple, be attached to the indwelling spirit, the real presiding deity. Search for God with every breath, in every action, and with knowledge, as described in the previous chapter.

This chapter beautifully explains that a life of self control is the gateway to divine love. Discriminating between the body and the soul, disciplining the mind, and having devotion to God will bring real joy to life.

As one loves one's own body, one must love the bodies of others. Love yourself, love others. When love becomes universal, life becomes divine. The entire universe is *kshetra* (field), and it is the playground of God.

This chapter discusses in detail the life of true devotion and knowledge through self discipline, self surrender, and self manifestation. It describes the play of the formless Self in the body form, the infinite in the finite body. This Self radiates divine joy and glory that is realized only by those who meditate and have right vision.

Arjuna's Inquiry

arjuna uvāca
prakṛtim puruṣam caiva
kṣetram kṣetrajñam eva ca
etad veditum icchāmi
jñānam jñeyam ca keśava

Translation

Arjuna asked:

***Prakriti* and *purusha*, the field and the knower of the field, I have the desire to know all of these, the knowledge and the knower of knowledge, O Keshava (Krishna)!**

Note: Many scholars of the Bhagavad Gita are of the view that this verse is not actually part of the Gita, but the following verses are a direct response to this question formulated by Arjuna, the seeker of truth.

Metaphorical Interpretation

In human life, there are alternating positive and negative waves; good and bad qualities and thoughts constantly arise, each in their turn. But a seeker, like Arjuna, wants to know how all these conflicting and opposite propensities can come from one source. That is why Arjuna asks, "O Keshava! What is *prakriti* (nature) and *purusha* (Self)? What is *kshetra,* the body field, and *kshetrajña,* the knower of this field? What is knowledge and the knower of knowledge? Please explain this to me in detail."

Keshava is another name of Krishna, but this word has a special significance. *Keshava* is made of *ka* plus *isha* plus *va*, meaning the creator, the preserver, and the destroyer. A thought is created, becomes manifest in the body and mind, and then is destroyed. These three processes are continuously occurring, at every moment, in every breath. And they are manifested from the top, that is, from the fontanel at the crown of the head.

Arjuna thus addressed Krishna, "O Keshava, the supreme soul in me! Please explain in detail all the aspects of creation and free me from all difficulties and doubts." Arjuna wants to know, because through the knowledge of the Self, God, the supreme almighty creator, he will merge in soul-consciousness, cosmic-consciousness, and ultimately in the wisdom that is divine love and emancipation.

Verse 1

śrībhagavān uvāca
idam śarīram kaunteya
kṣetram ity abhidhīyate
etad yo vetti tam prāhuḥ
kṣetrajña iti tadvidaḥ

Translation

The Blessed Lord said:

This body, O Kaunteya is known as the field (or land). He who knows this is called *kshetrajña* (knower of the field) by those who are wise in such things.

(Note: See I Corinthians 3:9: "Ye are God's field" or "building")

Metaphorical interpretation

"O son of the finest conception! (Kaunteya, son of Kunti)," says Shri Bhagavan, the blessed Lord, "This body is the fertile land." When a seed is sown in the earth, it produces a harvest according to the quality of the soil and the agricultural activity. Similarly, by sowing the seed of spiritual practice as taught by the realized master and through regular and sincere practice, there will be a spiritual harvest. The human body is a land that can be cultivated by removing the weeds, stones, and roots of delusion, illusion, and error, which are *maya*. By proper cultivation of the body-land, the practice of Kriya meditation—one can know the indwelling Self.

A good cultivator must take the following steps: First, collect good seeds for sowing; second, cultivate the land nicely; finally, remove all impediments to the harvest. Similarly, a spiritual seeker must first come to a realized master, learn the practice, and ultimately remove all obstacles to meditation and to leading a spiritual life. Then, surely success in spiritual life is at hand.

Verse 2

kṣetrajñam cā 'pi mām viddhi
sarvakṣetreṣu bhārata
kṣetrakṣetrajñayor jñānam
yat taj jñānam matam mama

Translation

Know also that I am the knower of the field in all fields, O Bharata (Arjuna). The knowledge of the field and of the knower of the field do I consider as true knowledge.

Metaphorical interpretation

Here Arjuna is called Bharata. *Bha* means divine illumination. *Rata* means to be engrossed and attached. Thus, Bharata is one who is always absorbed in the super-conscious state: divine illumination.

Here the blessed Lord is telling Arjuna, "O Seeker! I remain as the formless power behind every form, in the human body as well as in animals and in plants. I revealed my all-pervading form only to you (in Chapter 11). You are always engrossed in My divine illumination. You know that I am not only flesh, bone, marrow, blood, skin, and so forth; that I am not only the five gross elements (ether, air, fire, water, and earth); that I am not only the twenty-four elements that make up the human body land, but that I am the *kshetrajña*, the knower of each and every body land. I am beyond everything."

"You see the storm, causing havoc in the air outside. You also see the tumultuous breath in each living being. I am breathing all that air, creating the movement both inside and outside of the body; yet I am beyond it. I am the soul, *sa* (the indwelling Self), in every living form (body land). *Ham* is *kshetra* and *sa* is *kshetrajña*. *Ham* is the body land, the field, and *sa* is the knower of the body land. *Ham* is changing and perishable, but *sa* is changeless and imperishable. I am *kshetrajña*. *Ham* and *sa* are my two aspects. When you know my two natures *ham* and *sa*, and also that *ham* and *sa* are one, then you can know my all-pervading state." To know the distinction as well as the unity of *ham* and *sa*, *kshetra* and *kshetrajña*, body and soul, is the best approach to spiritual life.

Consider how butter is all-pervading in milk, but cannot be seen through the eyes. Once the milk is churned, the butter separates and does not mix with the milk anymore. Similarly, by the sincere practice of Kriya, one becomes aware of the indwelling Self that is pervading every thought and disposition, every moment, and every breath. This awareness is constant liberation. One realizes his false identity of body as Self and becomes free of all bondage and attachment.

Verse 3

tat kṣetram yac ca yādṛk ca
yadvikāri yataś ca yat
sa ca yo yatprabhāvaś ca
tat samāsena me śṛṇu

Translation

What this body field is, what is its nature, what are its modifications or evolutions, from where it came, what He (*kshetrajña*) is and what are His powers, you shall hear in brief from Me.

Metaphorical Interpretation

The blessed Lord is saying, "What is this *kshetra*, this body land? What are its qualities? How do *vikara* (all modifications and evolutions) affect this *kshetra* body of five gross elements and this material world? Please listen to Me, and I will tell you in short about *ham* and *sa*."

The conductor and the maintainer of the body is *kshetrañjna*—hiding in each living being. He is formless. He remains compassionately detached. He is imperishable and formless. He is free from and the director of the divine illusory force—*maya*. This body, this material world is pervaded by Him alone. Although many thoughts, desires, ambitions, dispositions, and modifications are recurring in the mind and senses, everything—good and bad—comes from Him. Without Him, there is nothing. Without breath, there is death. He breathes the breath of life from the top (the fontanel) in all living beings.

Verse 4

ṛṣibhir bahudhā gītam
chandobhir vividhaiḥ pṛthak
brahmasūtrapadaiś cai 'va
hetumadbhir viniścitaiḥ

Translation

The seers have sung it in many ways in various distinct sacred hymns, as well as in the definitive and well-reasoned Aphorisms of the Absolute (the Brahma Sutras).

Metaphorical Interpretation

How does one perceive the living presence of God in each human being as well as everywhere? This self-knowledge was revealed to the great seers (*maharishis*), the men of right vision. It was a spiritual revelation.

"O Arjuna! What I told you in the beginning (Chapters 1 to 6) was also explained by sages such as Vasishtha, Bhrigu, and others. It is beautifully presented in holy books such as Vyasa's Brahma Sutras."

Rishi means man of right vision. They are known as sages. The songs of the great seers and the writings of Vyasa (the Brahma Sutras[1] and others), are not merely words in books. These scriptures are the spiritual experiences of the great seers. They are the songs of spiritual life. *Brahma* means the all-pervading absolute, and *sutra* means thread or link. Thus, the breath is *brahma sutra,* the thread of the link to the absolute. Because of this breath, each living being can act in the divine play of God, but only humans can become aware of this connection. The all-pervading God is breathing the breath of life in every human being (See Genesis 1:27).

The spine of each human being is made of thirty-two vertebrae stacked one above the other, through which come all animal, rational, and divine propensities. But when a person cultivates the human body land with the help of the guru preceptor and through the power of God, all animal qualities can be overcome and divinity can be perceived. One can avoid darkness in life and perceive constant illumination.

People should not roam in the darkness of their life like animals. With the help of the realized masters of Kriya Yoga, they can transform their life, moving from the ordinary state to the divine state, from knowledge to consciousness, soul-consciousness, cosmic-consciousness, and even to the wisdom stage, which is *samadhi*.

The body land must be purified and cultivated with the help of the guru preceptor. Just as the professor in medical school teaches by both theory and practice and helps his students become qualified and efficient doctors, similarly the Blessed Lord says "I, the almighty father, am telling you that human beings should not remain in darkness. People in darkness cannot see anything as though they were blind; similarly, worldly people, who are unaware of the indwelling Self, are blind.

"Krishna is *sa* in every living being—the soul, the guru—and He is teaching you all. Please follow Him and achieve God-realization."

Verses 5 and 6

mahābhūtāny ahamkāro
buddhir avyaktam eva ca
indriyāṇi daśai 'kam ca

pañca cendriyagocarāḥ
icchā dveṣaḥ sukham duḥkham
samghātaś cetanā dhṛtiḥ
etat kṣetram samāsena
savikāram udāhṛtam

Translation

The gross elements: ego, and intellect; and the unmanifest: the ten senses; the one (mind), and the five objects of the senses,

ambition, aversion, pleasure and pain, the aggregate (the body), consciousness and firmness; this in brief constitutes the field with its modifications.

Metaphorical interpretation

A detailed explanation of the *kshetra* (the body land) is given in these two verses.

When the supreme being started creation, first ether (space) was created, then air, fire, water, and earth. These are the five gross elements. When they are combined in the proper way, they become the twenty-four principles of creation. So the five gross elements are the basis for the creation of living beings. Each human being has a mind, ego, intellect, memory, ten sense organs (five organs of action and five organs of perception), and five objects of the senses (sound, touch, sight, taste, and smell). All these along with the five gross elements add up to twenty-four. The aggregate of atoms, molecules, and elements make up the human body. Due to the presence of the imperishable soul, the body looks active and beautiful, full of awareness and consciousness. All these things are the *kshetra* (the body field), which undergoes constant change and modification.

In these verses Shri Krishna explains delusion in detail. How much delusion comes to each human being! The twenty-four principles are the roots of delusion. Everyone knows this, but people cling to ambition nevertheless. Ambition is the greatest enemy and is the most dangerous.

If you want liberation
Give up your ambition
Ambition will bring you complete destruction

Ambition refers to attachment and the desire to possess something; it is the result of sensory pleasure. Aversion comes from the experience of pain associated with some incident. *Sukha* and *duhkha* normally refer to pleasure and pain, but in Sanskrit the word *sukha* is composed of the prefix *su*, meaning beautiful, and *kha*, meaning ether; so *sukha* actually means the joy derived from remaining in the formless stage. *Duhkha* on the other hand means deviation from one's real state, coming from, *duh*, deviated, and *kha*, ether, *Duhkha* means to be engrossed in the lower centers, which breeds pain. People are shackled to *maya* by the chains of ambition, attachment, attraction, and temptation.

A fisherman can catch a big fish by covering the hook with bait and securing it to a thin thread. When the fish swallows the bait, it is reeled out of the water, which is its death. Similarly, God being all-pervading, all human beings are united with God. But due to attachment created by the five sense organs, they completely forget that they are a rational being, that they are God in a human form. Just like the fish, they are pulled out of the water, so they suffer. As a result their marvelous rational and divine qualities are lost.

This *kshetra* (the body field) is the cage that imprisons the soul. These twenty-four aspects of the field constitute the cause of all negative qualities—*maya*—the root of all delusion, illusion, and error, which exist in every human being. But anyone's life can be changed by remaining constantly in good company and in soul-consciousness, with the help of the divine guide—the guru preceptor. By cultivating the body land, one will get a divine harvest. The next five verses (Verses 7 to 11) list the good qualities that are necessary for God-realization.

Verses 7 to 11

amānitvam adambhitvam
ahimsā kṣāntir ārjavam

ācāryopāsanam śaucam
sthairyam ātmavinigrahaḥ

indriyārtheṣu vairāgyam
anahamkāra eva ca
anmamṛtyujarāvyādhi-
duḥkhadoṣānudarśanam

asaktir anabhiṣvangaḥ
putradāragṛhādiṣu
nityam ca samacittatvam
iṣṭāniṣṭopapattiṣu

mayi cā 'nanyayogena
bhaktir avyabhicāriṇī
viviktadeśasevitvam
aratir janasamsadi

adhyātmajñānanityatvam
tattvajñānārthadarśanam
etaj jñānam iti proktam
ajñānam yad ato 'nyathā

Translation

Absence of pride, freedom form hypocrisy, no maliciousness, patience, simplicity, love, and service of the guru preceptor, purity, steadiness, and self-restraint.

Detachment from the objects of sense, complete absence of egotism, and keeping in constant view the evils of birth, death, old age, and disease.

Non-attachment and absence of clinging to son, wife, house, and the like, constant balance of mind towards desired and undesired objects.

Unflinching devotion to Me with single-minded yoga, love of solitary living, and dislike for the company of people.

Constancy in the knowledge of the supreme Self, insight into the perception of truth in all. This is declared as true knowledge and anything contrary to it is but ignorance.

Metaphorical Interpretation

These twenty spiritual qualities are enumerated by the Lord and are to be cultivated, harvested, and preserved by each human being.

1. Absence of pride. Pride arises because of wealth, physical beauty (sex), food, and material status. Pride is a great obstacle in spiritual life. It brings body consciousness and delusion. Breath is the principal thing in human life. Everyone should be conscious of their own breath, inhaled and exhaled from the top by *sa*. This constant perception of the soul brings this state of no-pride. If one always feels: "I have come into the world empty-handed and I will have to leave it empty-handed—what can I carry when I am to leave this world?", then pride will disappear from the mind.

2. Freedom from hypocrisy and arrogance. Hypocrisy is to pretend to be more than what one is. In spiritual life, there should be no touch of hypocrisy. The rose shares its fragrance. It is its inherent nature. It is not the ego of the rose. Every spiritual seeker must carefully scrutinize his own nature and should not allow a hint of hypocrisy or arrogance—which brings pollution—to come into his life (see Matthew 7:5 and 7:15–20).

3. Non-maliciousness; non-violence; non-injury. Waves of thoughts arise from the ocean of consciousness, but you must avoid all negative, harmful, malicious, violent, and arrogant thoughts. Instead you should think, "I am born to love, to radiate and distribute love; I am an insignificant person. My life in this body is very short. I will spend every moment in serving and loving." This attitude is extremely helpful in spiritual life. Let not a thought, word, or action create pain in another.

4. Forbearance toward all people (patience). People who show forbearance, especially those endowed with the power to punish others, are the greatest in the eye of God. The life of Jesus is the best example. Even as he was being crucified he was praying, "Father, forgive them, for they know not what they do" (Luke 23:34).

5. Simplicity. Spiritual life is a life of simplicity and purity. As one progresses along the spiritual path, all complexities disappear. Human complexities are the source of all unhappiness. A simple person is a happy person.

6. Service to the guru preceptor (acharya-upasana). Two beautiful Sanskrit words are combined together to describe this spiritual quality. First, *acharya* means the master, preceptor, or the realized one, and second, *upasana* means to serve, to follow, to sit near, to be in constant company with. A spiritual seeker should serve his guru preceptor, which reduces his ego, and at the same time must follow his master faithfully and sincerely.

7. Purity. There are two types of purity—internal and external. Most people are concerned with external purity—cleaning the body, the clothes, the house, and so forth. This is good, but real purity is internal purity (See Katha Upanishad 1:3:7). One who constantly fixes his attention on the fontanel, on His presence, is really pure. One who remains conscious of the soul obtains purity. To make the mind clean is real purity.

8. Steadiness. Pleasure and pain, loss and gain, heat and cold, summer and winter, everything comes in turns. One must not be perturbed by these events. One must constantly follow the master and steadily proceed on the path of God-realization.

9. Control of body and mind. The body is the car and the soul is the driver. The body and mind instruments must be kept under thorough control. People become so engrossed in the physical body that they become its slave. But one must be the master of the body. One must be free from body consciousness, through meditation and a yogic lifestyle.

10. Detachment from the object of senses. Every human being has ten senses and ten objects of the senses. Because people are extremely attached to the senses, they think there is actual pleasure in sense objects. But enjoyment breeds disease. All satisfaction brings dissatisfaction. God has not given us senses to bring about our destruction through abuse of our senses, but so we can achieve God perception. One can perceive God's presence through all the doors of the senses.

11. Absence of egotism. Egotism is I-ness and self-doership. Everyone thinks, "I am the doer, I do everything. Without me, nothing can be done." But truly speaking, who is the doer? Can a dead man do anything? Everything, in everyone, is done by the breath, the living power of the formless God. One who loves God will see his ego disappear. Ego is bondage, and no ego is liberation.

12. Perception of the evils of birth, death, old age, disease, and pain. Birth is painful. Death is unpleasant. Disease brings much suffering. In old age, the body and senses become weak, and memory and intelligence decrease. So life becomes miserable. Therefore by thinking constantly about these endless problems, one gets more attached to God.

13. Detachment. One should be detached from the world and attached to God in every breath, thought, and deed.

14. Compassionately detached from affection and the clinging to family, home, and the like. One should live in the world like a lotus flower in water: born in water, floating in water, yet untouched by it. One may have a family, children, and a house, but one should feel that these are the living power of God. The best example is the life of Shri Shri Lahiri Baba.

15. A balanced mind in all circumstances. Feeling that "I am the actor and God is the director" fosters equal-mindedness. When one gets thorough control over one's own breath, one attains the state of equanimity. Regular practice of meditation bestows balance of mind.

16. Unflinching devotion to the Lord with single-minded meditation (yoga). Devotion is constant attachment to God, the supreme Lord, who is breathing from the top.

17. Living in seclusion. Seclusion is the price of greatness. Seclusion is not a place pervaded by extreme external silence, but a state of remaining free from all thoughts, tensions, and distractions. External seclusion is partially helpful, but what is really beneficial is to spend time in seclusion in meditation and soul culture.

18. Avoiding the company of people. The company of worldly people brings distraction in meditation. At the beginning of spiritual life, it is best to live in seclusion, in silence, and to spend every breath in God-consciousness.

19. Remaining constantly in soul-consciousness and cosmic-consciousness. God is all-pervading. He permeates everything. To perceive His living presence in every external object and in every internal thought—to be constantly in the fontanel—is the highway to Self-realization.

20. Search truth, liberation, and emancipation. Truth is the universal and all-pervading form of the almighty father. "He is in me and I am in Him. He and I are one and always have been one"—this must be perceived, conceived, and realized. This should be the core of everyone's life.

These twenty qualities pertain to the soul-consciousness and cosmic-consciousness state; all contrary qualities are ignorance. One should always watch and scrutinize one's own thoughts, moods, and dispositions in order to progress along the path of realization.

The sincere and regular practice of Kriya Yoga, combined with implicit faith, love, and loyalty for the master will make these twenty divine qualities blossom. By cultivating the body land and regulating the restless breath with the scientific technique of Kriya Yoga, one can achieve this stage. Let a garland of these twenty flowers be around the neck of every seeker at all times.

Verse 12

jñeyam yat tat pravakṣyāmi
yaj jñātvā 'mṛitam aśnute
anādimat param brahma
na sat tan nā 'sad ucyate

Translation

That which has to be known I shall narrate, knowing which one attains immortality. It is the beginningless, supreme Brahman who is said to be neither existent nor non-existent.

Metaphorical Interpretation

Shri Krishna is explaining *kshetra* (the field) and *jñana* (knowledge). Now the seeker is understanding the master, learning from him.

The Lord says, "I have described in detail the best qualities of a spiritual person, which are pure, perfect, and essential for God-realization. Read all these verses daily. Remember all these qualities. Do not forget. Watch all your negatives." Man must try sincerely to shun all negatives.

The almighty father, the supreme one, existed before creation. He will also exist after creation. He is in creation. He is within you. He is also without you. He is beginningless as well as endless. He is beyond existence and non-existence. He is beyond honesty and dishonesty. *Brahmavid brahmaiva bhavati.* "He is beyond all duality and changes. He is the unity in every thing and being."

Whatever is seen in this world is perishable. He Who is beyond everything is to be known. To know Brahman is to be Brahman. Knowing Him, the fear of death disappears. If one meditates very deeply, practicing the authentic Kriya Yoga technique according to the direction of the master, liberation is undoubtedly at hand.

Verse 13

sarvataḥpāṇipādam tat
sarvatokṣiśiromukham
sarvataḥśrutimal loke
sarvam āvṛtya tiṣṭhati

Translation

With hands and feet everywhere, eyes, head and faces everywhere, ears everywhere, He dwells in the world, covering everything.

Metaphorical Interpretation

People are confused: Is God formless, or does he have a form? The almighty God has no hands, legs, eyes, nose, or body, yet he has given His limbs to all. He exists in every living being. He is especially manifest in man—in the hands, legs, feet, eyes, ears, head, face, mouth, stomach, in the spine, in the whole body. Inside this invisible body, there is an invisible counterpart. In this body form, the formless God is hiding. Without the formless God, this body form is useless. Meditation brings Self-knowledge, the knowledge of the absolute—*Brahma vidya*. Alexander Pope wrote in his song, *Psalms of Life*,

"*Know thyself. Presume not God to scan.*
The proper study of mankind is man."

Perceive Him in every action, that is, through *kri* and *ya*. Watch Him in every breath. This is the easiest way to God-realization. He is within you and without you, day and night. He hears through your ears and speaks through your mouth. (See Matthew 13:16). He is the seer in all. He is the breath in all. He is the taste in the mouth. He is working through the hands. He is walking through the legs. He is inside. He is outside. He is all-pervading. He is everything; without Him, there is nothing.

Sarva khalvidam brahma. Sarvam brahmamayam jagat: "The whole universe is the form of Brahman—the absolute. He is everywhere. He is nowhere, but also He is right here, right now." This is the declaration of the great seers in the Upanishads.

Verse 14

sarvendriyaguṇābhāsam
sarvendriyavivarjitam
asaktam sarvabhṛc cai 'va
nirguṇam guṇabhoktṛ ca

Translation

He seems to have the qualities of the senses, yet He is without

the senses, detached, maintaining all, free from the qualities of nature (the *gunas*), yet experiencing these qualities.

Metaphorical Interpretation

The five sense organs are activated by the power of the imperishable soul and the almighty father who is the source of everything, who remains within man in every breath. If He does not inhale, the five sense organs and the whole body will cease to function. If he does not abide in the body, man is dead.

The Lord is detached from all five sense organs and the sense objects. He is attached and at the same time compassionately detached. When one knows Him, one will live in this world compassionately detached.

God gives realization and liberation to those who are after Him. Although He is manifest in the whole body, His special abode is above the pituitary, in the fontanel. He is beyond the triple qualities of *maya*, but His power allows man to operate in the material world. People become engrossed and attached to the material world, but He abides and breathes even in these deluded ones. Always, He remains compassionately detached. He has everything—He has nothing. The three qualities of nature come from Him, but He is free from them. He is ever pure, perfect, and the one without a second (see the Shvetashvatara Upanishad 3:17).

Verse 15

bahir antaś ca bhūtānām
acaram caram eva ca
sūkṣmatvāt tad avijñeyam
dūrastham cā 'ntike ca tat

Translation

He is outside as well as inside all beings. He is unmoving

as well as moving. He is too subtle to be known. He is very far, and at the same time very near.

Metaphorical Interpretation

These contrasts proclaim and glorify the beauty of God.

God is outside of man and all living beings as ether (sky), air, fire, water, and earth. He is also inside man as these five gross elements—manifest in the five lower centers. He remains everywhere in the world, in every part of the body, and in the whole universe. He is in the skin, flesh, bone, marrow, blood—everywhere. Everything is God. He is extremely subtle in the atom form; it is very difficult to know Him. He is very far—farther than the farthest. He is at the same time very near, nearer than the nearest. He is the dearest of all. He is in all; all is in Him. He is all.

People, being ignorant, do not perceive Him. They do not know His all-pervading form. They remain very far from God. Those who are in soul-consciousness and cosmic-consciousness always want Him; they watch Him in every breath and in every activity.

Verse 16

avibhaktam ca bhūteṣu
vibhaktam iva ca sthitam
bhūtabhartṛ ca taj jñeyam
grasiṣṇu prabhaviṣṇu ca

Translation

He is undivided yet He seems to be divided among all beings. He is to be known as the maintainer of all beings, destroying them, and creating them all.

Metaphorical Interpretation

One cannot separate the almighty creator from creation. Creator and creation are one, just as the ocean and the waves are one. To the eyes, the waves seem to differ in shape and size, to be separate from the ocean. But the ocean and the waves are inseparable. In creation, every thing and every being looks different, but all are nothing but God's presence. God is within all and maintaining all from their birth until their death.

Shri Krishna is saying, "O Arjuna! You should know Him and that He is always with and within you. He is breathing day and night. At the time of death, He stops breathing. If the mother does not inhale, she cannot conceive. The creator in her is inhaling. If the creator does not breathe in the male, he cannot have sexual enjoyment. He has no sperm. The life existing in the sperm is the power of God. Every human being is the living power of God, He gives satisfaction as well as dissatisfaction to all. He is the creator, maintainer, and destroyer of everything."

Deluded people ignore Him constantly. But if a human being searches for Him through the natural breath and through every activity, and perceives that He is present everywhere, that He is breathing and working through *ham*, the body (*kshetra*), as *sa*, the imperishable soul, then this person will get God-realization—the omnipresent God will seem to be hiding everywhere.

Every person will achieve realization today or tomorrow, because we are born to be realized. Through the practice of the scientific Kriya Yoga technique, even for a short period of time, one experiences God-consciousness in every breath, thought, and action. Through this, one can then give love to the almighty father who is in the *kshetra* (body field), in the *kshetrajña* (knower of the body field), and everywhere. This divine knowledge comes only through the practice of meditation.

Verse 17

jyotiṣām api taj jyotis
tamasaḥ param ucyate

jñānam jñeyam jñānagamyam
hṛdi sarvasya dhiṣṭhitam

Translation

He is the light of lights, and is said to be beyond darkness. Knowledge worth knowing and attainable through wisdom, He is seated in the heart of all.

Metaphorical Interpretation

In the sky, we see the sun. But God is not the sun. God directs the sun to shine. In the moon, stars, planets, lightning, and candle lamps, there is light. There is also light in the whole body, in the seven centers (*dakhsina agni* in the coccygeal center, *grihapati agni* in the sacral center, *vaishwanara agni* in the lumbar center, *ahavaniya agni* in the dorsal (heart) center, and so on). All these fires, even the powerful sun, are in each human body. One can know Him, the light of all lights, through the lights in each of the seven centers.

Ordinarily, people in the *kshetra* (*ham,* the body land) remain in darkness. As the blind cannot see anything, similarly, those who are ignorant cannot know the imperishable (*sa*), the almighty father. One must try to know Him through knowledge, consciousness, soul-consciousness and cosmic-consciousness—through deep meditation. Only human beings can know the almighty father who abides in all as the light of lights, illuminating everything in the world (see the Mundaka Upanishad 2:2:9), but it is not possible to perceive, conceive, and realize Him without the help of the realized master. One cannot become a doctor by merely reading medical books, and one cannot realize the Self simply by reading books (see the Mundaka Upanishad 3:2:3). The realized master enables the disciple to remove the darkness of ignorance and to perceive the indwelling Self.

Self-realization is our birthright. One must realize the indwelling Self (*kshetrajña*) who remains on the top of the body, whose energy permeates the whole body, who is constantly breathing for every living being. To achieve our birthright, soul culture is required, which is the scientific technique of magnetizing the spine and regulating the breath. By avoiding all slothfulness, one can remain constantly focused on the top and rotate the breath around the spine. Through sincere and regular spiritual practice, Self-realization is attainable. Waste time with none but God, and time will not be wasted.

Verse 18

iti kṣetram tathā jñānam
jñeyam co 'ktam samāsataḥ
madbhakta etad vijñāya
madbhāvāyo 'papadyate

Translation

Thus the truth about the body land and knowledge and the object worth knowing has been described comprehensively. My devotee who understands this enters into My state of being.

Metaphorical Interpretation

Sri Krishna is telling Arjuna: "As I told you in the beginning, each human being has two aspects: one is *ham* (*kshetra*, the body field) and the other is *kshetrajña* (*sa*, the soul), the conductor of the body. I clearly explained that the gross body land is made of twenty-four principles. According to one's age and ambition, one is engrossed in these principles in the extrovert stage, in the *kshetra.* I have also described the divine qualities (Verses 8 to 12)—knowledge, consciousness, soul culture—and how to remain compassionately detached and lead a life of purity. I also talked about the knowable (Verses 13 to 17) who remains in each human body. Everyone is born to know one's own divine Self."

The deepest desire for Self-realization is the principal qualification of the disciple. God has created everything—including will and woe. Through troubles, difficulties, diseases, wants, worries, and anxieties, people develop an extreme desire to know God. It is nature's law. Most people seek God through their troubles. Trouble is a blessing in disguise. Trouble is not for trouble's sake. Trouble can enable one to search for the indwelling Self—*kshetrajña*.

But there are many who according to their destiny have an automatic and intense desire for God-realization, who have many questions about God. Self-inquiry brings Self-knowledge.

In this verse, the Lord speaks of "My devotee" (*madbhakta*). Who is His devotee? One who constantly inquires about God and searches for Him—he is the real follower, the lover and the devotee of God. Continuous Self-inquiry is the quality of the devotee. Devotion is the foundation of God-realization.

There are many cults, sects, and traditions who teach people to know God through the five sense organs, through emotions, magic, hallucination, and so forth. But it is impossible to realize God in this way (see the Katha Upanishad 2:3:12). One must go beyond the domain of the senses, mind, thought, intellect, and ego to achieve Self-realization.

This is the scientific age. People should seek and search Him by this scientific process of soul culture. With the simple, shortcut Kriya Yoga technique, one can perceive God within a short period—through inner tranquility. This yoga is nonsectarian and free from all dogma. By learning the technique directly from a Self-realized master, everyone can proceed on the path of realization. Through God-realization, one will get the fulfillment of human birth and liberation.

Verse 19

prakṛtim puruṣam cai 'va
viddhy anādī ubhāv api
vikārāmś ca guṇāmś cai 'va
viddhi prakṛtisambhavān

Translation

Know that *prakriti* (nature) and *purusha* (soul) are both without beginning. Know also that the modifications and *gunas* (qualities) are born of *prakriti* (nature).

Metaphorical Interpretation

The Lord is describing the body nature and the indwelling soul. *Prakriti* (nature) has no beginning and no middle, but it does have an end. The indwelling Self being formless has no beginning, middle, or end. The soul is *kshetrajña* (the knower of the body field); *kshetra* is the body. The *kshetrajña* is the *purusha.*

This *purusha*, the soul, is hiding in each body and is beyond the triple qualities of *maya*. The imperishable soul, *kshetrajña*, is the letter "A." The soul is breathing for everyone and accordingly changing the dispositions of those individuals. In a living body, one can feel the existence of *purusha*, *kshetrajña*, the soul, from whom these changing negative and positive moods originate.

When that *purusha* comes below the pituitary, people are engrossed in their body nature—in money, sex, appetite, anger, pride, cruelty, many types of religious activity, many techniques taught by traditional teachers, and so on. People do all these things from their body nature, but it is made possible only because of the existence of the soul, *kshetrajña,* abiding in the body field.

People are extremely restless due to their many different dispositions and activities. But *kshetrajña* dwells above the five sense organs, in the *purusha,* in-between the two eyebrows, inside the pituitary; here, extreme calmness prevails. Then man is not engrossed in his body nature anymore. There is no restlessness. It is the state of freedom from all worldly qualities that evolve through the triple qualities of *maya*. When one goes above the pituitary, the fontanel, and even beyond to the all-pervading stage—one perceives complete freedom; no sense of the world remains. This is the door of wisdom, the state of *samadhi*.

Verses 20 and 21

kārya karaṇa kartṛtve
hetuḥ prakṛtir ucyate
puruṣaḥ sukhaduḥkhānām
bhoktṛtve hetur ucyate

puruṣaḥ prakṛtistho hi
bhunkte prakṛtijān guṇān
kāraṇam guṇasango 'sya
sadasadyonijanmasu

Translation

Nature is said to be the cause in cause and effect. The soul is said to be the cause in the experience of pleasure and pain.

The soul abiding in nature enjoys the qualities born of nature. Attachment to the qualities is the course of its birth in good and evil wombs.

Metaphorical Interpretation

Two things in human life must be clearly known. One is *kshetra,* which is *prakriti*, the body nature, also known as *ham*. The other is *kshetrajña,* which is the *purusha*, the imperishable soul. The soul dwells in this body field (nature). Anything one does, is done by the soul. The body is made of the twenty-four elements of *prakriti*, nature.

When one is in body nature, one needs the company of many beings and the association with many things. When one feels hunger, one needs money for food. People earn money—the cause is hunger. *Karana* is the cause in nature of the activity of earning money. But the *purusha*, the indwelling Self, is on the top, helping one to work. Food is the matter used to appease hunger. But without breath, one cannot prepare food. Or consider when one experiences the sex sense. This is the cause (*karana*) of someone wanting to marry. But sexual activity is conducted by *purusha*—if He does not inhale, there will be no sex sense.

The Lord breathes from the top, and because of this, people have different dispositions such as anger, pride, cruelty, joy, happiness, love, and so forth. Therefore on one hand, people can become furious, but on the other hand, a mother can have extreme affection and attachment for her baby. Any work the mother does is rooted in this extreme attachment and affection that we call "motherly love."

There are five gross elements, manifest in the five lower centers of the human body, which are governed by five deities as can be seen in the worship of the Hindus, for instance. In the sky (neck) center, there are the propensities for religion. The presiding deity of the sky center is Shiva, ruling the sense of hearing, the ears. The air (heart, the emotions) center is Vishnu (Rama, Krishna, Hari), governing the sense of touch, the skin. The presiding deity of the fire (navel, food) center is Surya, ruling the sense of sight, the eyes. The water (sacral, sex) center is Durga, Kali, Jagddhatri, Annapurna, Lakshmi, Saraswati, Manasa, Shitala, the goddesses, and so on, conducting the sense of taste, the mouth. Ganesha rules the earth (coccygeal, money) center and the sense of smell, the nose.

The cause of worship of the deities depends upon family tradition. If in a family somebody worships Krishna, all follow him, and Krishna, Shiva, Durga, and so on are different aspects of the One. In the Taittariya Upanishad (2:5), it says, *vijñanam sarve devah brahma jyestha upasate*—"All the Gods meditate on the first One, i.e. Brahman (soul)."

The five sense organs are conducted by breath. If there is no breath, then there is no Shiva, no Krishna. If a person worships any of the five deities, then he worships only the presiding deity of one sense organ. If one worships Krishna, then he worships the presiding deity of the skin only—all the other deities are left aside. And before all of this, the worshippers must perform rituals: *anganyasa* (God perception in the different limbs of the body), *karanyasa* (God perception in the fingers of the hand), and *pranayama* (breath regulation). It takes a long time. After that, they worship the deity by chanting with their mouth.

But by the practice of Kriya Yoga, one can perceive complete calmness in both the body and the mind in a few minutes. There will be inner transformation. One can change one's life force into an all-accomplishing divine force. There will be physical, mental, intellectual, and spiritual change. This is possible through breath control. Breath is the cause of all activities. Breath control is the key to the real life of every human being. Kriya Yoga helps us to achieve breath control.

If one concentrates calmly at a point in-between the two eyebrows, going in a straight line to the pituitary (the sixth center), one will perceive the *purusha*—the imperishable indwelling Self.

God inhales and we are born as a baby; with every breath the baby changes. From birth to death, the baby passes through ten successive stages. The perishable body changes every moment, but the soul is imperishable. All thoughts, dispositions, and activities come because of the soul in the body, but when we are all busy in the material world, we forget the indwelling Self, and as a result we feel happiness or unhappiness. God is the cause of the play of duality, but God, the conductor of everything, remains compassionately detached.

The *kshetrajña purusha* (indwelling Self) remains in the body land; thus, the *purusha* is enabling *maya* and its activities. People are good or bad according to the manifestation of the triple qualities of nature within them. Among the children born of the same parents, one may become a doctor by going to medical school, while another may become an engineer or a scientist—each according to their destiny and quality. According to the quality of the activity one pursues at any moment, one is reborn into a good or a bad state—a state of peace or suffering. People experience many changes during their lives. As they become engrossed in different activities, they acquire a new destiny.

So one is one's own friend or one's own foe. But by treading the royal path of God-realization through meditation, one can avoid all the distractions of material temptation and can reach the divine goal. Some people, due to their spiritual destiny, remain above the pituitary and the fontanel, perceiving their immortality in every breath, experiencing constant liberation, peace, bliss, and joy.

Verse 22

upadraṣṭā 'numantā ca
bhartā bhoktā maheśvaraḥ
paramātme 'ti cā 'py ukto
dehe 'smin puruṣaḥ paraḥ

Translation

The supreme soul in this body is called the witness, the true guide, the sustainer of all, the experiencer, the great Lord and the absolute.

Metaphorical Interpretation

Ham is the body nature that creates delusion, illusion, and error. *Sa* is *kshetrajña*—the indwelling Self—whose real abode is above the two eyebrows. *Sa* is *upadrashta*, meaning the witness. *Drashta* means seer; but *upadrashta* is the witness. He remains in the north of the body and from there watches everything—all the activities that are taking place in the south of the body.

He is *anumanta,* the guide. He gives orders and commands. If one person wants to do good things, He instructs him to do good. If one does bad, He allows it. But He is beyond everything, remaining compassionately detached.

He is *bharta*, the supporter who maintains the body and gives complete satisfaction. Without Him, human beings are dead.

He is *bhokta*, meaning the experiencer. He allows everyone to enjoy the material world and to get happiness. In the navel center, for example, He is present as the *vashvanara* fire. He provides four types of food: *charvya*, the food to be chewed; *choshya*, the food to be sucked; *lehya*, the food to be licked with the tongue; and *peya*, liquid food to drink. *Kshetrajña purusha*, the indwelling Self, allows the body to digest and to assimilate these four types of food.

The last part of the verse says that in this very human body, the supreme soul (*paramapurusha*) is hiding. He is Maheshvara, which means the great Lord—the conductor of life, the imperishable soul, the supreme father who is beyond everything. Being the king of kings, He abides in each human being and has been inhaling since each being's birthday, giving them the opportunity to realize the Self. Although human life is for Self-realization, people are ignorant and extremely absorbed in the material world. Only by introverting the five restless senses and going to the atom point can one perceive, conceive, and realize the indwelling supreme soul.

Verse 23

ya evam vetti puruṣam
prakṛtim ca guṇaiḥ saha
sarvathā vartamāno 'pi
na sa bhūyo 'bhijāyate

Translation

He who in this way knows the soul and nature, along with its qualities, though he acts in every way, he is not born again (he is liberated).

Metaphorical Interpretation

To realize God, one need not go to the forest, the mountains, or holy places of pilgrimage, but rather, one must dive within. That is essential. If one follows the instructions of a realized master and experiences this soul as the witness, the supporter, the experiencer, the great Lord, and the supreme spirit—then he is liberated.

This soul abides in this body, but those who are constantly engrossed in the body nature are constantly deluded by that nature. The Lord Who maintains the human body as well as all plants and animals grants free choice to all—between good and bad—giving the power for enjoyment. His abode is in the ten finger-width span from between the two eyebrows up to the fontanel. If one knows the indwelling Self in the pituitary and the triple qualities of nature: *sattva* (truth, calmness), *rajas* (activity), and *tamas* (sloth and also body nature, which gives constant delusion, illusion, and error), then one is liberated, enjoying constant peace, bliss, and joy.

When a person's experience remains below the pituitary, then he is in *maya*. But the soul enables him to go above the pituitary, to the spiritual state, beyond everything, to compassionate detachment. One must watch the imperishable soul and the supreme father. Thus one becomes emancipated and God-realized. This is the ultimate goal of each human being.

Verse 24

dhyānenā 'tmani paśyanti
kecid ātmānam ātmanā
anye sāmkhyena yogena
karmayogena cā 'pare

Translation

Through meditation, some perceive the divine Self in the Self by the Self. Others experience it by the path of knowledge, and still others by the path of action.

Metaphorical Interpretation

The Lord declares that there are many types of people who try for perfection and achieve the state of God-realization. Some meditate deeply and practice Kriya and remain in the pituitary; they go beyond body sense, mind, thought, intellect, ego, and even awareness of the world. Their third eye is opened. They continuously feel the living power of God abiding in their bodies. This is liberation.

Other people practice *samkhya yoga* (the path of knowledge), chanting mentally, remembering the almighty father in every breath, remaining inside the spine and watching the spine. With this practice, these people also achieve God-realization.

Others do work as a worship to God. In everything they see, they perceive that God is working through the body. They also realize that the work performed through all the different centers—the money, sex, food, passion, and religion centers—is possible only due to His presence in the body. They give oblation to the fire in each center. They become calm in their hearts. All extrovert dispositions disappear, and they achieve an introverted state and realize the indwelling Self. This is *karma* (action with love for God). In every breath, thought, and disposition, they feel that the soul is the sole doer in the body, and thus they attain God-realization.

Verse 25

anye tv evam ajānantaḥ
śrutvā 'nyebhya upāsate
te 'pi cā 'titaranty eva
mṛtyum śrutiparāyaṇāḥ

Translation

Yet others, not knowing this (path of yoga), hearing from other's worship, and even those who are devoted to what they have heard, cross the ocean of death.

Metaphorical Interpretation

There are many people who do not know how to meditate. They do not even chant the name of God or follow the path of *samkhya yoga* (the path of knowledge). They are idle and dull and have less wit. They have less ability to perceive or to understand the subtle spiritual truth. Then, they hear about God from the mouths of others. Afterward, they engage in spiritual practice and go to the realized master. They hear from the guru that God is working through their every breath, that without breath they cannot do any work. Following their master, they fix their attention in the fontanel and develop the short breath, and they become absorbed in super-consciousness and cosmic-consciousness. They forget everything, even their own body form; they achieve God-realization.

Some go to the master and, according to his instructions, try to hear the *aum* sound. They can learn to hear the *aum* sound day and night. They remain absorbed, forgetting their lower self, evils, and negatives, and they ultimately are liberated, free from death, in the state of immortality.

Verse 26

yāvat samjāyate kimcit
sattvam sthāvarajangamam
kṣetrakṣetrajñasamyogāt
tad viddhi bharatarṣabha

Translation

Whatever being—animate or inanimate—is born, know it as the union of the *kshetra* (body field) and *kshetrajña* (knower of the body field), O Best of the Bharatas (Arjuna).

Metaphorical Interpretation

In this world of matter, one sees land, hills, forests, animals, birds, insects, creepers, water, air, fire, earth, sky, and more. All of this is created by the supreme almighty father. Before creation there was nothing. It was His desire to create everything. He created the vacuum, air, fire, water, earth—deserts, hills, oceans, and so on. He created everything with the help of *prakriti* (nature), which is *kshetra* (the field), and He remains in everything as *kshetrajña* (the knower of the body field).

Wherever there is a little water deposited in the ground, one will find innumerable insects, germs, and bacteria underneath—it is teeming with life. In that life, there is also *prakriti* (nature) and *purusha* (the indwelling Self) because without the union of *prakriti* and *purusha*, there is no creation. In every creation, the creator—*purusha*—hides Himself. Everything, even ego, comes through *prakriti* and *purusha*, *kshetra* and *kshetrajña*, body and soul, *ham* and *sa*. So, one does not require external objects for God-realization. One must simply know that there is one almighty father, not two, pervading everywhere. *Sarvam brahmamayam jagat*: "In this world, whatever one sees or perceives is only one alone, the almighty father." This is declared in the four great instructions (*mahavakyas*) in the four Vedas:

Prajñanam brahma (Rig Veda): "Wisdom is the absolute God." This wisdom cannot be perceived by speech or any of the five sense organs, nor by suggestion, imagination, speculation, hallucination, or magic. It can only be perceived through deep meditation.

Aham brahmasmi (Yajur Veda): "I am the absolute God." Only rational and spiritual beings can try their utmost to realize this truth, which is similar to "Be still and know that I am God." (Psalm 46:10). In this state, one can perceive that everything is *kshetrajña*, God, hiding inside and outside of the body nature. By going to the north to infinity, to His presence, one can realize "I am the absolute God."

Tattwamasi (Sama Veda): "Thou art that." In every breath, in every vibration of life, one will feel that I and He are one and have always been one.

Ayamatma brahma (Atharva Veda): "This indwelling Self *(kshetrajña)* is He alone." In the whole universe, whatever one sees or feels in the vacuum, air, fire, water, earth—everything is the manifestation of God, His glory and glamour. However insignificant anything may be, it manifests the presence of God. The marvelous power of God is everywhere; this is the union of *kshetra* and *kshetrajña,* nature and Self, body and soul, *ham* and *sa*.

Verse 27

samam sarveṣu bhūteṣu
tiṣṭhantam parameśvaram

vinaśyatsv avinaśyantam
yaḥ paśyati sa paśyati

Translation

He who sees the supreme Lord present equally in all beings, never perishing when they perish, he alone truly sees.

Metaphorical Interpretation

Nature has no inner light. She is illuminated by the individual Self, *purusha*. The body cannot work without the soul. The supreme Lord abides everywhere, but His presence is more manifest in human beings. He allows the imperishable soul to breathe. The supreme Lord exists everywhere, in every human being, giving His marvelous power to all. When the human being dies, *kshetrajña*, the indwelling Self does not die. He is ever imperishable, immortal. He who realizes this is the true seeker of God. He will attain the real knowledge. Although the manifestation of God can be perceived more clearly in the beauty of nature, God is equally present everywhere. God has no partiality. The soul in each living being is the same.

Verse 28

samam paśyan hi sarvatra
samavasthitam īśvaram
na hinasty ātmanā 'tmānam
tato yāti parām gatim

Translation

Seeing indeed the same Lord present equally everywhere, he does not ignore the Self by the Self and ultimately goes to the supreme state.

Metaphorical Interpretation

By the practice of Kriya Yoga one can watch the imperishable soul in the perishable body. The soul is always detached. If one realizes this, constant liberation and realization will be achieved.

The person who searches to find the supreme Lord abiding everywhere in the formless state is never destroyed. He remains in the world, does every type of work, but is compassionately detached. The presence of the Lord resides equally in every name and form.

Below the pituitary is the play of the perishable world. Above the pituitary is the place of the imperishable soul. A true seeker does not search for the Self below the pituitary. He always searches the indwelling Self, above the eyebrows. He is free from all evils, negatives, and immoralities. Those who do not do this constantly destroy their own life.

Verse 29

prakṛtyai 'va ca karmāṇi
kriyamāṇāni sarvaśaḥ
yaḥ paśyati tathā 'tmānam
akartāram sa paśyati

Translation

And he who really sees that all actions are performed by nature (*prakriti*) only and (when one is above body nature) perceives that soul is not the doer, he alone really sees.

Metaphorical Interpretation

Ham, the body, is full of *maya.* Only the body nature has antecedents and consequences. This is how one is filled with delusion, illusion, and error. Delusion and restlessness arise from the body nature and the twenty-four gross elements. The gross body is either very active and absorbed in material work, or it is wasting time in idleness. The astral body is filled with emotion and thoughts. All these bodies are activated by breath energy—the living power of God. Always, the imperishable soul remains compassionately detached.

Through deep meditation, one goes to the state of complete detachment—where there is no work, no activity. The devotee who leads this type of life is the true seeker of God and achieves God-realization. In every breath, he feels the presence of the imperishable soul and is ever free, united with the supreme almighty father. He perceives "I am Brahman—I am the imperishable soul." Everything in the universe is Brahman. Wisdom is Brahman. This is the state of liberation.

Verse 30

yadā bhūtapṛthagbhāvam
ekastham anupaśyati
tata eva ca vistāram
brahma sampadyate tadā

Translation

The moment one perceives that the diversified existence of being is resting in the one supreme soul and spreads out from that alone, he attains Brahman.

Metaphorical Interpretation

In the material world, there are many types of people with many different dispositions. The Lord causes all human beings to be active. People work. They all work through the breath. People and their actions are different, but there is unity in the breath. As all the beads of the rosary are held together by a thread, similarly all human beings are alive and unified by the thread of the breath—the power of God. This thread, *sutra* in Sanskrit, is the Brahma Sutras, the thread of God. This thread holds everything together. The one abides in everyone. One soul hides in all. He is none but God. When one realizes this, he no longer discriminates between people. He feels that everyone is the power of God. He feels the touch of the supreme father. He perceives constant unity, and unity in diversity is divinity.

Verse 31

anāditvān nirguṇatvāt
paramātmā 'yam avyayaḥ
śarīrastho 'pi kaunteya
na karoti na lipyate

Translation

O Son of Kunti (Arjuna), this imperishable supreme soul is beginningless and without qualities. Although He remains in the body (in its reality), He is free from action and contamination.

Metaphorical Interpretation

The supreme Lord of the whole universe is called Purushottama in the Bhagavad Gita. He directs the imperishable soul to breathe. Breath is the cause of all activity.

The supreme Lord and the soul are not two; essentially they are one. The almighty father is one, there is no other except Him. Where is His beginning? He is the cause of everything. Nothing is the cause of God. He is beyond the triple qualities of *maya.* That is why He is formless. He abides in each human body as *kshetrajña*—the imperishable one. He does not do any work. He is not attached to any work. He is just like a mirror. If someone remains far from the mirror, he cannot see his own image. If he stands in front of the mirror, then he can see his own face, the clear and complete picture. If he sticks out his tongue, he will see his own tongue in the mirror. If he moves his head, he will see his head move in the mirror. Yet the mirror is completely detached. Similarly, the *kshetrajña*, the imperishable soul in the body land (*kshetra*), and the supreme almighty father, the conductor of the universe, remain completely detached. (See the Bhagavad Gita 15:8)

God is formless. He is beginningless—He is present before, during, and after creation. God is *nirguna*—beyond the triple qualities of *maya*. His presence is more manifest in the human body than anywhere else. By the practice of Kriya Yoga, a human being can remain above the eyebrows in the pituitary and even higher in the fontanel. He will feel nothing—no sense of the body, no sense of the world. He will feel extremely calm and will be compassionately detached. Such calmness and serenity is possible only through meditation. This is the state of Brahma and one can remain absorbed in it. At this time, the mirror is free from the image in the same way that *kshetrajña purusha*—the all-pervading supreme father—remains detached from the world.

A water drop on the lotus leaf moves like liquid silver, hither and thither, but remains unattached, unable to touch the leaf. In the same way, one's image does not touch the mirror. Through meditation, one will remain ever free. Meditation is the key to this freedom.

Verse 32

yathā sarvagatam saukṣmyād
ākāśam no 'palipyate
sarvatrā 'vasthito dehe
tathā 'tmā no 'palipyate

Translation

As the all-pervading ether (space), because of its subtlety, is not tainted, so the soul that is seated in the body is not tainted by the qualities of the body.

Metaphorical Interpretation

The mirror is always detached from the object it reflects. So it is for everything that dwells in space. Space is unattached. The body dwells in space. One cannot see space. It remains compassionately detached.

There are five gross elements: ether, air, fire, water, and earth. The air is formless; it permeates everywhere. The air moves in and out of the nostrils. But no one can touch or catch the air. Fire exists in each human body in the seven centers. The one fire becomes seven fires, activating the seven centers. Oxygen comes in and touches the fire, which is why the fire can burn and why we are all alive. But that fire does not burn the body. Consider another element—water. God cannot be drenched by water. Water cannot be drenched by water.

The power of God activates the five sense organs: the eyes, ears, nose, tongue, and skin. God is also in the five objects of the senses: sight, sound, smell, taste, and touch. But God is ever compassionately detached. There are certain types of fish that can live in mud underwater, but the mud does not cling to their body. Similarly the marvelous power of God remains in all, but He cannot be tainted by the activities of the world.

Each living body is made of the five gross elements and twenty-four principles. But each human body is full of fire that is the God fire—unknown and unseen —formless. That fire causes all activity through the agency of the triple qualities of nature.

Ordinary people cannot realize this. Only through the practice of Kriya Yoga, focusing one's full attention on the pituitary and fontanel beyond the sense of body, mind, intellect, and ego, can one perceive the imperishable supreme father who is all-pervading.

Verse 33

yathā prakāśayaty ekaḥ
kṛtsnam lokam imam raviḥ
kṣetram kṣetrī tathā kṛtsnam
prakāśayati bhārata

Translation

O Bharata (man of illumination, Arjuna), as the sun illuminates this entire world, so does the Lord of the body field illuminate the entire field.

Metaphorical Interpretation

In this verse, the Lord clearly explains the power of this soul in the body by using the sun as an example.

When the sun rises, darkness disappears. One can see everything by sunlight. The whole world becomes active by the power of the sun. But the sun is compassionately detached.

Similarly, in the body *(kshetra),* the Lord of this body—the imperishable soul, the formless one—breathes. By the light of the breath one can see one's own life and all five centers of the body—the money, sex, food, emotion, and religion centers.

Like the almighty father permeating the universe, like the sun illuminating the earth, the soul activates the body. All the body centers receive the light of the soul, and as a result, people have many types of dispositions and activities. When the sun is not in the sky, then everything is dark. Nothing is visible. Similarly, when the imperishable soul does not breathe through someone's nostrils, immediately that person is dead: no family, no home, no wealth—death of the body. Although the almighty soul sun abides in the body, one must go to the realized master to learn how to control the breath and ultimately the mind, in order to see this divine sun within. Breath control gives self control. Through self control, one can realize one's own Self and the supreme father, the formless illumination of God. Every single human being is born to achieve this; those who don't do it are leading the life of animals.

Verse 34

kṣetrakṣetrajñayor evam
antaram jñānacakṣuṣā

bhūtaprakṛtimokṣam ca
ye vidur yānti te param

Translation

Those who realize by their eye of wisdom the distinction between the field, the knower of the field, as well as the liberation of beings from nature (*prakriti*), they go to the supreme.

Metaphorical Interpretation

One must know three things:

1. What is the body nature and its qualities,
2. Who is *kshetrajña*, the knower of the body, and where does one find Him, and
3. How to be liberated from the activities of body nature

One who knows these things can lead a life of detachment. Just as human beings can do work by the power of the sun; similarly, by the power of *kshetrajña*, the imperishable soul in the body, people can do many types of work. *Kshetrajña*, the Lord of the body, remains detached like the mirror. One can easily know the difference between the body field and the knower of the body field, by which one can become liberated. But to achieve liberation, one needs the body.

Undoubtedly, the gross body is full of delusion, illusion, and error. Just as the sun rising in the sky enables the whole world to become active, the presence of the soul sun in the body makes people restless. But people with a restless body and mind can go beyond all restlessness and enter into the imperishable soul with the help of the realized master. They can go to the supreme almighty Lord who remains like the coating on the back of the mirror.

If they can fix their attention in the pituitary, then by the power of the guru they will be free from mind, thought, intellect, ego, body sense, and world sense. They will attain the supreme state. At that time, they cannot feel where they are sitting. Gradually, they will merge with the almighty father and attain the pulseless stage, *samadhi,* the ultimate goal of human life.

Instead of leading the life of the animals, human beings must, by the practice of the Kriya Yoga techniques, become a little more introverted. Then they will feel the marvelous power of God that exists in every human being and in the entire universe. This is the purpose of human life.

As a road has two sides, so the spiritual path has two sides: one side is the words of the master, and the other is the words of the scriptures. If one lives according to the words of the master and the scriptures, and with implicit faith in them, one will be liberated while still abiding in the physical body (*jivanmukti*).

The path of divine knowledge leads to the goal of liberation.

Summary

This thirteenth chapter of the Bhagavad Gita is known as the "Yoga of the Body Field and its Knower." It is comprised of thirty-four verses. Although many authors do not accept the first verse as part of this chapter, it provides an initiation into the chapter, revealing the cause of its narration. So Arjuna's query about *prakriti* (nature), *purusha* (the indwelling soul), *kshetra* (the field), and *kshetrajña* (the knower of the field) is the real beginning of this chapter.

This chapter explains in a systematic way that the human body is a field to be cultivated. God has given every human being a beautiful body land in which His marvelous and formless power is hiding. God is not far away, above the sky, in heaven, or in paradise; he is in every atom, cell, and tissue of the human body.

As the farmer obtains a bountiful harvest by the cultivation of his land; similarly, by cultivating this body land, one will reap the divine harvest of God-realization. In order to cultivate the land, the farmer needs to have knowledge. Work is done by knowledge, and knowledge is matured and concentrated by action and experience.

Knowledge and love are inseparable. Divine knowledge has many prerequisites. Verses 8 to 11 of this chapter describe beautifully the twenty qualities of knowledge. Knowledge is not the result of merely reading books or hearing discourses. Knowledge brings inner transformation and change. As a tree bends when laden with fruit, similarly the properly cultivated body land yields the divine harvest of humility in human life. A man of real wisdom is free from vanity, ego, arrogance, and hypocrisy. Knowledge breeds love. Divine love brings a real change in human life. This chapter discusses the twenty qualities of real knowledge. A man of knowledge must try to cultivate these qualities in his own life.

A tree provides shelter to birds and animals, shade where a man can rest, fruit to the hungry, and maintains ecological balance by breathing in gases like carbon dioxide and giving off oxygen. Animals can't breathe and exhale pure oxygen that they can live on. A tree gives its body to man for many uses. The tree's life is a life of sacrifice. Likewise, the life of a spiritual person is for all.

Reading the scriptures or simply hearing the talk of the master will not give one spiritual knowledge. One must proceed down the path of realization, cultivating the twenty spiritual qualities daily, regularly, and sincerely, to move quickly on the path. These twenty aspects of knowledge are the stepping stones to real spirituality.

Verses 13 to 17 of this chapter explain very nicely that which must be known and realized. People believe that God is unknown and unknowable, but in Verse 13 the Lord says that one must know Him. Although He is formless, the formless and invisible counterpart of God hides in this body form. A real seeker of truth tries to realize Him in every breath, in every moment of life, throughout all human activity and endeavor.

Without the formless one, the body form is inert, dead, and useless. God is beyond the limited perceptual capacity of the senses. His marvelous power enables the senses to activate. These verses also reiterate nicely the Upanishadic truth about the formless and the absolute: "He is the nearest of the near and the farthest of the far. He is inside. He is outside. He is knowledge. He is knowledgeable through knowledge. He is the supreme knowledge, which is wisdom."

Swans can separate the water from the milk by secreting a chemical from their beak. It is a special feature of swans. Every spiritual seeker is a swan who can fly into the sky of spirituality from the neck center up to the fontanel and even beyond. And also like the swan, a spiritual seeker can swim in the ocean of the world. In Sanskrit, swan is *hamsa*. *Hamsa* consists of two syllables: *ham* and *sa*. This is *prakriti* and *purusha*, body nature and the indwelling Self, attachment and detachment. Verses 20 to 24 beautifully explain the distinction between *prakriti* and *purusha*.

Real knowledge dawns in man when he is able to distinguish and discriminate *kshetra* from *kshetrajña*, body from soul, *prakriti* from *purusha*. By this knowledge, all attachment and attraction to the mundane world diminishes. One becomes free from pleasure and pain, gain and loss, all the dualities of the world. One who realizes the indwelling Self is one with the supreme Self—he is liberated.

In Verses 25 and 26, there is a discussion about so-called different paths for soul culture and God-realization. Although people find apparent distinctions between the paths of *yoga*, *karma*, *jñana*, and *bhakti*, they are in fact inseparable; they are correlated and causally connected. Kriya Yoga is the essence of all these different spiritual practices; it is the integration of *karma* (action), *jñana* (knowledge), *bhakti* (devotion) and *yoga* (meditation). The end of this chapter describes the play of *prakriti* (nature) and the state of realization. *Prakriti* gives the illusion of diversity and multiplicity, but in fact there is unity in all. Just as the thread passing through all the beads of the rosary provides unity, similarly a sincere seeker of truth perceives the constant unity of the supreme Self in every thing and every being. The Brihadaryanaka Upanishad (4:4:19) and the Katha Upanishad (2:1:10) declare, *mṛtyuḥ sa mṛtyum āpnoti ya iha nānyeva paśyati*: "One who perceives many enters the world of mortality."

But by the regular and sincere practice of Kriya Yoga, one can perceive the state of unity. This chapter concludes with a discussion of the analogy between the body universe and the universe. The body is the microcosm and the entire universe is the macrocosm. God is all-pervading in the whole universe, and is so in the entire body as well. The easiest and quickest way to perceive God is to see Him first in the whole body and then in the universe. That is what Kriya Yoga teaches.

---

[1] Note: The Brahmasutra is one of the three prominent holy books of India called *prasthana trayi*—the three sacred books for liberation, viz. the Upanishads, the Brahmasutra and the Bhagavad Gita.

Chapter 14

Guṇatraya vibhāga yoga

The Yoga of Discrimination of the Triple Qualities of Nature

Introduction

In the previous chapter, the divine master Lord Krishna explained that the spiritual treasure is not to be found outside of ourselves; it is our innermost divine nature. The soul is hiding in every human being. Similarly, the Shvetashvatara Upanishad 6:11 says, *eko devaḥ sarvabhūteṣu gūḍhaḥ sarvavyāpī sarvabhūtāntarātmā:* "The same deity remains hidden in all beings and is all-pervasive and the indwelling Self of all beings." But to discover this soul, one must penetrate the veil of nature (*prakriti*). *Purusha*—the soul that abides in the body—is the royal secret. It is to be perceived, conceived, and realized by the supreme scientific technique of Kriya Yoga.

Now the question inevitably arises in the mind of the seeker: if *prakriti* (nature) acts under the direction and the power of the almighty father, how can it cover the *purusha*, the indwelling Self? The answer is very simple. As a little cloth can cover the human body, so can the body nature cover the soul. Or, consider how the sun causes water to evaporate. The vapor turns into clouds, which then cover the sun, its creator. In this way the soul sun is covered by the cloud of body consciousness.

People of clear conscience and pure mind can comprehend the presence of the soul. The *prakriti* that appears to cover the soul is determined by the preponderance of its three qualities or *gunas*. Nature has three qualities that are enjoyed by the supreme soul, who is beyond the *gunas*—the soul is *nirguna*. One who practices yoga must know this nature and its qualities, just as a warrior must know the strengths and weaknesses of his enemy. *Prakriti*, the body nature, is an obstacle to meditation, but through the power of meditation a person with strong determination can perceive the ever pure, illuminating soul.

This chapter is called *gunatraya vibhaga yoga*: "The Yoga of Discrimination of the Triple Qualities of Nature." This chapter beautifully explains nature's three qualities and their impact on practical life.

Verse 1

śrībhagavān uvāca
param bhūyaḥ pravakṣyāmi
jñānānām jñānam uttamam
yaj jñātvā munayaḥ sarve
parām siddhim ito gatāḥ

Translation

The Lord said: I shall further narrate the highest knowledge, the best of all knowledge, having known which the sages (*munis*) have gone from this world to the highest perfection.

Metaphorical Interpretation

Verse 22 of the previous chapter described how the union of *purusha* (the indwelling Spirit) and *prakriti* (the body nature) accounts for all activity in life. This is the world. People are born in the world to realize God through meditation. The same thing is proclaimed in the Bible in James 2:26: "The body without the spirit is dead. Faith without works is dead."

The Lord is describing the highest knowledge. What is the highest knowledge? It is the knowledge that brings liberation from all human suffering. As has been explained previously, *tapa svdhyya īśvara-pranidhanani kriya yoga*, which means *tapah* (meditation), *svadhyaya* (self-study), and *ishvara pranidhana* (love for God) are the different aspects of Kriya Yoga. If one watches the imperishable soul constantly, in every breath, one will be constantly liberated. With breath consciousness, one's breath will become very short, so short that it will not even come out of the nostrils. When one watches the imperishable soul in every breath, the super-conscious or cosmic-conscious state will automatically arise.

Muni does not mean one who does not speak. A *muni* is one who seeks truth. *Muni* is the man of meditation. All the *munis* who have complete control over the mind perceive that the supreme almighty father and the imperishable soul are one, and that they are constantly present in the body. These *munis* ultimately attain *samadhi*. *Samadhi* is the highest yogic attainment, so it is called *parama siddhi*. Unfortunately in spiritual life, people who get a little *siddhi*—a little achievement—often forget the highest goal.

Fortunate indeed are those who can enter into the *samadhi* stage through constant effort. This is the only real achievement, the rarest in human life.

Verse 2

idam jñānam upāśritya
mama sādharmyam āgatāḥ
sarge 'pi no 'pajāyante
pralaye na vyathanti ca

Translation

Gaining this divine knowledge and having arrived at a state of identity with Me, they are not born at the time of creation, nor do they feel disturbed at the time of dissolution.

Metaphorical Interpretation

If a person meditates, develops the slow and feeble breath, searches for God in every breath and perceives His living presence in the fontanel and above, he will reach the state of divine knowledge. This state cannot be achieved by reading books or by intellectual pursuits. This state of inner detachment is the cause of liberation.

People should try to develop spiritually from their childhood. Such are the lives of the realized masters. An analysis of their lives clearly shows that they are calm and quiet from their infancy. They are free from anger, ego, pride, and cruelty. Unlike other children they are not restless, but are constantly sweet, kind, and loving. They are constantly conscious of their super-Self. They try to lead a special life; they are always after truth, soul culture, and God, and they want a higher study of the Self. As they advance in age, they radiate even more divine love and spirituality. A real spiritual life is being free from all ambition and aspiration, enjoying constant liberation while in the body and even when leaving the body. After the death of the physical body, these individuals merge in God. Creation and dissolution is a cosmic, divine play. Ordinary people cannot understand and accept it easily. But people with high spiritual enlightenment maintain a balanced state in all situations.

Verse 3

mama yonir mahad brahma
tasmin garbham dadhāmy aham
sambhavaḥ sarvabhūtānām
tato bhavati bhārata

Translation

Great Brahma (mother nature), is My womb, in it I place the seed of all life. The creation of all beings follows from that, O Bharata (Arjuna)!

Metaphorical Interpretation

Sarva khalvidam brahma: "The whole universe is Brahman." The almighty father abides in the whole universe. If one can remain in that state of awakening, then any touch sensation in the body is the touch of the almighty father. In fact, every sense organ is the womb of God. The womb is the place of creation. The mouth is the womb from which speech is created. Any talk that comes out of the mouth is the talk of God. The eye is the womb of God; all the sights of creation arise from here. Every part of the body is the womb of God.

God made male and female in His image. He breathes through the nostrils the breath of His life only to propagate the human race. The almighty father abides in both males and females. Through that power, both male and female enter the youthful stage. "It is also My stage," the Lord says, "I give My power to them. So, if I do not inhale in the male, the sperm is not created. That sperm cannot enter into the womb of the female if I do not breathe in her. All babies are born from My seed."

Every person is God in a human being and a human being in God. This is why one sees the multiplicity of the divine being in the material world. The Lord is saying, "I abide in them, constantly breathing through their nostrils; that is why they are all alive and active. I am hiding just behind the pituitary, where the atom point of life remains in the formless stage." The Lord creates ambition and attachment from that place. The *maya* (delusive force) of the body is the field of propagation, and it is also a manifestation of the divine power from which the whole universe is created.

Verse 4

sarvayoniṣu kaunteya
mūrtayaḥ sambhavanti yāḥ
tāsām brahma mahad yonir
aham bījapradaḥ pitā

Translation

Whatever forms come from any womb, O Son of Kunti (Arjuna), the great Brahma is their womb and I am the father who sows the seed.

Metaphorical Interpretation

"O Arjuna, you are the son of Kunti." Kunti means sharp intelligence, and the finest conception. With this quality, remain in the pituitary and listen.

The Lord continues, "You see many children born daily in this material world. This is My body. If I do not inhale in the parents, they cannot enjoy sexually. So I am the father, I am the mother, I am the breath in the nostrils of both. This is how the seed is created—*aham bijapradah pita*. Mothers become pregnant because of My breath. A dead body cannot conceive and become pregnant.

"I am the seed of everything. I am Brahma, the almighty creator. I am the Brahma in animals, insects, and whatever is born. My marvelous power is called *mahad-brahma*, which refers to the great Brahma, the *prakriti* in every human being. *Prakriti* is the womb for all My creation and through the breath I give power to the whole creation, the entire universe.

"I am the Creator. I am creation. I am in creation. Creation is in Me. Perceive everything as My living presence."

Verse 5

sattvam rajas tama iti
guṇāḥ prakṛtisambhavāḥ
nibadhnanti mahābāho
dehe dehinam avyayam

Translation

The three qualities *sattva* (good and spiritual), *rajas* (desires, activities, and restlessness), and *tamas* (idleness and sloth) born of nature (*prakriti*) bind the body fast, O Mahabahu (mighty-armed Arjuna), the imperishable indweller of the body.

Metaphorical Interpretation

Here the Lord addresses Arjuna as Mahabahu, the mighty-armed. The arm is the symbol of agility and activity, which must lead to purity and truth. Arjuna, due to his noble and divine quality, has the company of Krishna, who is the soul.

The Lord explains that there are three qualities of nature in every human body. A particular quality predominates when the breath flows through any of the three main astral nerves: *Ida, pingala,* or *sushumna.* These qualities exist in the spine. *ida* is idleness, *pingala* causes extreme activity and agility, and *sushumna* is the source of truth and all good qualities. All those qualities come from food. Arjuna is the food minister who remains in the food (navel) center. Food gives either extreme energy and vitality or idleness and sloth.

Shri Krishna, the soul, dwells on the top in the sixth center, in the pituitary. Arjuna does not remain in the navel center; he rises up to the top and is free from all idleness. Despite his tremendous strength and bravery, his delusion made him unwilling to fight. When the sun is covered by clouds, there is darkness. To overcome the state of delusion, one must come to the touch of the realized master. Then one can perceive that the marvelous power of God abides in the whole body.

Generally people are extremely attached to the material world. Engrossed in the material world, they are not able to go beyond the activities of the three qualities of nature. But Arjuna's mind is fixed on the father, the divine conductor of the body chariot. When the mind becomes still, calm, and quiet, then one can know God.

Verse 6

tatra sattvam nirmalatvāt
prakāśakam anāmayam
sukhasangena badhnāti
jñānasangena cā 'nagha

Translation

Of these, *sattva*, being free from impurity, causes illumination and freedom from disease. It binds by attachment to happiness and by attachment to knowledge, O sinless one (Arjuna)!

Metaphorical Interpretation

The Lord declares that if people can remain in truth and lead a truth-oriented life, they will achieve all-around development with absolute peace, reality, oneness with God, and liberation.

When people enjoy extreme happiness and prosperity in *rajo guna* —which is a supremely extroverted stage—they want to spend money in an unbalanced way. They want to have rich food, rich and costly drinks, and they spend valuable time in friendship and amusement. As a result they damage their liver and body and they die early. There is disease and suffering.

But those who want to live a life of righteousness and truth come to receive the touch of the realized masters for guidance. They learn practical techniques for spiritual progress and practice with love and loyalty. They lead a very simple life and watch God in every breath. By learning the science of breath—the extremely slow and feeble breath—one perceives energy from the pituitary to the fontanel, one constantly touches the imperishable soul, the indwelling Self. They practice remaining alert during every breath. The Kriya Yoga technique is very simple and the sincere seekers can quickly learn how to remain in super-consciousness and cosmic-consciousness. They feel the marvelous power of God in every center, day and night. They watch the soul and the breath simultaneously. They perceive God in every activity. Their lifestyle in the practical world is therefore moderate.

When they develop an appetite, they think of God and thank Him. They purify their hearts. They do not allow anger, pride, ego, or hypocrisy in themselves. Those who maintain awareness of the imperishable soul, *sa*, have no negative qualities. They maintain love for every human being and all religions. They try to live at the door of God. Every moment they watch the marvelous power of God breathing within them. They perceive God in the pituitary and above, and as a result they merge into the formless stage and godhood. Meditation with a moderate lifestyle brings freedom from disease and inner peace.

This kind of life makes one free from all impurities. This is the life of truth and light. In the Bible it says, "I am the light of the world. Whoever follows me will never walk in darkness, but will have light of life." (John 8:12) By practicing Kriya Yoga and leading a pure life, you will enjoy perfect health, long life, peace, bliss, and joy. This is the promise of the Lord to Arjuna.

In this verse Arjuna is addressed as Anagha, which means the sinless one, the one who is living the truth and following the soul. Krishna is sinless and pure. Without these qualities, it is impossible to be free from all negatives.

Verse 7

rajo rāgātmakam viddhi
tṛṣṇāsangasamudbhavam
tan nibadhnāti kaunteya
karmasangena dehinam

Translation

Know that *rajas* is characterized by passion (attraction) arising from desire and attachment. It binds fast, O Son of Kunti, the indwelling Self in the body, by attachment to action.

Metaphorical Interpretation

The metaphorical meaning of *rajas* is the "cause of birth," or "to make colorful" in the sense that something is attractive and tempting. Attraction, attachment, affection, and so on are the characteristics of *rajas*. Rajasic people are full of activity and restlessness. They try to earn money to become rich; as a result, they have extreme passion for sex, food, anger, and pride. Accordingly, they do many types of work for enjoyment. The satisfaction of desire breeds more desire. The more they chase after sex, the stronger is their desire for sex. In this way, their minds always remain focused on food, vanity, ego, pride, and arrogance. They are engrossed in many worldly things. External show and fashionable style is their main activity.

This attraction and attachment is the great bondage. People in the rajasic mode of nature are always charged with passion, ambition, and desire. They rarely enjoy the taste of freedom and liberation. Here the Lord calls Arjuna "Kaunteya"—the son of sharp intelligence. Without the finest memory and intelligence, one cannot be free from rajasic nature.

Verse 8

tamas tv ajñānajam viddhi
mohanam sarvadehinām
pramādālasyanidrābhis
tan nibadhnāti bhārata

Translation

Know clearly that *tamas* (dullness) is born of ignorance, which confuses all living beings. It binds fast with negligence, indolence, idleness, and sleep—O Bharata (Arjuna)!

Metaphorical Interpretation

In Verses 6, 7, and 8, Arjuna is addressed in three different ways: "Anagha" (sinless one), "Kaunteya" (child of finest conception), and "Bharata" (one engrossed in illumination), which are correlated with three qualities of nature and how to be free from three qualities.

Tamas is characterized by darkness. So Shri Krishna calls Arjuna "Bharata," (i.e., "who is engrossed in illumination") he who can easily be free from all tamasic qualities of darkness because he loves the light, illumination.

Here, He says, "O Arjuna! You are conscious of the super-Self. There are a lot of people who are idle, lazy, and procrastinating. They become extremely deluded in their whole body. There are even tamasic people who want to spend a long time in sleep, for which they do not hesitate to drink wine or take narcotic drugs."

Although man is rational by nature, tamasic people want to live like animals. They are full of whims, doubt, and confusion. Being extremely idle, they spend more time in sleep.

They are not after truth. Many worldly people are like this. They do not lead a human life, but a subhuman life. They have no clear conscience. Not only do they neglect their life, they waste their life in useless ways.

Verse 9

sattvam sukhe sañjayati
rajaḥ karmaṇi bhārata
jñānam āvṛtya tu tamaḥ
pramāde sañjayaty uta

Translation

***Sattva* (goodness) causes attachment to happiness, and *rajas* (passion) to action, O Bharata (Arjuna), but *tamas* (dullness) clouds wisdom and knowledge, overpowering goodness and action.**

Metaphorical Interpretation

It has been mentioned previously that there are three *prana* channels inside the spine. They are *sushumna, pingala,* and *ida*. They correspond to the three qualities of nature, which are *sattva*, *rajas,* and *tamas*.

There are also fifty kinds of *prana* or vital air, manifesting as different kinds of breath in human beings. Among them, there is one air called *udana,* which is a special breath taken with an extremely calm, short, and slow respiration. If you inhale slowly, perceiving divine energy from the pituitary to the fontanel, and experiencing the living presence of the imperishable indwelling Self, you can remain compassionately detached from the body and the world.

Watch God in every breath. Your breath will change so that it will not come out of the nostrils (also see the Gita 5:27–28). Then, without any talk, any thoughts, any body sense, or any worldly sense, find God in the fontanel and above the fontanel in the infinite north, where the imperishable almighty father abides in the formless state, then you will experience real calmness, which is Godliness. This is the real *su* (completely beautiful) and *kha* (ether), also known as *sukha* (happiness). If one can remain within the state of complete vacuum nothingness, then one will get peace, bliss, and joy. At this time, the breath flows through the *sushumna*.

There are also many kinds of breath coming through the *pingala* channel inside the spine. These breaths create extreme passion, desire, and restlessness. People overpowered with this kind of breathing do many kinds of work to earn money and constantly watch their material gain and remain busy with worldly enjoyments—always restless and always filled with temptation. These people love activity. Sometimes, they spend money for a noble cause. Being extremely restless, they have less aptitude for meditation. Such qualities are called *rajasic* qualities. They are always fond of tip-top dress, a fashionable lifestyle, material prosperity, and exhibitionism, but they are constantly forgetting God. They think that money is God. They even criticize spiritual people at times.

There are also many types of breath that bring sloth, idleness, drowsiness, and sleep. When people sleep, they take an entirely different breath. This breath can also cause snoring at times. People with such a tamasic nature are nervous, idle, fearful, and procrastinators. They lose spirit and enthusiasm. They do not have love for God or any good qualities. Many prefer to take narcotic drugs and wine, which are undoubtedly harmful to their body, brain, and mind. They do not have any drive for study or material advancement. They are always engrossed in sleep, sloth, and idleness. As a result, their life is poor and unpleasant. They do not get a real position in material life. Their dress, demeanor, and culture underscore their nature and habits. They are not liked by others.

Verse 10

rajas tamaś cā 'bhibhūya
sattvam bhavati bhārata
rajaḥ sattvam tamaś cai 'va
tamaḥ sattvam rajas tathā

Translation

O Bharata (man of divine illumination)! Overpowering *rajas* and *tamas*, *sattva* prevails; overpowering *sattva* and *tamas*, *rajas* prevails; likewise, overpowering *sattva* and *rajas*, *tamas* prevails.

Metaphorical Interpretation

Many people suppress their worldly activities and idleness trying to make real spiritual progress and to evolve. But real spiritual life is not suppression, it is a sublimation of the lower nature for a higher purpose. Spiritual seekers should come to receive the touch of the realized master and learn how to control the breath and thereby regulate their lives. They must try their utmost to maintain a meditative state.

Sometimes they will be in the mode of idleness and will not practice Kriya properly, forgetting the teachings of the master. Sometimes they are in the *sushumna* canal, with a short breath. At other times they go to the *pingala* canal, with long and restless breaths, therefore engaging in extreme activity. Yet at other times they become idle when the breath comes through the *ida* canal. Their activities and attitudes differ due to changes in their breath.

The stars and planets also have a profound effect; their positions in one's astrological chart empowers or impedes one's life and work, as do solar and lunar eclipses. But if they come to the realized master and follow him, they can learn how to overcome the impact of rajasic and tamasic qualities and at the same time be free from all the bad effects of the stars and planets. Through this, their spiritual power will increase.

If one does not pay extremely close attention to the master and follow his directions accordingly, one will fail in life. Spiritual and divine qualities increase when one is associated with good company and a good teacher. With the company of the realized master and with deepest desire and ceaseless effort, one can change all the negatives of life, and criminals like Ratnakar or Sage Valmiki[1] can be completely transformed and become highly realized saints. The constant companionship of the realized master enabled them to forsake all their debauchery and immorality.

When the sun rises, the light of the stars and planets is automatically suppressed. Similarly, when a special quality like *sattva, rajas,* or *tamas* dominates, the other qualities become powerless. Everyone should try to reach the *sattvic* stage to be truly fit for realization and the life divine.

Verse 11

sarvadvāreṣu dehe 'smin
prakāśa upajāyate
jñānam yadā tadā vidyād
vivṛddham sattvam ity uta

Translation

When the light of knowledge shines through all the gates (doors) of the body, then it should be known that *sattva* (goodness) is predominant.

Metaphorical Interpretation

Every human body is like a house with nine doors or gates. Each human being becomes engrossed in the extrovert stage through these body gates. Each sense organ leads to temptation and attachment. Each gate is the doorway to evil.

The eyes lead to debauchery, the ears to ignorance, the tongue to maliciousness and foolish and godless talk, and so forth. People perform many devilish actions by associating with bad company. Their lives exhibit anger, pride, ego, and cruelty. The nose likes good fragrance. The skin is enamored by the touch sensation of the opposite sex, which causes people to gradually proceed closer and nearer to each other, mixing, touching, hugging, kissing, which then creates extremely alluring excitement. That is why sex is always so dominant. Sex prevails.

Due to irregular and unbalanced food and eating habits, people develop problems in their digestive system in the colon and small intestine, and thereby get many diseases. They also get hypertension and heart trouble.

But if people are well trained under masters such as Swami Shriyukteshwarji, they can take a turn from all negative and dark activities to a life of light and divinity. So everyone should carefully guard each door of the body. Ordinarily there are nine doors: two eyes, two ears, two nostrils, one mouth, one anus, and one uro-genital passage. But every point in the body is also a door. One should know how to control and regulate all the doors of the body.

If people come to the doctors of spiritual life, the highly realized Kriya Yoga masters, they can learn the proper technique of self-control. With the help of the master, the teacher, good people, and good company, they will develop thorough control over their sense organs.

Previous verses in the Bhagavad Gita (5:13 and 8:12) also emphasize the importance of controlling the nine doors. The process of regulating, controlling, and channeling the energy of the nine doors is called *jyoti mudra*, or *navadwara-ruddha mudra*. It is a scientific technique for controlling the nine doors and cultivating the body land. By thorough control of the breath, one will touch the imperishable soul in the pituitary and the fontanel. The seeker will perceive divine illumination.

God has given these doors to man not for distraction or delusion, but for God perception and calmness. By practicing of the scientific technique of Kriya Yoga, one can perceive the divinity in each door of the body. Every sight will be divine. Every taste will give

God perception. Every talk will be the talk of God. Every work will be His worship. Every moment will give the taste of reality and truth. With utmost caution, calmness, and introverted senses, the light of knowledge will then shine in each door.

Verse 12

lobhaḥ pravṛttir ārambhaḥ
karmaṇām aśamaḥ spṛhā
rajasy etāni jāyante
vivṛddhe bharatarṣabha

Translation

Greed, activity, and the undertaking of actions, restlessness and desires—these are born when *rajas* is dominant, O best of the Bharata dynasty (Arjuna)!

Metaphorical Interpretation

In this verse, the Lord describes the qualities of rajasic people, their habits and endeavors.

Desire has no end. The satisfaction of one desire breeds another desire, and this is the cause of greed and extreme attachment. Temptation is the greatest enemy for every human being. This is God's desire. It is written in the Bhagavad Gita (15:2), *adhaś ca mūlāny anusamtatāni*: "Human beings tend to come down in the lower portion of the body, to get absorbed in money, sex, food, and restlessness." Money is extremely tempting; it is needed for many things. So is sex. However, sex prevails. Whatever their age, people are engrossed in it. Most people's desire and dispositions are always directed towards sex. They work hard and earn a living for a little sex enjoyment. They have many desires and temptation. One temptation comes, then another, and so on—in an unending chain. Temptation dooms them and keeps them far from truth. They are extremely attached. This attachment invariably increases their greediness and desire to do many things—making them restless.

Think of a man's stomach. It has a limited capacity. With a little simple and spiritual food, one can maintain one's life. But people want rich, rajasic food, which is neither good for their health, nor for peace. For a little sex satisfaction, people undertake many types of work; some even commit murder, become pickpockets, thieves, and spoil their lives. It is death to them.

Work, ambition, restlessness, passion, possessiveness, and so on are all signs of the rajasic quality. A rajasic nature causes constant dissatisfaction, fans the flame of temptation, and leads to a multitude of activity. During this time, the breath flows in the *pingala*, through the right nostril. A variety of ambitions, desires, and temptations causes man to roam from place to place, from country to country—but peace of mind eludes him. Peace of mind depends upon the rest of *prana*, the life force, which is externally manifested as breath. Being extremely restless and full of activity, a person faces death quickly.

Temptation can better be understood by using a fishing metaphor. The bait, which conceals a hook inside, tempts the fish. A big fish swallows the bait and with it, the deadly iron hook, which becomes embedded in its mouth. By means of a very thin thread, the fish is brought out of the water, which is death to the fish. So everyone should be extremely careful with temptation.

Verse 13

aprakāśo 'pravṛttiś ca
pramādo moha eva ca
tamasy etāni jāyante
vivṛddhe kurunandana

Translation

Darkness, inertia, negligence, and confusion, these arise O Arjuna (joy of the Kurus) when *tamas* (idleness) is dominant.

Metaphorical Interpretation

Here Arjuna is addressed as Kurunandana. (See the Bhagavad Gita 2:41) Man's life must be well regulated and thoroughly controlled. But man, engrossed in activity, is full of restlessness. Man does not know how to control his turbulent mind. If a person is not able to judge what is good and what is bad, it will mean death to him. Insects looking at the brilliant blazing fire think that it is beautiful and sweet, so they jump into the fire and die. Man should not be an insect ruled by instincts.

Many children do not have the desire to read. If their parents, relatives, and teachers do not take good care of them, they will certainly not have any success in life because they will not be properly educated and trained. They will remain uneducated and uncultured. Their whole life will be poor and miserable, and they will maintain their livelihood with the greatest difficulty.

If on the other hand the family members, parents, elderly people, and teachers take the utmost care of the children, their interest for study will increase.

Many young people at this growing and formative stage are addicted to drugs. They spend their life in sleep and idleness, which makes their life miserable. They should be very careful. They cannot judge whether something is right or wrong. They commit mistakes and as a result have trouble in their lives. They run after falsehood.

When the breath flows through the *ida* canal, people feel sloth and inertia, and develop a habit of neglect. People also get many types of diseases, due to their lack of desire for activity and study. They are full of delusions. As they do not perform their own duty, they suffer. Out of idleness, they even neglect to clean their body, their clothes, or even their mouth. Cleanliness is an essential part of divine life.

Always seeking confusion, dullness, and idleness, they suffer continuously. If they come to the touch of the realized master, follow his instructions, and lead their lives according to the teachings of the Gita, the Bible, or other spiritual books, they will change their lives. By regulating and channeling the breath, restlessness and idleness will disappear. They will be able to enjoy peace, bliss, and joy. They will be free from all idleness, sloth, and addictive, overpowering drugs. They will lead a real divine life.

Verses 14 and 15

yadā sattve pravṛddhe tu
pralayam yāti dehabhṛt
tado 'ttamavidām lokān
amalān pratipadyate

rajasi pralayam gatvā
karmasangiṣu jāyate
tathā pralīnas tamasi
mūḍhayoniṣu jāyate

Translation

When an embodied being enters the state of dissolution while under the dominance of *sattva*, he attains the pure world of those who know the highest.

He who goes to dissolution when *rajas* is predominant is born among those attached to actions. If he is dissolved when *tamas* prevails, he is born in the wombs of the deluded.

Metaphorical Interpretation

Three qualities are present in each human being:

1. *Sattva*: spiritual qualities of goodness and calmness
2. *Rajas*: material qualities of extreme activity and passion and calmness
3. *Tamas*: idle qualities of extreme sloth and inertia

These three qualities constantly fluctuate in their predominance. Sometimes one is very spiritual, calm, and quiet. At other times one is restless and active. Sometimes one is very idle, dull, and inactive.

Each human being also goes through ten stages in life. This is called *dasha dasha*:

1. *Infancy:* This is a stage of complete ignorance. The baby knows only the parents, only sucking the breast of the mother and sleeping on her lap in extreme helplessness. Up to the age of seven months, a baby is unable to distinguish or recognize people or things. Sensory discrimination is inactive. Everyone is a friend to the baby.
2. *From 7 months to 2 years:* The baby gains strength of the body and develops the senses. He can recognize objects and people, and can speak a little. The Oedipus complex develops around the age of two.
3. *From 2 to 6 years:* Children get busy with toys, balls, and balloons. They are attracted to colorful things. They spend their time mostly in play.
4. *From 6 to 12 years:* At this age the nature of friendship changes. These children love books and are eager to know more. They are extremely inquisitive.
5. *Teenage years:* This is the youthful stage, characterized by restlessness. The attraction for the opposite sex manifests. Teenagers are romantic, dreamy, and experiment with sex. They are learning, too.
6. *Twenties:* There is a desire for marriage, to have children, and to work hard to make every dream materialize.
7. *Adulthood:* More responsibilities, people are overburdened with the problems of life.
8. *Old age:* The passions increase, but the body does not cooperate.
9. *Extreme old age:* The senses become weak, but desires still dominate.
10. *Death*

In the Bhaja Govindam, Verse 7, Acharya Shankara said: "Boys are always busy with money, Youths are playing with male or female (the opposite sex), Old men are full of worries, thoughts, and apprehensions, But no one is after God!"

Changes in human life are natural. When one stage is completed, another begins, and so do the activities associated with that new stage. The death of one stage gives birth to the next. There is birth and death at every stage. Unless a stage dies, the next stage cannot be born. If a boy is spiritual, he becomes more spiritual when he grows into a young man.

Likewise, there is death and birth in every breath. Every exhalation is death and every inhalation is birth. If there is no further inhalation after exhalation, this is the final death. But usually the power of God inhales from the top immediately after the exhalation, thereby giving a new life. This is how human beings get new dispositions. The mood, propensity, or intellectual activity dominant at the time of exhalation is magnified with the following inhalation, thereby determining one's destiny.

Human beings are different from each other due to their destiny. Some are very calm and quiet, more spiritual; they are in the *sattva* state. They perceive death and rebirth in every exhalation and inhalation.

If in every exhalation (death) and every inhalation (birth), and according to their destiny, people busy themselves with worldly activities, money, and pleasure for the senses, but not with spirituality, this is the state of *rajas*. Although they change with every exhalation and inhalation, they do not get spiritual change very quickly because they like to remain in their old destiny and habits.

Those who always seek idleness, who do not learn well from infancy, will not be able to get a proper education as they advance in age. They mix with bad company and develop bad habits of addiction and intoxication. They live and grow in poverty. This is the *tamas* state. Throughout their life they are poor and far away from enlightenment. They keep all their bad habits throughout life, even in their old age, and are neither active in the material world nor in spirituality. They always remain silly, uncultured, and dishonored.

But people who have the desire to make progress on their spiritual path can change their life through self-transformation, by regulating their breath under the guidance of a realized master. Meditation techniques such as Kriya Yoga quicken human evolution, change the qualities of nature, and make a person truly spiritual.

Verse 16

karmaṇaḥ sukṛtasyā 'huḥ
sāttvikam nirmalam phalam
rajasas tu phalam duḥkham
ajñānam tamasaḥ phalam

Translation

It is said that the fruit of sattvic action is good and without impurity. But the fruit of rajasic action is pain, and the fruit of tamasic action is ignorance.

Metaphorical Interpretation

People with a spiritual destiny are always after God. They are pure and their activities are pure. They want more purity and truth. They search for God in the pituitary, inside the cerebral cortex—constantly feeling the moving sensation of the imperishable soul, going ever higher in the vacuum in the sky above the heavens, trying to open the door of the supreme almighty father, humbly requesting that He let them in, in other words, attain realization, *samadhi.*

These people feel the extreme calm. During meditation they have no sense of the world, no sense of the body, resulting in purity, perfection, joy, and bliss. They can reach *samadhi* during any stage. This is top-grade meditation.

Those who are extremely absorbed in activity and material prosperity spend money in irrelevant ways—for sex, or for a variety of rich and costly foods. The more they run after sensual pleasure, the more they have restlessness and dissatisfaction, because their ambition and desire increases. They are not after truth. Many also give money to the needy, educate the poor, provide help to people in distress, and give food to the hungry and medicine to the diseased. By doing this, the pain and dissatisfaction of rajasic people is somehow decreased. But they usually do it for their own aggrandizement and publicity.

Those who are idle lead a miserable life. They can neither serve their parents, nor can they take proper care of their children. They are obstinate, wild, and extremely rough. Many of them seek intoxication. They love to sleep for a long time. Their whole life is a life of poverty and suffering. They become more ignorant. They are neither after material success nor after God. Due to their foolishness, they experience innumerable troubles in their life.

Verse 17

sattvāt samjāyate jñānam
rajaso lobha eva ca
pramādamohau tamaso
bhavato 'jñānam eva ca

Translation

From *sattva*, knowledge is born. From *rajas*, desire (greed) is born. From *tamas*, doubt (negligence), delusion, and ignorance are born.

Metaphorical Interpretation

In this verse the Lord again highlights the three qualities of nature and their fruits and results.

By leading a life of consciousness, super-consciousness, and cosmic-consciousness, if one seeks the imperishable soul (*sa*), Who is constantly inhaling through the nostrils, Who is the cause of life and activity, one will attain the state of wisdom. Wisdom is the result of a strict spiritual and sattvic lifestyle. Wisdom cannot be achieved by intellectual pursuits, but by going to a state beyond the reach of the senses. Wisdom can be realized in the atom point. This is the state of *samadhi*. Through that power, one can maintain continuous God-consciousness. All day and all night, one will feel that He and I are one and always have been one; that He is in me and I am in Him; that He is all-pervading, in the sky, air, fire, water and earth, in the five sense organs, in the whole body, in the whole universe, in every breath, thought, word, and action. This is the divine state.

Rajasic people have extremely active lives. They are always busy in the material world, earning more to spend lavishly, mixing with an ever increasing number of people. They have endless desire, ambition, and greed; and this leads to a completely unbalanced, restless life, which can even result in many physical disabilities.

Tamasic people are idle, engrossed in matter; they do not want any education or culture. They are always sleepy, but at the end they repent. It is their madness. Having no consideration of consequences or discrimination between good and bad, they exist only in delusion. This is the result of ignorance. Ignorance breeds either idleness or the performance of a multitude of bad actions. Their troubles multiply due to the sloth and darkness of *tamas*.

By the practice of a scientific meditation technique like Kriya Yoga, one can overcome the impact of nature's different modes: *tamas, rajas,* and *sattva*. One can go to the state beyond the three qualities of nature and become free.

Verse 18

ūrdhvam gacchanti sattvasthā
madhye tiṣṭhanti rājasāḥ
jaghanyaguṇavṛttisthā
adho gacchanti tāmasāḥ

Translation

Those who abide in the quality of *sattva* rise upward, the rajasic remain in the middle, and the tamasic established in the lowest qualities go downward.

Metaphorical Interpretation

The human body can be divided into three parts—the upper, middle, and lower. The power of God is more manifest from the pituitary to the fontanel, inside the cerebral cortex. This is the upper part. Those who are spiritual always give love to the invisible supreme almighty father. In the Bhagavad Gita (15:1), it says that each human body is a tree. The root of the ordinary tree remains in the ground sustaining the whole trunk, branches, leaves, and roots. The roots support and maintain the tree. But the root of the body tree, which is the marvelous power of God, remains on the top. People talk, hear, smell, speak, taste, and touch from the top. People should perceive God by keeping their concentration on the top.

The seer, seeing, and the sight are one. Speech is not mere words, it is the talk of God. "Man shall not live by bread alone, but by every word that comes from the mouth of God." (Matthew 4:4). Speech comes from the fontanel. Those who are spiritual see Him in *ham* and *sa*. Each human being is *hamsa*. *Sa*, the formless one, abides in the *ham* body, compassionately detached, without Whom no one can work or even live. Every spiritual person should seek Him (*sa*) in this *ham* body. This is what it means to say that sattvic (spiritual) people go to the top. At the top there is illumination, calmness, and love.

Those who are in the mode of *rajas* are engrossed in thoughts, emotions, extreme activity, and restlessness. They remain in the heart center and food center. They are always chasing after temptations, attractions, attachments, multiple activities, and they are driven to earn money. Their material minds do not want to rise above, to the top.

The minds of those living in *tamas* are at the animal level. Like animals, they eat, drink, enjoy sexually, give birth to children, quarrel with each other. They are constantly busy in arguments and litigations. Their mind is in the lower centers—money, sex, food—and the lower propensities of life. They always have negative moods. They do not have any proper ambition. They are extremely engrossed in delusion, illusion, and error. They are lost and groping in the darkness of *maya*. Their minds always sink downward.

Verse 19

nā 'nyam guṇebhyaḥ kartāram
yadā draṣṭā 'nupaśyati
guṇebhyaś ca param vetti
madbhāvam so 'dhigacchati

Translation

When the seer perceives no doer other than the qualities and also knows that which is higher than the qualities, he attains My being.

Metaphorical Interpretation

There are three qualities in each human being:

1. Spirituality or calmness
2. Extreme activity
3. Idleness and inertia

Human beings associate with the company that corresponds to their innate qualities. All of their activities are guided by these qualities. Work and activity is caused by the living power of God abiding within. So those who have a spiritual nature always feel that "I am not doing any work. By my spiritual destiny and with the help of a spiritual teacher (who teaches the technique of going to the imperishable power of God), I perceive that I am just an instrument, and He is the operator. He is doing the work."

When the sun rises, people go to work. Similarly, people should undertake all activities while watching the almighty sun, the almighty father who created male and female, animals, insects, plants, trees, and creepers, and Who abides everywhere while remaining compassionately detached from everything. By perceiving the formless power of God, a true seeker gives love to the imperishable soul. Practicing like this with the guidance of the teacher gives spiritual seekers the experience that "I am not the doer—He allows me to do."

The teacher is the medium that makes students well educated, meaning spiritually realized. When students follow the teacher with sincerity and love, they quickly evolve spiritually. They will always be free from bad work. They will be in truth, free from all negatives, immorality, and hypocrisy. Sincere students always try to be free from the power of *tamo guna* (idleness and sloth), and *rajo guna* (extreme activity and restlessness). They try to be in *sattva guna* (spirituality), and even beyond that.

Those who are sincere search for God in every activity and get the power of the guru and God. They become highly realized, constantly perceiving oneness with the almighty father.

Verse 20

guṇān etān atītya trīn
dehī dehasamudbhavān
janmamṛtyujarāduḥkhair
vimukto 'mṛtam aśnute

Translation

When the embodied soul transcends the three qualities that have caused the body, it is free from birth, death, old age, and pain. Such a being attains immortality and is free from all sorrow, perceiving supreme bliss.

Metaphorical Interpretation

These three qualities, *sattva*, *rajas*, and *tamas* exist in every human body.

With the help of the guru or spiritual master, using the scientific meditation technique of Kriya Yoga, and by practice and implicit faith, one can feel the imperishable soul. It is the spiritual destiny of all people to realize Him constantly. If people seek Him in the infinite north (in the pituitary and the fontanel), breathing a short breath, watching Him during every breath, they will automatically be emancipated and in Godhood. They will be free from all the negatives of life and they may even forget all body sense.

As the drunkard who has drunk strong alcohol forgets everything and falls unconscious on the ground, or as worldly people forget the whole world during sleep, similarly realized people become free from everything—even from the cycle of birth and death. Exhalation is death and inhalation is birth. During this process of breathing the true seeker watches the marvelous power at the top. Breath-consciousness is God-consciousness. These people enjoy good health and are free from all disease. They forget their body sense and the sense of the world while meditating. They remain free. Like intoxicated people, they are free from their body consciousness and the worldly sense. They enjoy extreme divine peace, bliss, and joy. When there is no restlessness, no human stage, no sense of the body, they attain the state of wisdom: *samadhi.*

When one is beyond the play of the three qualities of nature, one is completely free from all the limitations of life, merged in God. This is the state of liberation.

Verse 21

arjuna uvāca
kair lingais trīn guṇān etān
atīto bhavati prabho
kimācāraḥ katham cai 'tāms
trīn guṇān ativartate

Translation

Arjuna asked:

What are the marks of he who has transcended these three qualities of nature, O Lord? What is his conduct? And how does he go beyond these three qualities?

Metaphorical Interpretation

In this verse, Arjuna addresses Shri Krishna as Prabhu, which means the manifested one. Krishna is unmanifest, and He is manifest. By perceiving His presence everywhere, one attains Godhood.

Here Arjuna asks the Lord three questions:

1. What are the signs of a person who has gone beyond the three qualities of nature?
2. What is his way of life?
3. How does he reach that state?

Arjuna is always seeking truth. When a person treads the path of truth, he wants to cross all the hurdles and obstacles of life. So when various thoughts and motivations arise depending on the qualities of his nature, the seeker of truth wants to go to the source, the cause of all these thoughts. He even wants to go beyond it. That is why he asks what are the indications of a Self-realized person, what is his disposition, and how does he manage to go beyond the triple qualities of nature to reach the almighty father?

Verse 22

śrībhagavān uvāca
prakāśam ca pravṛttim ca
moham eva ca pāṇḍava
na dveṣṭi sampravṛttāni
na nivṛttāni kāṅkṣati

Translation

The Lord answered:

O Pandava (manifest divine knowledge) Arjuna! He hates not light, activities nor delusion when they arise, and desires them not when they have ceased.

Metaphorical Interpretation

The indwelling Self answers the questions of the real seeker of truth—Arjuna.

One who seeks truth is beyond all the activities of nature. The *sattva* quality is light, *rajas* is activity and restlessness, and *tamas* is ignorance and delusion. These qualities create different tendencies in man. But one who is above the pituitary and even higher in the fontanel and beyond is not affected by any of these qualities. He is beyond the dualities of nature.

The sun rises in the sky, but it remains compassionately detached in the sense that when people work under the light of the sun, the sun is not affected by their activity. Similarly, by rising above the work of the different qualities of nature, one is not the least attracted or distracted by the work of these three qualities.

A person who is really free from the activities of nature is compassionately detached. He does not repent. He is free from sorrow, sufferings, unhappiness, and restlessness. He is free from delusion. This state is called *gunatita*—beyond the play of the different qualities of nature.

Verse 23

udāsīnavad āsīno
guṇair yo na vicālyate
guṇā vartanta ity eva
yo 'vatiṣṭhati ne 'ngate

Translation

He who is seated as one indifferent, undisturbed by the qualities, knowing that the *gunas* alone move among the *gunas*, he is established in identity with God and never falls from that state.

Metaphorical Interpretation

The three qualities affect all human activities and vice versa. The activities of the five sense organs bind people to the material world. Nature works through the three qualities, but one can remain compassionately detached like the sun. One who is not concerned with anything, who is not perturbed by the qualities of *maya* (delusion, illusion) is free from all the activities of nature.

Through the agency of the indwelling Self people do work and become attracted and attached to everything. But the Self remains detached. The electric current flowing through a red bulb produces a red light, and through a yellow bulb, a yellow light—but the electricity cannot be seen.

When the spiritual quality is dominant, one does spiritual work. God helps indirectly. Some work extremely hard at earning money but become so engrossed in this pursuit that they are not aware of God. God is helping them to work but remains detached like the sun. Many are idle and lazy.

Everyone works according to their predominant quality with the help of the indwelling Self, who remains detached.

He who practices a meditation technique like Kriya Yoga can remain compassionately detached. He is a witness, not affected by the qualities of nature. He is constantly united with God. He never comes down. He never forgets God. This is a state of perfect calmness.

Verse 24

samaduḥkhasukhaḥ svasthaḥ
samaloṣṭāśmakāñcanaḥ
tulyapriyāpriyo dhīras
tulyanindātmasamstutiḥ

Translation

Pain and pleasure are equal to him, for he dwells in the Self. A clod, a stone, and a piece of gold are of equal worth to him,

because he is established in wisdom. The pleasant and the unpleasant are alike to him, for he is steadfast. Blame and praise are the same to him.

Metaphorical Interpretation

The ordinary man is always affected by the dualities of *maya*: by pleasure and pain, loss and gain, sun and rain—by the play of nature through her qualities. But when a person practices Kriya Yoga meditation and proceeds on the path of spirituality and realization, his activities will be very divine. He will lead a life like Shri Lahiri Baba did—remaining in the family, doing office work, passing through all the trials and tribulations of life, but always remaining detached.

As the Isha Upanishad declares in mantra 2:

kurvann eveha karmaṇī jijīviṣec chatam samāḥ
evam tvayi nānyatheto 'sti na karma lipyate nare:

"If you work in this world according to this knowledge (that God is all-pervading), you attain immortality, constant salvation, and freedom from all bondage. You will have no alternative except perception of God."[2]

He who is equal in happiness and sorrow, who constantly remains absorbed in God, feels that "I am not the doer." To this person gold is not attractive, nor is a stone useless. A clod of soil, a stone, or a piece of gold are of equal value. Everything is of the earth and its modifications. Until a person achieves extreme God-realization, he cannot experience this state of equanimity.

He who is equal toward favorable and unfavorable persons, who remains free from the play of the five sense organs, who is beyond praise and blame, who is always feeling that God is more precious than anything else—he is above the three qualities of nature. He is free from illusion, delusion, attachment, and attraction. He is just like a baby who cannot appreciate either gold or stone. Neither are attractive to him. He loves the colorful balloon more than anything else.

The more a person meditates deeply and becomes like a baby, the more he becomes pure and divine. He is always in God. His concentration and awareness is always on the top of the body, in the fontanel, in the almighty father. He is free from the triple qualities of *maya*. Money is not money. Gold is not gold. He constantly feels the love of God in every situation.

Verse 25

mānāpamānayos tulyas
tulyo mitrāripakṣayoḥ
sarvārambhaparityāgī
guṇātītaḥ sa ucyate

Translation

To whom honor and dishonor are equal, who is the same to friend and foe, and who has renounced all initiative of action, he is said to be beyond the influence of the qualities of nature.

Metaphorical Interpretation

A truly spiritual person is not after praise or blame. If anybody speaks highly of him, he does not inflate himself like an empty balloon; he knows that he is an insignificant bug. Neither is he affected by malicious words aimed at him. He is not unhappy or angry if someone hates him. He feels the same in all circumstances, just like a baby. Enemy and friend are equal to him.

The spiritual person is always extremely calm and inwardly detached, constantly perceiving that his breath can stop at any time. He has given up all initiative in action—*sarvarambhaparityagi* (See the Bhagavad Gita 12:16). He has no ambition. He is free. He is pure. Anything that comes to us—good or bad, sweet or sour—is due to our destiny. A truly spiritual person neither accepts nor rejects it. He works at the office or at home like a machine—only for duty's sake, not out of personal ambition or attachment. His life is a life of thorough control and complete detachment like Shri Lahiri Baba.

He operates within the triple qualities, but is detached from them. He is free from everything. He is constantly absorbed in the almighty father.

Verse 26

mām ca yo 'vyabhicāreṇa
bhaktiyogena sevate
sa guṇān samatītyai 'tān
brahmabhūyāya kalpate

Translation

He who serves Me with the yoga of exclusive devotion, transcending these three qualities, is ready and eligible for absorption in Brahman.

Metaphorical Interpretation

Churning milk produces cream. Churning cream while applying heat yields butter oil or *ghee*. If one churns the mind, he will produce intellect. Churning the intellect by the process of meditation gives successively knowledge, consciousness, super-consciousness and cosmic-consciousness. Churning cosmic-consciousness and going to the extreme end of the human stage yields wisdom—meaning that one is constantly united with the almighty father. At this stage, one will know real love for God.

Sant Tulsidas said, *kāmi hi nāri payāri jimi:* "The passionate husband who loves his wife extremely wants to spend all his time with her." They want to drink the love of passion, constantly feeling physical oneness. Thus, does a true lover of God want constant association with Him, the supreme almighty Lord, the real lover.

In India, the wife serves the husband and works ceaselessly for his welfare. She does not keep her mind on any other person. She loves her husband with unwavering faith. Similarly, the husband gives love to his wife and serves her to his utmost capacity, even at the cost of his life. He does not keep his mind on any other woman. Likewise, the person coming to receive the touch of the guru, the realized master, bows to him and serves him with love. He humbly asks the guru to bestow upon him the science of soul culture, and he serves the guru wholeheartedly. The guru also tries his utmost to teach and to serve the disciple. This is the example of a real divine relationship without any selfish motive.

The disciple also meditates according to the instructions of the master and tries to find God in every breath and in every action. He then gradually progresses from super-consciousness to cosmic-consciousness and eventually enters into the state of wisdom. Wisdom means oneness with the almighty father—expressed as the unflinching love for God and guru.

This disciple becomes free from all three *gunas* (qualities of nature). He forgets his little self and attains *samadhi*. He perceives *ayamātma brahma*: "Myself and the almighty father are one, and *aham brahmāsm:* "I am Brahma," meaning that the whole human stage is really God's stage, as exemplified in the guru. Then he feels *sattva khalvidam brahma*: "Wherever I turn my eyes, I feel the power of the almighty Lord," and finally *prajñānam brahma*: "I feel intensely that the marvelous power of God is in me." This individual will attain the pulseless, formless stage, with no sense of the body and no sense of the world. His field is ready for real peace, bliss, joy, and all-around development.

Verse 27

brahmaṇo hi pratiṣṭhā 'ham
amṛtasyā 'vyayasya ca
śaśvatasya ca dharmasya
sukhasyai 'kāntikasya ca

Translation

For I am the abode of Brahman, the immortal and the imperishable, of eternal spiritual life and of absolute bliss.

Metaphorical Interpretation

If one meditates by practicing the different stages of the higher Kriyas, gradually proceeding on the path of spiritual experience, he feels constant oneness with the indwelling almighty father. He perceives that the marvelous power of God is within. In this stage, he tastes immortality and gets emancipation. When he is immortal, he is free from the fear of death.

"I cannot die, I am peace. I am the vacuum. The almighty father is all around me. He envelops me. I am inside Him." Through this perception, one remains constantly alert in every breath. He has no negatives in him. He does not know the meaning of death.

So the devotee feels constant joy, divine peace. He cannot talk. He cannot move. He cannot sing. He does not know whether he is hungry or not. He cannot feel the motion of urine or stool. He is like an infant, free from fear or shame. He does not know whether he has clothes on or not. He remains in constant bliss. He does not even know of his own existence. His entire body becomes the real peaceful abode of God. He knows essentially that only God permeates the entire universe. This is the ultimate goal—the state beyond creation where there are neither positive nor negative qualities. This is the state of reality, realization and Godhood. Shri Chaitanya Mahaprabhu attained that stage while living in his Ashram Gambhira (Puri). He was completely and constantly absorbed in God-consciousness.

---

[1] Sage Valmiki, the author of the epic Ramayana, was a criminal who changed his life after he encountered Narada, whom he accepted as his spiritual guide.

[2] For a detailed explanation, please see the metaphorical explanation of the Isha Upanishad by the author.

Summary

External nature and body nature are the playground of the divine. The nature of the body is the field, and the soul, God, the formless one, plays constantly in it. In twenty-seven verses, Chapter 14 of the Bhagavad Gita explains the secret behind the creation of everything and every being, every thought and every activity. In the previous chapter the Lord, Krishna—the divine master—discussed *prakriti*, *purusha,* and their divine play. Nature is the womb of God from which everything emerges. Each human body is the womb, from which all thoughts, words and activities come. Chapter 14 elaborates on the ideas presented in Chapter 2 and Chapter 13.

God is the supreme father and nature is the mother. The whole creation is the union of God the father and mother nature. Although the father and the mother are the physical cause of the birth of the baby, the real cause is the breath. Without breath the father cannot give his seed, and the mother cannot conceive. Similarly in each human body, there is a body nature and a father nature. The union of the two allows all creative work to proceed.

This body nature has three qualities: *sattva, rajas,* and *tamas*. *Sattva* is the symbol of calmness, peace, and light. *Rajas* is extreme activity, and *tamas* is the quality of idleness, sloth, and inertia.

These three qualities of nature are born of nature and God, yet they seem to cover the indwelling Self and turn human life into bondage. People attached to the sattvic quality think "I am learned. I am happy. I am peaceful." This is spiritual ego.

Rajasic people are engrossed in extreme activity. Due to passion and the thirst for achievement, material comfort, and pleasure, people work day and night to fulfill these dreams. And they suffer.

The *tamas* quality brings idleness, sloth, inertia, laziness, and procrastination.

These three qualities of nature are present in each human body in different proportions. One quality is always predominant and suppresses the other two. One quality overpowers man, then another, in endless cycles. When the sattvic quality is predominant, there is light, divine illumination in all the doors of the body. When the rajasic quality becomes powerful, man is extremely restless. When the tamasic quality is the strongest, he is forgetful, and his memory and activities decrease. The fruit of sattvic nature is happiness; rajasic nature brings suffering; tamasic nature yields ignorance. At the end of this chapter, the Lord explains how to go beyond the qualities of nature. A person who meditates and follows the instructions of the scriptures and the master can lead a life of extreme detachment and equanimity and can be free from all the dualities of nature: pleasure and pain, praise and blame, gain and loss, heat and cold, and on and on.

Leading a life of truth and spirituality, with implicit faith, love, and loyalty for the guru and God, remaining free from all the negative qualities of life, one will continuously feel the presence of God in every breath, in every moment, in all activities, and during every disposition. To perceive the formless, one must go to the formless state. To realize God means to be God. It is possible only through deep meditation and by avoiding all the negative qualities of life as well as the attraction and play of the triple qualities of nature.

This chapter concludes with the Lord's description of the divine perception of immortality—the imperishable quality of the eternal cosmic law and absolute bliss.

Chapter 15

Purushottama yoga

The Yoga of the Supreme Self

Introduction

Chapter 15 is the most beautiful chapter in the Bhagavad Gita. Among the eighteen chapters of the Bhagavad Gita, Chapters 13 and 15 are the shortest, consisting of only twenty verses each. Chapter 15, *Purushottama Yoga*, "The Yoga of the Supreme Self," is also one of the few chapters that contains only discourses from the Lord—there are no questions from Arjuna. This small chapter is memorized and chanted by monks in many ashrams in India before meals.

This chapter explains the concept of the trinity, a central concept in many religions. In Christianity, it is expounded as God the father, Jesus the son, and the holy spirit. In this chapter, it is termed *kshara* (perishable), *akshara* (imperishable), and *purushottama* (supreme Self).

Every human being is a living scripture. Every human being is a Bhagavad Gita. Everyone is potentially divine. Realization of one's divinity through soul culture is the birthright of each person. It is not dependent upon age, sex, race, language, nationality, or religion—it is the foremost duty of every person to do his best to realize his own Self. Alexander Pope wrote in his *Psalm of Life*:

Know thy Self, presume not God to scan.
The proper study of mankind is man.

Every human being has three bodies: gross, astral, and causal. These three bodies altogether are the temple of the almighty God. The imperishable soul and the supreme almighty father exists in the perishable body, and one must perceive, conceive, and realize this truth.

Each human body is like a tree. A tree absorbs energy and transforms it into beautiful leaves, buds, flowers, and fruits. A tree is known by its fruit. The fruit of each human body bears witness to the quality of one's life. In the Bible (Matthew 7:17–20), there is a metaphor about the body tree, which is easy to understand. "A good tree cannot bear bad fruit and a bad tree cannot bear good fruit. Every tree that does not bear good fruit is cut down and thrown into the fire. Thus, by their fruit, you will recognize them."

Chapter 15 of the Bhagavad Gita begins with the description of the body tree and its beautiful features. Both good and bad qualities exist in each human body tree, but every rational individual should go to the root of all activity, the breath, give up all the bad qualities, and ultimately proceed to the supreme almighty father. God is all-pervading, but the presence of God is more manifest in man, which is why man is called the supreme creation. Man, by his rationality, can achieve the state of divinity and God-realization.

To realize God, one need not go to a cave, the mountains, or the jungle, but must go into the cave of the cranium where it is possible to realize one's own Self. It is at hand.

Verse 1

śrībhagavan uvāca
ūrdhvamūlam adhaḥśākham
aśvattham prāhur avyayam
chandāmsi yasya parṇāni
yas tam veda sa vedavit

Translation

The Lord said:

They speak of the eternal *ashvatthama* (peepul tree) as having its roots above and branches below. Its leaves are the Vedic hymns and he who knows this is the knower of the Vedas.

Metaphorical Interpretation

The blessed Lord is describing in detail the abode of God and the kingdom of heaven. He begins His divine gospel by declaring, "They speak of the eternal *ashvattham* tree." In this instance, "They speak" means as narrated in the mantras of the Vedas and the Upanishads. The same phrase is found in the Katha Upanishad (2:3:1) and is presented in virtually the same words, *ūrdhvamūlo 'vākṣākha eṣo 'śvatthaḥ sanātanaḥ:* "This is the tree called the eternal *ashvatthah* (peepul tree) whose roots are above and branches below."

This is a simple but beautiful allegory. The root of the tree remains in the ground. Most people can't see the root; only the trunk, branches, and leaves. Similarly, each human body is a tree, but its root remains hidden on the top, inside the head, in the cerebral cortex.

If you take a small tree and hold it upside down with the roots above and the limbs below, you will see that there are numerous branches going downward and many branches pointing upward. Each human body is like this tree, which is the Tree of Life and the Tree of Knowledge (See Genesis, Chapters 2 and 3, and Revelations, Chapters 2 and 22, and their metaphorical interpretation in *The Torah, the*

Bible and Kriya Yoga by Swami Prajñanananda). Each human being has many good propensities going upward, the sattvic qualities; many types of extroverted tendencies, extreme engagements, which are the rajasic qualities in the middle; and a lot of downward-pulling qualities, which are tamasic (See the Bhagavad Gita 14:18).

The Sanskrit word for the peepul tree, *ashvattha*, is made of three parts: *a* plus *shva* plus *ttha*. *A* means "not", *shva* means "until tomorrow," and *ttha* means "to exist." The complete meaning of *ashvattha* is therefore "it will not last until tomorrow." This tree of life, *ashvattha,* is only temporary. Although man knows full well that his body is constantly decaying, he nonetheless remains completely absorbed in activity, not in God. This body tree lives only for a few years–a short period of time.

From the neck to the pituitary in the human body tree there are many branches and leaves representing the divine qualities, the good and moral attributes, which lead human beings towards God. Below the neck are the demonic qualities. In the heart center there is an extreme desire to always make more money and to engage in many types of work. Although people know that they may die at any moment, they do not seek God or Self-realization. They have extreme ambition in the heart center. Although overburdening the heart may cause heart failure, many run from east to west and from west to east trying to earn enormous wealth by relying on lies, falsehood, and hypocrisy, by cherishing crookedness and by misbehaving with many people while behaving nicely with others for their own selfish gain. They continuously find trouble—day and night—and are constantly preoccupied with doing business. Being extremely restless, their mind flows down toward rich foods, money, and sex. If they suffer a loss, they experience extreme restlessness and unhappiness and cannot sleep at night. They live a life of corruption and lies. The more money they earn, the more unfair means they use to spend it. They drink alcohol. When they cannot sleep due to anxiety and tension, they take tranquilizers. This strain and stress may result in heart trouble. These people do not know that the almighty father abides in the body temple. They do not know that breath is their life and that by controlling and regulating their breath, they can change their life.

The leaves are the beauty of the tree. A tree without leaves is not at all beautiful. The leaves of the body tree are unlimited and as a consequence, human beings utter many types of speech: talk of money, sex, food, emotions, sweetness, kindness, lovingness, cruelty, dishonesty, and hypocrisy, as well as talk of religion, the scriptures, and spirituality. In total, good and bad talk. "Talk" in Sanskrit is usually given as *vak,* but in reality it is *avankvak*, which means "the talk of the formless." When people stop talking, they can hear the inaudible talk of God. This is the metaphorical explanation of the leaves of the body tree. A *vedavid* is a person who thoroughly knows the body tree, knows essentially what is real.

Words about God, Krishna, Rama, Kali, Moses, Jesus, Buddha, Mohammed, Zoroaster, and so forth are all good. But God cannot be perceived by speech. One must search for Him not with the mouth, but in the pituitary, in the fontanel, and even above the fontanel. The Kena Upanishad 1:5 says, "That which speech cannot reveal, but Who reveals the speech, know that alone to be God, not what people worship here." One must feel that man's speech is God's speech. A dead man cannot talk.

In the Bhagavad Gita 2:50 it says, *yogaḥ karmasu kauśalam*: "Skill in action is the real spiritual technique that will lead the people from the lower centers to the top of the body." The human body can be compared to a seven story building. First, one must come up from the first floor to the sixth floor, to the soul center (inside the cave of the cranium near the pituitary), and then one must go above to the seventh floor—to the fontanel, where the formless life of God abides in the cerebral cortex. One can even go above this to the infinite, to the abode of the almighty father.

The downward-flowing propensities in each human life are the branches that grow away from the root—they are extroverted, restless, and destructive. Most people busy themselves in the lower centers, not in the neck or above, up to the root of the body tree, which is the real life in the body.

The lower part of the body tree starts from the navel down. The navel center is the food center. Food is the marvelous power of God. The fire within digests the food. This food is transformed into energy. In ordinary people, that energy goes downward. Energy has a tendency to flow downward. If one throws something out of the window, even a small, extremely light piece of paper, it will not go up, but down. Food is the principal thing for the existence, maintenance, and functioning of the human body. People who take the spiritual food described in the Bhagavad Gita (6:17 and 17:8), as well as in the Upanishads and Smritis, will get all-around development. It is said, *jīrnam annam prasamsriyat*: "The food that can be easily digested is the real food."

Further down is the sex center. Sex prevails and dominates human life. Babyhood and childhood are very brief. When the youthful stage comes, God gives the sex drive to human males and females. It is so attractive and alluring that sexual passion dominates them from the teenage years to old age. From this, people develop extreme bondage. When a dog is chained, it cannot go hither and thither. Similarly, conjugal life is an extremely strong chain linking together husband, wife, and children, giving them constant delusion, illusion, and error. This bond is so powerful that they are not willing to break it.

The lowest center is the center of material activities and possession of wealth.

The two highest centers from the pituitary to the fontanel are the roots where the invisible power abides. If people seek Him there in every breath and every activity by learning and practicing the beautiful technique of Kriya Yoga, then they will be *vedavid*, the real knower, the person of knowledge. Work *(kri)* is worship *(ya)*. They can remain in the material world while simultaneously feeling that their real support and strength is from the power of the breath, the power of God. If they truly practice the scientific technique of Kriya Yoga, they will all be *vedajña purusha*, highly realized people. So the Lord says, *yastam veda sa vedavit*: "If one really knows all the propensities of the body tree, one is truly spiritual and educated."

Verse 2

adhaś co 'rdhvam prasṛtās tasya śākhā
guṇapravṛddhā viṣayapravālāḥ

adhaś ca mūlāny anusamtatāni
karmānubandhīni manuṣyaloke

Translation

Its branches spread below and above, nourished by the qualities (of nature), with the objects of the senses as the sprouts (shoots), and below its roots stretch forth in all directions, binding the soul according to the actions performed in the human body.

Metaphorical Interpretation

A tree has some branches that extend down and other branches that stretch upward. Similarly, man has many dispositions, thoughts, and activities that bring his mind down due to his rajasic and tamasic qualities, while some divine qualities move him upward.

The downward activities done when one is overpowered by a desire for money, sex, or food, or by arrogance and ego, are associated with the lower four centers in the spine. In addition, people with tamasic qualities do not work and are always slothful by nature; poor and idle, they are not after God. On the other hand, the upward branches are the divine qualities that enable one to search for the almighty Lord by practicing Kriya Yoga. This kind of person's destiny will be good. By the virtue of good company and the guidance of the realized master, spiritual people search for the almighty father in the fontanel while breathing the slow, rhythmic breath.

What are the roots of the tree? Some roots are very deep: inside the brain, there are numerous specialized nerves called neurons that spread like roots in the soul. These nerves spread from the pituitary to the fontanel. There are also many shallow roots, bringing one down into worldliness.

In the human body, there are twelve pairs of cranial nerves; eleven pairs are inside the head and one pair (the vagus nerves) reaches down the chest and trunk, constantly giving delusion, illusion, and error. This is *maya*. Because of *maya*, people cannot raise themselves above worldly concerns.

The general tendency of all human beings is to make money, enjoy sexually, eat delicious rich foods, drink wine—in other words to remain in the lower four centers from the coccyx to the dorsal (heart) center. The cervical (fifth) center is the vacuum center. People with love for religion and philosophy remain there.

People who are truly spiritual search for the almighty father through the breath, the formless air. The body undergoes constant change, but the indwelling soul does not. Those who are sincerely seeking the realization of the indwelling Self seek the company of the realized master and learn the spiritual way directly through personal contact. Beyond the pituitary is nothing but the inner sky experienced in meditation. The imperishable power of God abides here, in the fontanel. This is the formless state. Through deep meditation, everyone must rise to this formless state to become completely realized.

The three types of activity come from the three *gunas*, the qualities of nature (see chapters 13 and 14). The body nature is *kshetra*-the land that must be cultivated and maintained to reap the desired harvest. But the general tendency of man is to go downward. For this reason the Lord says, *adhay ca mulany anusamtatani:* "Good company makes one good, and bad company makes one bad." A man inherits the nature of his company. Spiritual people should always seek good company.

This chapter is entitled *Purushottam Yoga*, "The Yoga of the Supreme Self," which is about contact with the supreme almighty Father. How does one go to the supreme almighty Father? How does one become liberated and taste immortality? How does one find real peace, bliss, and joy? This verse and the previous one clearly explain it. Those who search in the imperishable soul will surely realize the formless almighty father. If one can go to the root that is inside the brain and spreads up to the fontanel, then one will realize the formless state, which brings unity with the almighty father. (See also the explanation in the Bhagavad Gita 11:34.)

The almighty father is everywhere. His formless presence fills the whole universe. This formless quality pervades the entire human system, from the toes to the top. There is an invisible formless counterpart for each body part, which will be explained in the following verses.

A deep desire to know one's Self and sincere meditation are essential for the disciple to receive the teaching and the direct touch of the divine master, who will help and lead the disciple to perceive the formless God. But one must follow the master faithfully and practice the technique with love. The technique is essential. Every work is based on a specific technique, and Kriya Yoga is the essence of all techniques.

Since the formless God is hiding in the whole body, one must search for His presence in every body part—in the fingers, nails, everywhere. These are the parts of the body tree. Those who practice Kriya Yoga can feel in two minutes the presence of the formless God in every body part.

In the Vedic *karma kanda* (also called the *puja viddhi*), which contains vedic ritualistic ceremonies, this process is also known as *anganyasa* and *karanyasa,* which means to perceive God in the five body parts and five fingers. Next is *matrikanyasa*, which means to experience calm and God perception throughout the whole body. Then there is *pranayama*—breath control. Those who busy themselves with formal worship only chant mantras. But by practicing the Kriya Yoga technique, one can feel the sensation of God moving in one hundred body parts immediately or within a short period of time. One can feel and realize the formless God in the whole body.

One must perceive the ceaseless vibration of God, the divine sensation, as long as one's breathing continues. God is not only in the body, He is everywhere. He was before creation. He is in creation. He will be after creation. He can also remain without creation. One cannot see God, touch or drench God, because He is everywhere and formless. But one can realize Him through practice.

This human body is extremely temporary and may not exist in the next moment. That is why it is called an *ashvattha* tree. The root of the tree is the almighty father, whose presence is more readily perceived inside the brain, in the fontanel. One can feel this presence by fixing one's attention in the fontanel and experiencing Him with a slow and feeble breath. One can hear the *aum* sound constantly and in a variety of ways.

Verse 3

na rūpam asye 'ha tatho 'palabhyate
nā 'nto na cā 'dir na ca sampratiṣṭhā
aśvattham enam suvirūḍhamūlam
asangaśastreṇa dṛḍhena chittvā

Translation

Its real form is not perceptible here in the world, not its end, nor its beginning, nor its existence. Cut down this deeply rooted peepul tree with the strong ax of detachment.

Metaphorical Interpretation

One must change one's life. One must cut off all the bad qualities—evils, debauchery, immorality, and so forth—which grow quickly in the shade of bad company. If one can remove, avoid, and be free from all the negatives of human life by practicing the scientific technique of Kriya Yoga, human evolution will be quick. Kriya Yoga is the stepping stone of all religions and the essence of all spiritual practices.

The lower centers are full of *maya*, attraction to the material world through the illusory force of nature. In order to rise up from the lower centers to the upper centers, one must practice the technique with the help of the realized master. Just as the professor in medical college teaches anatomy to the students by performing dissections while the students follow these teachings with extreme concentration to become qualified doctors, similarly, if the student and the spiritual master live together and practice the scientific technique of Kriya Yoga, the student will become educated and will achieve extreme calm. He will gradually come up from the lower centers to the top, to the root.

To become a successful doctor, one must read and practice diligently. Likewise, to be successful in meditation, one must go to the deep root at the top in the fontanel—then one will get to the *samadhi* stage. As a doctor is always a doctor, similarly, a realized person is always realized. He will always feel the *kshetrajña* in the *kshetra*—the imperishable soul in the perishable body. He will always be grateful, constantly praising, "O Lord! You are the creator of everything. You are the ancient Father. You are the support of the whole universe. You are the knower and the knowable."

The realized person can constantly feel that the creator and the creation are one, and that the seer, the seen, and the sight are one.

Verse 4

tataḥ padam tat parimārgitavyam
yasmin gatā na nivartanti bhūyaḥ
tam eva cā 'dyam puruṣam prapadye
yataḥ pravṛttiḥ prasṛtā purāṇī

Translation

Thereafter the goal must be sought from which, having gone, no one returns. "Thou art the primeval being. I take refuge in Thee from Whom the flow of this beginningless creation has proceeded."

Metaphorical Interpretation

In this verse, the word *pada* means the feet of God, the goal of life. Everyone must seek the divine goal in the fontanel. The play of *maya*—nature and the world—is below the pituitary and down to the toes. It is very attractive. Most people are engrossed in it, forgetting the real purpose of human life. But if a seeker sincerely tries to reach the goal of Self-realization with the guidance and help of the realized master, he will certainly succeed. Once he has reached that stage, he is free. Realization brings a complete change in life.

When realization is attained, one constantly feels love for God and extreme gratitude toward Him. He perceives that all *pravritti* (attractive delusive desires) flow from the top. A realized person is in a state of *nivritti* (extreme detachment). This state comes through deep meditation.

Once butter is separated from the milk, it won't mix with milk again. It floats on the top. Such is the condition of the realized person. He never again gets entangled in the play of *maya*—the world drama.

Verse 5

nirmānamohā jitasangadoṣā
adhyātmanityā vinivṛttakāmāḥ
dvandvair vimuktāḥ sukhaduḥkhasamjñair
gacchanty amūḍhāḥ padam avyayam tat

Translation

Those wise men who are free from arrogance and delusion, who have overcome the evils of attachment, who are in eternal union with God with desires and ambitions extinguished, who are released from the dualities such as pleasure and pain, these undeluded people reach that supreme immortal state.

Metaphorical Interpretation

A realized person such as Lahiri Baba has no vanity, delusion, or illusion. He is free from all negative qualities, always seeing that the soul is the sole doer in the body. He is not doing anything. He watches the living presence of God in every breath. In every step of life, he feels that "I and He are one. I must lead this type of spiritual life. Constantly I am in touch with the almighty father, the imperishable soul in me."

Humility is the stepping stone to spiritual life. Through humility one can avoid bad company, one is not tempted by the objects of the senses, one is free from all carnal as well as material desires, and one always feels that the marvelous power of God is constantly manifested in the body.

This person is also free from all the dualities of life. Duality is death, unity is immortality. Duality is delusion, unity is liberation. The dualities of pleasure and pain, loss and gain, heat and cold, winter and summer, friend and foe disappear from his life. The realized person constantly feels the presence of God in everything and in every being.

Through inner experience of the Lord, one remains detached during every activity. God gives the appetite. God is in the food. God is in the taste of all food. God digests the food. The spiritual person feels that "I am not eating. I am giving oblation to the fire in the navel center."

The spiritual devotee constantly feels that he is beyond everything in the material world. He is neither foolish nor ignorant. He is always compassionately detached. He isn't happy because of pleasurable things. He isn't heartbroken in painful circumstances. He sees God in everything, by which he gets constant liberation. He is always in soul-consciousness and cosmic-consciousness. He finally attains complete realization through *samadhi*, which means he is in touch with the almighty father—merged and engrossed in God-consciousness. When he returns to the material world, he has a life of complete freedom.

Verse 6

na tad bhāsayate sūryo
na śaśānko na pāvakaḥ
yad gatvā na nivartante
tad dhāma paramam mama

Translation

Neither the sun, nor the moon, nor even fire can illumine that supreme Self-effulgent state, attaining to which they never return to this world. That is my supreme abode.

Metaphorical Interpretation

The sun, the moon, and fire give illumination through the direction of the supreme almighty father. In the Katha Upanishad (2:2:15), Mundaka Upanishad (2:2:10), and Shvetashvatara Upanishad (6:14), it says that neither sun, moon, nor star can give any illumination, nor can even lightning or the spirit of electricity. How can a little light or fire illumine Him, who is the source of all light? "O supreme one, You illumine everything. I bow to Thee."

The *Gayatri mantra* describes seven *lokas* and seven suns, but the supreme being, the almighty father gives light to everything.

The seven fires inside the body are as follows:

Money center: *dakshina agni* (fire remaining in the south)

Sex center: *grihapati agni* (fire used in household activities)

Food center: *vaishvanara agni* (fire of digestion)

Heart center: *ahavaniya agni* (fire of welcoming good and evil)

Neck center: *samidbhavanama agni* (fire of religious ceremony)

Pituitary: *brahma agni* (fire of the soul)

Fontanel: *vishvarupa mahana agni* (fire of the cosmic form)

Under the direction of the supreme almighty sun fire (*bhargah*, as written in the *Gayatri*), all these fires, the seven suns, radiate light in this body universe. But God is the real sun. He directs the sun and the moon to shine. He is the illuminator of everything.

Through deep meditation with love and devotion, one can go to that *bhargo*—the almighty father, the real sun of the universe. A man of meditation is merged in Him, is one with Him, and is realized. Having attained the state of total God-consciousness, he does not come back to the ordinary level of body and world consciousness. Although he remains in the body form, he realizes the formless father within, all the time.

Verse 7

mamai 'vā 'mśo jīvaloke
jīvabhūtaḥ sanātanaḥ

manaḥṣaṣṭhānī 'ndriyāṇi
prakṛtisthāni karṣati

Translation

The eternal soul in this body, in the world of living, is a fragment of Myself. It is that alone which draws to itself the five senses and the sixth sense, the mind, that exist in material nature (*prakriti*).

Metaphorical Interpretation

That imperishable supreme almighty father, having created the whole universe, abides everywhere. God is infinite and formless. His invisible counterpart remains in each living body.

God and his fragmentary existence can better be understood by the simple example of the ocean and waves. The ocean is vast, formless, and beyond the sphere of vision. In this formless ocean, waves arise. These waves are born in the ocean, live in the ocean, and merge in the ocean. Waves exist only in the ocean. The ocean is the total and the wave is an insignificant fragment. Ocean and waves are one. This is the relationship between God, the supreme Self, and man, the individual self.

God made man and woman in His image and breathed the breath of His life into their nostrils. That is why man became a living being. All human beings are God in the form of a human being.

The Lord is saying, "I abide in the whole universe. I am also the abode of the whole universe. I am in the body universe. I have given five senses to every person so they can perceive. I have also given them a sixth sense—the mind. I have created the triple qualities of nature (*maya*). I remain in *kshetra* and *kshetrajña* as *ham* (the twenty-four gross elements) and *sa* (the imperishable soul). Through *ham*, the gross body, and *maya*, people are attached in the material world, engrossed in delusion, illusion, and error. They are also bound by the *triguna* (the triple qualities of nature): *sattva* (spiritual nature), *rajas* (material activities), and *tamas* (slothful state). But just as a piece of paper is paper, and a piece of gold is gold, similarly, I am one. I am the multiplicity and I am the unity. People see and enjoy multiplicity through the veiling power of *maya*, and people see unity in everything through meditation and inner detachment. They receive My divine power everywhere and thereby attain liberation."

Verse 8

śarīram yad avāpnoti
yac cā 'py utkrāmatī 'śvaraḥ
gṛhītvai 'tāni samyāti
vāyur gandhān ivā 'śayāt

Translation

When the Lord acquires a body and when He departs from it, He takes them along (the senses and mind) like the blowing wind carries scents from their sources.

Metaphorical Interpretation

God has created human beings out of His own desire. The human body is so beautiful and divine because He, the formless power, the king of kings, has entered into each human body and breathes from above from their birth. This is how each person is alive and active in the material world.

Man must know that the imperishable power of God remains in each human body. He must try for God-realization. To do that, he must receive the touch of the realized master, who will try to make him realized. Man is born only for God-realization. God has granted this human life span for a short period only. One day, He will not breathe through a person's nostrils and this person will have to immediately leave all his property and prosperity, ego and vanity, wealth and family, friends and relatives—

everything. He came alone and he must go alone. The moment the almighty father thinks "I will not stay in this body, because this person is extrovert, not searching for Me. He is restless and reckless. He does not follow the golden rule so that he will live one hundred years. He is committing many mistakes." This is death to any human being.

Man must be extremely cautious, careful, and attentive. All the work that he performs determines his destiny. A spiritual person with sattvic qualities does noble things. All the effects of spiritual activities are stored in the midbrain, constantly accumulating in him. These qualities go with the soul when it leaves the body. Those who are after rajasic qualities *(rajo guna)* are striving for wealth, activity, and attachment. All these qualities, which they have earned, will follow them. Those who are slothful, who do nothing, who do not cultivate the body land, will inherit all their tamasic qualities after death.

The flower blooms with a beautiful fragrance. The air carries the scent of the flower, although air itself has no odor. Similarly the destiny, the accumulated balance sheet of all activities performed, whether mental or physical, that are created and earned in the material world will accompany the soul when it leaves the body and goes to the astral plane. So man must be very careful when he does any work. Negative work will create a negative result in his destiny.

Man is his own friend and his own foe. Everyone creates his own destiny. By sincere effort, one can become realized and be free from his destiny.

Verse 9

śrotram cakṣuḥ sparśanam ca
rasanam ghrāṇam eva ca
adhiṣṭhāya manaś cā 'yam
viṣayān upasevate

Translation

Presiding over hearing, sight, touch, taste, and smell, as well as the mind, He (the fragment of the Lord, the indwelling Self) enjoys the objects of senses.

Metaphorical Interpretation

The body is inert and mortal. If God does not breathe, then the body cannot do anything. The ear cannot hear. The tongue cannot talk or taste. The eyes cannot see. The nose cannot smell. People enjoy this material world through the imperishable soul, with the help of the mind.

The sun rising in the sky makes the whole world active and energetic, yet it remains detached from all these activities. Similarly *dehi*, the indwelling Self, gives enjoyment to everybody with the help of the sense organs and the mind.

Without the human body, which is made of twenty-four gross elements, man cannot enjoy anything. And without the presence of the indwelling Self, this body is inert and dead. Each human being is *hamsa*—*ham* (body) and *sa* (soul) together. It appears that the imperishable, indwelling soul is doing the enjoying, but when people look at a flower and enjoy it with the help of the sun, this enjoyment does not go to the sun. The sun remains detached. For example, a father gives his son in marriage. The son lives a marital life with his wife, but the father does not enjoy their conjugal bliss. The father is compassionately detached. This is a very common picture in India.

The imperishable soul abides in the body from infancy, causing man to be alive and constantly engrossed in delusion, illusion, and error. The soul in the body makes every enjoyment possible, but the soul is compassionately detached.

Verse 10

utkrāmantam sthitam vā 'pi
bhuñjānam vā guṇānvitam

vimūḍhā nā 'nupaśyanti
paśyanti jñānacakṣuṣaḥ

Translation

When the soul departs, remains, or enjoys (the sense objects) while accompanied by the qualities (of nature), the deluded (ignorant, fools) do not perceive Him. Those with the eye of knowledge are able to realize Him.

Metaphorical Interpretation

Here the Lord classifies all people into two categories: *vimudhah,* the extremely dull, foolish, deluded, ignorant, materialistic, and spiritually blind, and *jñanachakshushah,* those with the eye of knowledge, who have the third eye open. *Muddha* is a dull state of mind explained in detail in the Yoga Sutras of Patañjali.

Man is alive, but in delusion. He is not after God. He is after money, sex, food, ego, vanity, and so forth. But nothing belongs to him. Man comes to the world empty-handed and must leave it empty-handed. When man enjoys money, sex, food, or friends, he is not seeking God. It is foolishness. These are the symptoms of delusion. Man is engrossed in the five sense organs and material world, constantly ignoring and forgetting God.

Man must learn to perceive God in every part of the body and everywhere in creation. Man must search for God in everything. Man's body is the temple of God. This is real education. But man is foolish; he does not search.

Man is not a mere animal. Man is rational and potentially divine. Those who are truly intelligent search for Him with the help of the realized master. Practicing a scientific meditation technique such as Kriya Yoga opens their third eye. They become absorbed in knowledge, consciousness, soul-consciousness, and cosmic-consciousness. They proceed forward, always trying their utmost. With their spiritual eye they see, perceive, and realize the Self while remaining in the body and enjoying the objects of the senses (the five objects of sight, sound, smell, touch, and taste). They are even conscious when the soul leaves the body. This is their conscious *samadhi*, which is possible through the good company of the realized master, constant meditation, and a God-conscious life.

Verse 11

yatanto yoginaś cai 'nam
paśyanty ātmany avasthitam
yatanto 'py akṛtātmāno
nai 'nam paśyanty acetasaḥ

Translation

The yogis who strive (meditate) will realize that He is established in the Self. But the ignorant, whose inner being is not disciplined, strives, but cannot perceive Him.

Metaphorical Interpretation

Those who try sincerely—by thoroughly controlling their inner life and avoiding evil and bad qualities—proceed upward. They do not deviate from their goal because of the so-called attraction of the lower centers. They follow the master sincerely and practice the technique with implicit faith, love, and loyalty, and they become free from all restlessness. By controlling their breath, they get thorough control of their inner Self. They go beyond body consciousness. They get realization.

Those who read many books think they are intelligent. But by reading books one cannot achieve spiritual progress, just as chanting the name of food will not fill one's stomach, and uttering the name of a medicine will not free one from disease. Similarly one must seek to get the touch of the master to see the indwelling Self.

Two types of people are striving. One is a yogi and the other is a fool. The yogi follows the path directed by the master and his third eye opens—the eye of knowledge, reality, and truth. This is the third eye. Once someone enjoys the state of bliss, he seeks sincerely to be merged in divinity.

Only through the practice of the Kriya Yoga technique under the guidance of a realized master, and by leading a self-disciplined life, can one develop an intuitive force: the power to perceive distant objects and even things that will happen in the future. But the sincere seeker is not attracted by these yogic powers (*siddhis*). He is free and is only after the truth.

The yogi who is constantly striving awakes, arises, and strives constantly and sincerely until he is realized. He even acquires the power of divine perception (See Chapter 11). He can perceive the all-pervading father covering the whole world. His life becomes the divine life. If he can proceed sincerely and steadily; he can attain *samadhi*.

Verse 12

yad ādityagatam tejo
jagad bhāsayate 'khilam
yac candramasi yac cā 'gnau
tat tejo viddhi māmakam

Translation

The brilliance that resides in the sun and illumines the entire universe, that which shines in the moon as well as in the fire, know that to be Mine.

Metaphorical Interpretation

The sun shines in the sky. People can see the entire world by the power of the sun. At night there is no sun, but there is the moon. The light of the moon is nothing but the reflection of the light of the sun. Millions of stars cannot be equal to the light of the moon. A flame and the brilliance of fire also manifests the same principle of the sun.

God is the light of lights. Open your eyes. See the whole world. It is nothing but the manifestation of the glory of God. The life force existing in every part of the body is the light and power of God. Every spiritual seeker must try to see the unmanifest in every manifest object. The almighty sun gives light to the solar sun and moon.

Think of this entire cosmos so systematically and beautifully arranged. It is nothing but the order of that almighty sun—*bhargo deva*.

One who perceives God's power, loves God's glory, and depends on the almighty father is empowered by Him to perceive everything as God. This state is attainable by deep meditation and love.

Verse 13

gām āviśya ca bhūtāni
dhārayāmy aham ojasā
puṣṇāmi cau 'ṣadhīḥ sarvāḥ
somo bhūtvā rasātmakaḥ

Translation

And permeating the earth, it is I who supports all creatures by My vital power, and having become the nectarine (watering) moon, I nourish all plants.

Metaphorical Interpretation

The Lord is saying, "I am formless. It was my desire that I would be many. I thought—I shall be many with My power. I created the whole universe. I made all creatures including human beings—males, females, and even eunuchs." (See the Taittiriya Upanishad 2:6:1)

"When I started creation, I first created the sky, then air, fire, water, and earth, then fungus, insects, plants, animals, and rational human beings. Having created everything, my power permeated everywhere—I am the all-pervading supreme Self.

"Externally, I am inside the herbs, plants, and trees where there is the marvelous power of medicine. By the power of the moonlight, I give My power to the herbs as medicine.

"I am the life of all human beings. I hide in them. I breathe in them, day and night. I work through their body. Without My presence, they cannot work. I am the creator. I am in the creation. I and My creation are one. Without Me, there is nothing. There are many people who are not after Me. They do not know Who I am. Still, they are my children."

In this verse two things are indicated in a very subtle way. By referring to earth and water, God is speaking of the bottom center and the second center. All the activities of the lower centers are activating by the power of God.

Verse 14

aham vaiśvānaro bhūtvā
prāṇinām deham āśritaḥ
prāṇāpānasamāyuktaḥ
pacāmy annam caturvidham

Translation

Having become the vaishvanara fire in the body of all living beings, I live. Going outward (*prana*) and inward (*apana*), I digest the four kinds of food.

Metaphorical Interpretation

The Lord said, "I remain in each human being as seven fires in the seven centers." (See Verse 6). God is now discussing the navel (third) center.

"I am the digestive fire, *vaishvanara,* that abides in the navel center and is active in the stomach. I give people appetite. They eat and take the food with great relish. I give them more respiration to digest the food. Just after eating, the breath is changed. They get deep respiration. More blood is coming to the stomach, which provides more pressure in the stomach to digest the food. Through this, they get strength and vitality. Through food they can seek the ultimate Truth, which is real education, or debauchery—good or bad. If they take spiritual food (See the Bhagavad Gita 6:17 and 17:8), they will experience reality.

"There are four types of food: *charvya*, the food to be chewed; *chosya*, the food to be sucked; *lehya*, the food to be licked; and *peya*, the food to be drunk. People consume these four types of food, but I digest all these foods."

The digestive power diminishes with advancing age. If people take a lot of rich food like butter, cheese, cream, and even fish and flesh, it affects their liver badly. They get liver trouble. They cannot live long. Many die early because of incorrect food habits and a defective lifestyle. In the Isha Upanishad (*mantra* 2), it says, *jijīviṣecchatam samāḥ*: "Your lifespan is to be a hundred years." A long and healthy life directed toward God-realization is successful living.

"I am the *vaishvanara* fire that digests the food well by regulating the *prana* (exhalation) and *apana* (inhalation). Through the circulation of blood, I give good health to all living beings. If this fire is weak, the body becomes weak. *Prana* and *apana* is the oblation in the soul fire. The four types of food are the oblation in the *vaishvanara* fire. Food is the fuel. Excess fuel makes the fire weak as does insufficient fuel. Fuel must be moderate to keep the fire glowing and active."

So if all human beings are very careful about moderation in food and their lifestyle, they can live longer and even achieve God-realization.

Verse 15

sarvasya cā 'ham hṛdi samniviṣṭo
mattaḥ smṛtir jñānam apohanam ca
vedaiś ca sarvair aham eva vedyo
vedāntakṛd vedavid eva cā 'ham

Translation

I have entered into the hearts of all beings. From Me came memory, knowledge as well as their loss. I alone am that which is to be known in all the Vedas. I am the author of the Vedanta and the knower of the Vedas.

Metaphorical Interpretation

The Lord has discussed earth, water, and fire—the lower three centers. Now the Lord discusses the heart center.

The Lord is saying, "I abide in every human being as *kshetrajña*, the knower of the body field, but I remain extremely detached. Although I play and manifest in all centers, the heart is the place where people harbor more delusion, illusion, and error through attachment and infatuation.

"I work in the brain as well as in the heart. I am in the memory of each person. Everything remaining as memory in the storehouse of the brain is My power. Because of matter and this memory, and with the help of the five sense organs, people get absorbed in the material world. Those who do not remain in the soul center and come down to the heart center easily become victims of their emotions, temptation and so on. In the heart, people experience delusion, illusion, and error. But, if they practice meditation and come up to the fontanel, all their negative memory can be diminished.

"I am the source of knowledge." Knowledge is of two types: *apara vidya* (material knowledge) and *para vidya* (spiritual knowledge). Most people have material skills, but they are not after the truth or reality. In the Mundaka Upanishad (1:1:4), one reads that it is necessary to be very efficient in both *para* and *apara vidya*. But people with material knowledge are ignorant of God and live in a state of extroversion. When, due to extremely extroverted and restless activity, they lose their memory of the indwelling Self, they cannot understand and realize God.

There are four Vedas (Rik, Yajur, Sama, and Atharva). These holy scriptures teach the essence of spiritual life. The Vedas are the most ancient scriptures in the world. The Vedas come from the root word *vid,* which means "to know," in the sense of knowing the indwelling Self, knowing the all-pervading Brahman. The four great sentences of the Vedas—"Thou art that"; "I am Brahman"; "Wisdom is Brahman"; and "Everything is Brahman"—describe the topmost, cosmic-conscious state in human beings. People with spiritual knowledge experience God's presence. All this is described in the Vedas. To know the Lord, people should take the help, assistance, and guidance of a realized master. The Lord is in the body of the realized masters. With God's help, people can know the Vedas and Brahman.

"The Vedas are My breath. People should realize this. They are born only for God-realization. If they have the deepest desire, they can know Me in a moment's time. I will help them to be free from *maya.* One who knows Me constantly feels that I am in Him and he in Me."

Vedanta does not only mean the numerous books that teach about God-realization; the real meaning of the word *vedanta* comes from *veda,* knowledge and *anta,* end, namely the end of knowledge is wisdom. This is the state where nothing more remains to be known. "I am the author of the Vedanta" means "I am the absolute truth. I am the knower of the Vedas." One who knows the indwelling Self becomes all-knowing.

Verse 16

dvāv imau puruṣau loke
kṣaraś cā 'kṣara eva ca
kṣaraḥ sarvāṇi bhūtāni
kūṭastho 'kṣara ucyate

Translation

There are two *purushas* in this world, the perishable and the imperishable. All beings are perishable, but kutastha (the unchanging) is called the imperishable.

Metaphorical Interpretation

In this world, there is the perishable and the imperishable. Whatever is visible is perishable. Behind all these perishable objects, things, and beings is the imperishable power of God.

This also applies to every human being. The ten stages of human being are discussed in detail in Chapter 14: the child is born; babyhood lasts for some time, but with the passage of time, the baby stage disappears followed by childhood with its extreme attachment to the parents; then comes the teenage youthful stage, and so on. All the stages come in their turn and are characterized by different activities and dispositions. These ten stages of change from birth to death in each human body are called *kshara sharira.* This is *ham* or *kshetra* or the perishable body stage. The gross body of every human being is perishable.

But in each human being is also *akshara sharira,* the imperishable one. This imperishable counterpart remains inside the perishable body. This imperishable being is called *sa* or *kshetrajña*—the one who is the director, conductor, evolver, and protector of the body. This imperishable being, called *kutastha,* is the principal component of human life. *Kuthastha* is a place about three inches deep from the midpoint of the two eyebrows. The imperishable soul abides there. By the divine company of the realized master, people can fix their attention in the *kutastha* and perceive the marvelous divine power there.

Without this imperishable being (*sa*), the perishable (*ham*) body is dead. The *ham* body is the gross body of man, also called the body nature. It is the cause of delusion, illusion, and error.

The material world enters every human being through the five sense organs. Man is more deluded due to the company of people. There are three types of company, according to the three qualities of people: spiritual company (sattvic), materialistic company (rajasic), leading to extreme activities, and idle and evil company (tamasic). The qualities existing in every person become more prominent according to the company he keeps. Their destiny motivates them to seek it.

God is always giving pleasure and pain, happiness and unhappiness in turns. Due to poverty, unhappiness, death in the family, and so forth, people become heartbroken and are in great distress. Those who commit extremely grave misdeeds also have much unpleasantness. But if these people come to the good company of the realized master, they can change their lives.

For soul perception, one first needs extreme desire for inner transformation, and second, one must find good company in order to be transformed from dishonesty to honesty, from darkness to light, from falsehood to truth, from impurity to purity, and from mortality to immortality.

Verse 17

uttamaḥ puruṣas tv anyaḥ
paramātme 'ty udāhṛtaḥ
yo lokatrayam āviśya
bibharty avyaya īśvaraḥ

Translation

But the supreme person, who is still other than these, is also called the supreme Self who, entering into the three worlds as the eternal Lord, supports them.

Metaphorical Interpretation

In the previous verse, the Lord explained in detail the *kshara* (the perishable) and the *akshara* (the imperishable in the pituitary) in each human body. Apart from these two, there is another being who is called *purushottam*, the highest spirit, the supreme almighty father, the cause of everything.

This *kshara* (perishable), *akshara* (imperishable), and *purushottama* (the supreme almighty father) are symbolically represented by three letters. The supreme almighty father is "A"; the imperishable *akshara brahma* is "U"; the perishable gross body is "M." These three taken together are AUM.

If a person can meditate very deeply like Arjuna, who saw the all-pervading form of Shri Krishna (see the Bhagavad Gita, Chapter 11), we will experience real love for God and can progress spiritually. Every human being should try to be like Arjuna, fit for soul culture and Self-realization. Arjuna is trying sincerely to be free from all negatives. He is constantly fighting with all the evil propensities of life. Although the triple qualities of *maya* (nature) are in every human being, generating delusion, illusion, and error, a person with ardent desire for God-realization can overcome *maya* with the holy company of the realized master and the scientific practice of the extremely effective meditation technique of Kriya Yoga.

Through regular deep meditation, one can easily experience the supreme almighty father as formless. He is all-pervading, omnipresent, omniscient, and omnipotent. He is in the whole universe, He abides everywhere, but His presence is manifested more in human beings. He is the invisible counterpart of every body part and even beyond that. Although He is everywhere, He remains compassionately detached.

The more the devotee meditates and practices higher Kriya, the more he can constantly remain in the state of cosmic-consciousness. This is the stage of wisdom. *Prajñanam brahma*: "Wisdom is God." Wisdom cannot be perceived by the five sense organs. It can only be realized by going to the atom, in the fontanel. In the Upanishads it says, *Brahmavid brahmaiva bhavati*: "When a devotee enters into this state, he becomes free, detached from the body sense, merged in the almighty father."

Verse 18

yasmāt kṣaram atīto 'ham
akṣarād api co 'ttamaḥ
ato 'smi loke vede ca
prathitaḥ puruṣottamaḥ

Translation

Since I am beyond the perishable and even superior to the imperishable, therefore I am known as Purushottama, the supreme person in the world as well as in the Vedas.

Metaphorical Interpretation

In this world, people are always engrossed in the perishable form (*kshara sharira, kshetra*). They are excessively body-conscious; extremely attached to the body and the material world. If, by the practice of deep meditation, they can go to the imperishable (*sa*) state, then they can proceed from delusion to dis-illusion.

If one practices and proceeds further using the *neti, neti* discrimination technique ("not this, not this"), he can go to the *purushottama* state. The more one practices Kriya Yoga and meditates very deeply, the more one can see the *purusha* inside. *Purusha* comes from *puryam shete iti*: "The one who is resting in the house." Each human body is a house with nine doors. In this house, the imperishable *akshara purusha* is resting constantly. He is the real body in this gross body. He has no form. He is formless. But wherever one touches the body, from top to bottom, this touch sensation is possible because of *purusha*, the indwelling Self. This *purusha–sa* is the life principle in the body, constantly breathing through the nostrils. By the practice of Kriya Yoga, one can constantly feel the presence of the soul, *sa,* and can be free from all evil, wrongs, debauchery, immorality, anger, and pride. People can perceive constant purity, righteousness, and truth.

The more one goes to the top, to His presence in the sixth center, in between the two eyebrows, the more that devotee will be free from all the play of *maya*. By the practice of higher Kriya, one will go beyond the restlessness of *prana*. He will be still. In the Bible (Psalm 46:10), it says, "Be still and know that I am God." In the opening invocation of the Prashna Upanishad it is written, *sthirair angais tuṣṭuvāmsas tanūbhiḥ*: "By making every part of the body still, calm, and quiet, one will be free from the mind." When one is still, one can gradually go up—above the pituitary—to get divine joy, peace, and bliss. Then one can proceed farther in the fontanel, where "A," the supreme almighty father, resides.

Gradually, one will attain the wisdom stage, which is beyond *kshara*, the perishable, and also beyond the imperishable, *akshara*. This is to merge in the absolute, the supreme being. The wisdom stage is the best stage of life, where the supreme almighty father dwells. This is the egoless, formless state, the state of extreme detachment. This is the stage of revelation, the pulseless and the breathless state through which one can know that the creator who has created the whole universe is one with the Self. This state of complete union, oneness with the supreme almighty father, is called *purushottam*. In this state, life is truly fulfilled. This is real education.

To reach this state, one has to overcome the obstacles arising out of the triple qualities of *maya* that exist in every human body as *sattva*, *rajas*, and *tamas*. Because of the veiling power of *maya* and its three qualities, many people are completely absorbed in the material world and are not seeking God. Although they are rational, they are in darkness. Their life from top to bottom is that of animals, always after food, sex, money, quarrels, ego, and arrogance. They do not perceive that their body, life, and all activities are the combination of three things: A, U, and M.

The supreme almighty father in the fontanel is "A," the formless one, the causeless cause of everything. Although He is in the whole universe and more manifest in the body universe, He is beyond everything—changeless, the supreme Lord, the highest Self.

Through deep meditation, when one goes to the astral plane, causal plane, and even beyond, one will gradually achieve the stage of knowledge, consciousness, super-consciousness, and cosmic-consciousness, the "U" stage. This is the *sa* body. Each human being should know his own Self. It is his birthright.

This gross body is constantly undergoing change, but the imperishable form does not change. As the sun shines and makes the whole world active, similarly the soul in the body makes the whole body active through breath. This is how the gross body works. This is "M." Breath is the life of man. This breath is inhaled and exhaled by *sa*, from the pituitary (*kutastha*). But no one knows how long the breath will continue in the body, how long one will remain in the world. This body is *ashvattha* —"not to stay until tomorrow." By the help of the three bodies, gross, astral, and causal, one can remain compassionately detached from all evils, wrongs, and immorality, watching the soul sun. One can hear the "A" plus the "U" sound constantly while meditating, even day and night, which will give calm and peace.

When one is working in the material world, one can see that "U" and "M" are activated in the body by the power of "A." Those who are truly spiritual know "A," the supreme almighty father, *purushottam*, the formless one, in every breath, in every moment.

The Lord, being the king of kings, having created male and female, inhales from the day of their birth. To be breath-conscious is to be God-conscious. By the help of the realized master and through the practice of higher Kriya, one can realize the formless almighty father and can achieve the *samadhi* stage in this very life. This is the time to earn God. Do not think that it is too late, just try now. As one touches the bare electric wire, one immediately feels the electric current in the whole body; similarly by the practice of Kriya Yoga, one will perceive His living presence constantly, day and night, which will bring the state of *purushottam.*

Verse 19

yo mām evam asammūḍho
jānāti puruṣottamam
sa sarvavid bhajati mām
sarvabhāvena bhārata

Translation

O Bharata (Arjuna)! He who, thus undeluded, knows Me as the supreme person, knows all and worships Me constantly with his whole being.

Metaphorical Interpretation

Here the Lord addresses Arjuna as *bha-rata*, which means one who is completely engrossed in cosmic-consciousness, in the wisdom state, in illumination.

Those who have the deepest desire to be free from the delusive force of nature must come to the touch of the realized master and follow him. By practicing the technique, they can touch the imperishable soul who is the indwelling Self, who abides constantly in the body and remains compassionately detached.

In each human body, there are three bodies:

1. The perishable body, which changes from infancy. Through every activity in the perishable body (*ham*), one can know the imperishable soul (*sa*).
2. The imperishable soul is the *akshara purusha*—the knowledge body, which knows everything.
3. *Purushottam*—the supreme almighty father, who is beyond the perishable and the imperishable, better than the two. He abides in the whole universe. He is the all-in-all in the universe, constantly in the perishable as well as in the imperishable body. He is the invisible counterpart in each human being. The person who knows Him with scrutiny, without any doubt, and who seeks Him calmly will realize Him in every breath.

If anyone practices higher Kriya and realizes Him, he will be all-knowing and loved by all people as was Shri Lahiri Baba. He will remain in the material world but will perceive the imperishable soul through every activity. He will perceive the activities of A, U, and M. He who watches Him in every breath will be constantly alert and will get Godhood and the *samadhi* state.

One who perceives God in every breath, in every activity, in every thought will worship Him through love. His whole life is meditation. His work will be worship, *kri* and *ya*—constant perception of God.

Verse 20

iti guhyatamam śāstram
idam uktam mayā 'nagha
etad buddhvā buddhimān syāt
kṛtakṛtyaś ca bhārata

Translation

O blameless, sinless Arjuna! Thus, this most secret doctrine has been taught by Me. By grasping it in essence, a man becomes wise and his mission in life is accomplished.

Metaphorical Interpretation

Lord Krishna, the master incarnate, the supreme Self, is telling Arjuna:

"O Arjuna! You are free from sin. You are spotless. You have constant desire for God-realization. From the very beginning you have constantly asked Me about spiritual progress and God-realization, the stage one can attain after death. You are always questioning Me. You are a true seeker (*jijnasu*). You truly want to be free from sin, worldly activity, anxiety, and evil—for that reason, I call you 'Bharata.' You are constantly busy in super-consciousness and cosmic-consciousness. Your real complexion is white. (In deep meditation, one perceives the entire cosmos covered with milk-white light.) So I told you in detail about life."

What is human life? Who really exists in this body house with nine doors? The soul, *sa,* is the indwelling spirit, remaining compassionately detached. The imperishable soul is the life of each person. But Who is above the imperishable soul? He is *purushottam.*

Purushottam is made of two words: *uttama* and *purusha. Uttama* means the supreme, the highest, the best. *Purusha* means the one who remains in the kingdom. *Uttama purusha* or *purushottam* is the supreme Self, the highest spirit, the supreme almighty father, the super power of life. He is formless. He covers the whole universe. He is the king of kings. He is beyond conception and perception.

Unless people have a special destiny, until they get real guidance from their infancy and have the deepest desire, they cannot realize *purushottam*. This is the most secret doctrine. It is very difficult to reach this stage. Until man gets the stage of wisdom, he cannot know the supreme almighty father. Wisdom cannot be perceived by the five sense organs, nor by magic or hallucination, nor by imagination or speculation.

Those who practice the Kriya technique and follow the master sincerely and faithfully can go to that stage, as did Vivasvan, as mentioned in the Bhagavad Gita 4:1.

"O Arjuna! you are my dearest disciple. You are advanced and divine. That is why I taught you this secret doctrine of God perception. If you practice it deeply, then you will achieve the formless stage. You will be free from everything. You will never have any body sense or world sense. You will be completely merged in Me and gradually you will feel that I am the life of all living beings, including inferior creatures such as animals, insects, birds, even the grass and plants. I am even in the five gross elements—earth, water, fire, air, and sky. As fire makes everything fire, fire is the symbol of extreme purity. Fire purifies everything. I am the supreme fire conducting the sun, the moon, and the fire to illumine. I am the cosmic life, the supreme life, the conductor of all life. You can perceive it. I am the invisible counterpart of all the visible universe."

If you realize this, you will be the wisest of the wise. You will be completely divine.

Summary

The Mundaka Upanishad (3:1:1), one of the most important Upanishads, declares, *dvā suparṇā sayujā sakhāyā samānam vṛkṣam pariṣasvajāte...*: "There are two birds living in a tree, embracing each other." This tree is the tree of the body with the roots above and the trunk spreading downward. This is the gross body. This body is perishable. Inside the structure of the perishable body, two birds are living, one is the soul (*akshara*) and the other is the supreme Self (*purushottam*). These two birds are also called *jivatma* and *paramatma*. This verse is the foundation of this chapter.

In Chapter 14, the Lord described the play of *maya* with its three qualities and how their restlessness affects the life of each person. But those who want to go to the state of perfection must go beyond the triple qualities of nature.

Each chapter of the Bhagavad Gita is the continuation of the previous one. Each chapter is another step that takes us beyond the previous one. To go to the state of perfection, *nishanga* (complete cessation of all activities, the pulseless, breathless stage), one must use the weapon of *asanga* (detachment), as described in Verse 3.

Detachment comes through discrimination. Discrimination is the quality of differentiation between good and bad. In a tree, some branches go up and others go down; similarly in each human being, there are good and bad qualities, a mixture of opposites—rice and stone. With the power of differentiation (discrimination), one will attain detachment (*asanga*). For this detachment and discrimination, one needs the constant company of the wise—the realized master, the holy scriptures—these are a person's good company, his *satsanga*.

If one develops from animality to rationality and then from

rationality to divinity, one will proceed quickly on the path of perfection.

In this chapter, one of the great declarations of the Lord is *mamaivamsa jiva*: "The individual self is part and parcel of the supreme Self." There is no difference between the two. This is unity of the Self in the multiplicity of creation. One who constantly perceives this unity attains liberation.

Man is guided by destiny. Destiny is nothing but the aggregate balance sheet of past activities. Man is not slave to his fate or destiny. He is the maker as well as the breaker of his own destiny. Man, by his sincere effort, can change all the negative effects of past actions and can overcome all the trials and tribulations of human life. To do this, he must use his God-given potential for rationality and divinity. Each rational individual should try to go to the cause of creation, to the root, the seed, and even to the state before creation.

Spirituality is not the words of the scriptures or the analysis of intellectuals, rather, it is the inner experience and realization of true seekers under the constant guidance of a realized master. God is the cause of everything. He is the source of all energy, not only in people, but also in all the stars, planets, sun and moon, plants and creepers, birds and animals, however insignificant they may be.

"I am the fire, the supreme fire present everywhere as the source of life. I am the omniscient Lord present in the cave of the cranium in each person. I am the cause of illusion and enlightenment, darkness and light. One who follows Me attains liberation. One who forgets me roams and gropes in darkness, losing the way." This is the declaration of the Lord Himself.

Revelation is realization. God reveals His glory to His devotee. In this chapter, God reveals His glory as the supreme almighty father, who maintains the entire universe.

God is the knower and the knowable; God is also declaring indirectly that He is always near the seeker in the form of the realized master (See the Bhagavad Gita 15:15). "I am the knowable as written in the Vedas. I reveal the meaning of the scriptures (*vedanta*). I am the author of all the scriptures." Also, "I am the way. I am the goal and I am the truth."

"I am the imperishable body. I am the imperishable soul. I am also beyond the perishable and the imperishable. I am the supreme almighty father, known as *purushottama*." Each person, as a soul, is *purusha*. But each *purusha* must achieve the state of *purushottama* by deep meditation and by faithfully following the realized master. Then the disciple will constantly feel that he is in the form, and beyond the form, form and formless together.

"I am popularly known as *purushottama*. I am in each human form. I am in the universal form. But I am the formless form. I incarnate. I am beyond incarnation. "

This doctrine of *purushottama* is extremely secret. This is a *guhya tama* scripture. *Guhya* is the hidden secret in each human being.

If one practices a meditation technique such as Kriya Yoga that is taught by a realized master and directly follows all the instructions as taught in the Bhagavad Gita, then one will lead a blameless life. One will be truly wise and will be realized. One will attain constant God awareness and liberation.

Chapter 16

Daivāsura sampad vibhāga yoga

The Yoga of Discrimination Between Divine and Demonic Qualities

Introduction

This chapter, like the previous one, contains only the sermons of the supreme divine master, Lord Krishna, delivered to his loving disciple Arjuna. The Lord's teachings are encapsulated in twenty-four beautiful verses.

Ancient Indian mythology is full of stories of battles between gods and demons. On the surface they seem to belong to the realm of fantasy, but these narrations depict the battle of life in this world. The gods and demons are not outside, they are in each human being. Human life is a battlefield—an external struggle and an inner war. The inner battle is a fight against all the weaknesses of being human. Good and bad qualities, virtue and vice, positive and negative dispositions, and divine and devilish natures exist in every human being. Everyone knows their own weaknesses.

The scriptures reveal the moral standard that one should aspire to achieve for Self enfoldment by eradicating the negative propensities of life. Perfected beings such as Buddha, Rama, Moses, Jesus, and so on had to struggle to overcome all the weaknesses of human life. Satan came to Jesus. Mara came to Buddha. Kama came to sages and saints. But they could stand undisturbed, in divine glory. The spiritual journey is a voyage through struggle. One who is well equipped with divine qualities and who has acquired the blessings of the master can win this battle.

The yogic scriptures state, *abhayam sattvasamśuddhir*—through the purification of mind one gets freedom from fear.

Verses 1 to 3

śrībhagavān uvāca
jñānayogavyavasthitiḥ
dānam damaś ca yajñaś ca
svādyāyas tapa ārjavam

ahimsā satyam akrodhas
tyāgaḥ śāntir apaiśunam
dayā bhūteṣv aloluptvam
mārdavam hrīr acāpalam

tejaḥ kṣamā dhṛtiḥ śaucam
adroho nā 'timānitā
bhavanti sampadam daivīm
abhijātasya bhārata

Translation

The Lord said:

Absolute fearlessness, perfect purity of mind, constant fixation in the yoga of meditation for the sake of self-realization, charity, self-restraint, sacrifice, study and teaching of the scriptures, austerity, rectitude (uprightness),

Non-violence, truth, absence of anger, renunciation, serenity, calmness, aversion to fault-finding, compassion to all beings, freedom from desire, gentleness, modesty, and absence of fickleness,

Vigor, forgiveness, fortitude, purity, freedom from malice, freedom from pride. These are the marks of he who is born with divine qualities, godly gifts.

Metaphorical Interpretation

In Chapter 13, the Lord described twenty spiritual qualities while He was explaining knowledge. Here, the Lord lists twenty-six spiritual qualities, which are the gifts of God. Man is potentially divine.

Every person has a multitude of divine qualities but these remain dormant. Through the practice of living a divine life, these are manifested. God-realization is possible when one has good and spiritual habits. Every spiritual seeker must try to cultivate these divine qualities in daily life. The divine qualities are the parameter and indicator of one's own spiritual nature.

1. *Abhayam*: fearlessness

Fear is the greatest enemy of spiritual life. Man is afraid of losing happiness and is afraid to face death. These two basic fears make man sorrowful. When a person realizes that he is the soul, the birthless, deathless, living power of God, and that the soul is the source of everything and is always free, then all fears disappear. The Upanishads exhort us, *ma bhai*: "never be deluded by fear."

When the realized master is approached by a person who is full of fear, the master gives him courage and consolation. He says, "My son, when one enjoys too much sexually, there is a constant fear of disease. When a person is wealthy, he fears theft or tax. When a person has physical beauty, he fears old age. When a person has physical strength, he fears rivals. A learned man is afraid of those more learned. A body-conscious person always fears death, but a God-realized person, endowed with the power of discrimination, detachment, and dispassion, is fearless. My child, be fearless."

When the disciple follows a master and proceeds toward the goal of realization, he gradually becomes fearless. A spiritual seeker is a brave warrior in the battle of life.

2. *Sattvasamshuddis:* extremely spiritual (perfect purity of mind).

Every person is a mixture of the three qualities of nature: the sattvic (spiritual), rajasic (material), and tamasic (slothful). These three qualities rule every center up to and including the pituitary. When one is truly pure, one's mind, thoughts, and actions are pure.

3. *Jñanayogavyavasthitis:* well established in yoga and knowledge

Yoga is the perception of constant unity with the almighty father during every breath and every activity. To attain this state, one must practice meditation and lead a spiritual life under the direct guidance of a realized master; one must not deviate from this practice from temptation of trivial pleasure. One who is always perceiving *hamsa*, (i.e. *ham* is the perishable body and *sa* is the indwelling imperishable soul) will reach *jñana* (knowledge), and will remain in illumination, not in ignorance or darkness.

4. *Danam*: charity

Helping needy people is an important virtue. A river flows for others. A tree gives fruit, flowers, shelter, and even its whole body for others. Self-sacrifice is charity, but charity must be free from ego. To give food to the poor, medicine to people afflicted with disease, money to poor students for their education, and courage to the heartbroken, and above all to spend money, time, and energy for noble and spiritual work, is charity. Charity purifies bad deeds. Charity broadens the mind. It is the real ornament of the hand. A charitable man's hand is always higher than the receiver's hand. Giving a spiritual education to others is the best form of charity.

5. *Damas:* self-restraint

According to the classical spiritual texts, self-control means control of the sense organs. Man has ten sense organs—five organs of action (*karmendriyas*): speech, feet, hands, rectum, and genitals, and five instruments of perception (*jñanendriyas*): eyes, ears, mouth, skin, and nose. These sense organs are extroverted and restless; they prevent the mind from roaming in the higher realm of spiritual experience.

When one follows the master and practices a scientific technique such as Kriya Yoga daily, regularly, and sincerely, complete control of the sense organs is gradually acheived. These sense organs are given to man by God for man's spiritual evolution, not for his destruction. Untrained wayward senses are troublesome, disciplined Godward senses increase spiritual progress, allowing every sense perception to create higher soul consciousness. Through the practice of breath control, one can purify the mind and body.

6. *Yajña:* sacrifice

Ordinarily *yajña* is a religious ritual where people offer an oblation of ghee to a ceremonial fire, but there are many types of *yajñas* (sacrifices) described in the Bhagavad Gita (4:28). The *smritis* (scriptures of moral rights) describe the *panca yajñas*—the five types of oblation: *rishi yajña* (study of the scriptures), *deva yajña* (meditation and prayer), *nriyajña* (serving people), *bhuta yajña* (taking care of plants, animals, and so forth), and *pitri yajña* (praying for the liberation of diseased and departed souls, especially the parents).

The real and metaphorical explanation of a *yajña* is knowing the indwelling self and offering the oblation of every breath into the God fire of the seven centers of the spine. Watching the soul during every breath is the real oblation.

7. *Svadhyaya*: study of the scriptures

The simple meaning of *svadhyaya* is the study of the authentic scriptures from the mouth of the realized master. In Indian culture, the most authentic scriptures for God-realization are grouped under the term *prasthana trayi*, "the three great spiritual texts for realization or final exit": the Upanishads, the Bhagavad Gita, and the Brahma Sutras. Along with these, one must read the scriptures of all the religions: the Torah, the Bible, the Tripitaka, the Guru Granth Sahib, the Koran, and so on. These are all authentic scriptures, but the meaning of the scriptures can be understood only with the help of the realized master and deep meditation.

The metaphorical meaning of *svadhyaya* is *sva* (soul) plus *adhyaya* (culture or study). Study your own self—that is soul culture. Watching God in every thought, in every disposition, even when enjoying money, sex, food, emotional activities, religious feelings, and even above the pituitary—that is soul culture and *svadhyaya.*

8. *Tapas*: austerity, penance

Tapasya means to meditate sincerely and roam in the *tapaloka* (pituitary). The *gayatri mantra* mentions the *sapta loka*, "the seven planes": *bhuloka,* the money center; *bhuvaloka*, the sex center; *svarloka*, the food center; *mahaloka,* the emotion center; *janaloka*, the religion center; *tapaloka,* the soul center (pituitary); and *satyaloka,* the formless (fontanel). *Tapaloka* is the place of austerity in the pituitary. Searching for the soul fire in the pituitary with every breath and praying to the Lord, "Please lead me to realization, not down the path of delusion and temptation. Make me free from all evils."—this is *tapasya.* Keeping the awareness in the pituitary is real *tapasya.* The body heat (*tapa*) is maintained by the breath of God. To love God with every breath is *tapas*—austerity.

9. *Arjavam:* rectitude, straightforwardness

A spiritual person is completely free from all crookedness, all shrewdness. His inner self and outer self are one. He is like a child, free from hypocrisy. When one feels that God is all-pervading, *sarvambrahmamayam jagat:* "that only God abides in the whole universe, there is no duality, only unity, then one will constantly be in the state of *ayamatma brahma:* 'my soul is God.'"

10. *Ahimsa:* non-violence, non-injury

Non-violence is in thought, word, and deed, maintaining love for all. Avoid jealousy and maliciousness and the mood to torture anyone. *Ahimsa* is experienced through equanimity. A person who perceives God everywhere is no doubt free from violence. Delusion, illusion, and error disappear. Everyone is forgiven. If the teeth bite the tongue, the tongue does not seek revenge on the teeth. When man feels God in all, there is equanimity.

11. *Satyam:* truth

God is truth and truth is God. Truth always triumphs. The Mundaka Upanishad 3:1:6 declares: *satyameva jayate nanritam* "Truth alone triumphs, not falsehood." The life of the sincere seeker is established in truth. There is no chance of falsehood. Every spiritual person should try to speak the truth; every action must be established in truth. Truth in word, truth in action, and truth in life enables one to realize the truth absolute—God. To remain in the soul is the real practice of truth.

12. *Akrodha:* absence of anger

While truth and rectitude are positive virtues, non-violence and absence of anger are virtues negating the lower self. Passion is the cause of anger. When passion is not satisfied, anger is born. (See the Bhagavad Gita 2:62–63 and 3:37.)

Anger is the second door leading to hell. (See the Bhagavad Gita 16:21) Anger is a sign of weakness, which over-stimulates the nerves, veins, and arteries, and strains the brain, heart, and lungs. When people get angry, they deviate from truth and reality. A spiritual person is ever compassionate, free from anger, ego, and vanity.

13. *Tyaga:* renunciation

In the Isha Upanishad (mantra 1), it says, *tena tyaktena bhunjithah,* which means "To enjoy in the sense of detachment and renunciation." If one reverses the word *gita*, it becomes *tagi*, which means to renounce. We all are in the world. We may leave it at any moment. Nothing is permanent. So everyone should remain compassionately detached. Attachment is death. Detachment is liberation. One must live in the world, but be prepared to leave the world. This is inner renunciation. Outer renunciation is less important than inner renunciation. Outer renunciation is putting on a monk's colored cloth. Inner renunciation means to color the mind in the true spirit of renunciation. A renunciate is the best of men. (See Bhagavad Gita 18:4)

14. *Shanti:* serenity, peace

When crookedness disappears, simplicity comes. Through simplicity, one gets tranquility of mind. When the waves are many, the ocean is restless. When ambitions are many, the mind is restless. Through the practice of breath control, one learns to control and regulate the life force, which leads to constant peace, bliss, and joy.

15. *Apaishunam:* aversion to fault-finding

Fault-finding is a negative quality. Everyone is eager to see the faults in others, but not to see one's own defects. By seeking faults in others, one becomes full of defects and negative qualities. That is why Jesus said, "You fool, you have a beam in your eye, but you see sawdust in the eye of others." Be mindful of your own defects, mistakes, and faults. Be compassionate and forgiving to others. Do not blame others.

16. *Daya:* compassion

Compassion (kindness) is an important virtue that should be cultivated by everyone. In spite of many mistakes, God forgives. God provides us with endless opportunities to rectify our faults. God is ever compassionate. People should be compassionate and kind to others. With meditation and love for God, one's heart becomes extremely soft and pure, and one will desire to help people in many ways.

17. *Aloluptvam:* freedom from greediness and desire

Man's inherent nature is to acquire more and more, even beyond necessity. A greedy man is a needy man because desires multiply. Many people think they can satisfy their desires, but desire is an unquenchable, insatiable fire. Although we should be mindful of our own needs, we must watch our minds carefully. To possess more than we need brings trouble in daily life. If we eat more than we need, innumerable health problems will befall us. Similarly, greediness in daily life breeds numerous troubles and difficulties.

18. *Mardavam:* gentleness

A divine man is well polished, sweet, kind, and loving—always ready to help others. He is not rough; he is open and free from all duplicity.

19. *Hrih:* modesty

People who are truly divine lead a pure life, free from all blemishes. They are always careful not to engage in any sinful work. They are afraid of committing any wrong deed or even the slightest mistake for which they will have to repent. Leading life according to the injunctions of the scriptures, they are always pure and free.

20. *Acapala:* absence of fickleness

Fickleness can be seen in unnecessary movements of the limbs, unnecessary talk, restlessness of the eyes, and an extremely restless breath. A divine person regulates his body, senses, talk, and breath. Remember, breath control is self-control, and breath mastery is self-mastery. By thoroughly controlling one's breath, one can be free from restlessness.

21. *Tejas:* vigor

Vigor does not mean the strength and vigor of the body. Animals have a lot of strength and vigor. A man of vigor is one who constantly depends on God, whose mind is always absorbed in God-consciousness, whose life is full of peace, love and harmony. His body and mind radiate divine love, peace, and joy. He has no fear of proceeding forward. This is vigor.

22. *Kshama:* forgiveness

Even if a person has the ability to punish, he must forgive and excuse others. To forgive others is the greatest virtue. Jesus, after his humiliation and torture, prayed on the cross, "Father, forgive them, for they do not know what they do." (See The Bible, Luke 23:34)

23. *Dhritih:* fortitude

To stand firm, to be steady and resolved in any situation, and to prevent weakness from overpowering the body, the senses, and the mind—this is fortitude.

24. *Shaucham:* purity

Most people practice external purity, which is good. The practice of cleaning the body and putting on clean and fresh clothes is no doubt hygienic and healthy, but until and unless one attains inner purity, one cannot achieve realization. What is inner purity? How can one achieve this stage?

A person with inner purity is always in truth. His thoughts, words, and deeds are pure. Only by meditating and leading a God-conscious life can one get inner purity. According to the Katha Upanishad (1:3:8), "One who is always in the super-conscious and cosmic-conscious state, watching the indwelling Self" has inner purity.

25. *Adrohah:* freedom from maliciousness

Maliciousness is the by-product of jealousy and intolerance. A spiritual person is constantly seeking God and truth, and never creates problems for others.

26. *Natimanita:* freedom from pride, humility

One must not think of oneself as an extremely respectable person. One should be humble. Humility is the greatest virtue. A lover of God is ever humble. Pride, ego, vanity, or arrogance cannot enter the mind of a person who seeks God.

These are the twenty-six qualities of spiritual beings who watch the formless indwelling Self and become realized. Although these twenty-six divine qualities and the twenty qualities of the man of knowledge (see Chapter 13) are similar, some subtle differences exist. In the thirteenth chapter, the Lord speaks of these qualities as the weapons to fight with evil and negative aptitude of devilish habit.

At the end of the third verse, the Lord says, "O Bharata! (O lover of divine illumination) These qualities are inherent in a truly spiritual person."

Verse 4

dambho darpo 'timānaś ca
krodhaḥ pāruṣyam eva ca

ajñānam cā 'bhijātasya
pārtha sampadam āsurīm

Translation

O Partha (Arjuna)! Hypocrisy (fraud, deceit), arrogance, pride, anger, harshness, and ignorance are the marks of those born with a demonic nature.

Metaphorical Interpretation

After explaining the twenty-six divine qualities, the Lord describes the six devilish qualities, the satanic forces.

1. *Dambhas:* hypocrisy

People with demonic qualities maintain a double standard. Outwardly, they seem very spiritual, but inwardly they are not so. In the Bible it says, "Beware of false prophets. They come to you in sheep's clothing, but inwardly they are ferocious wolves. By their fruits you will recognize them" (see Matthew 7:15–16). Devilish people say one thing but do another. They are extremely deceitful and fraudulent.

2. *Darpas:* arrogance

Arrogant people are those who think they are very intelligent, wise, advanced, rich, and honored. These people make an outward show of worshipping. Materially, these people work extremely hard to earn money, doing many things to achieve that end, even cheating people. They ignore others. They are full of hatred. They always try to prove that they are the best. At the slightest contradiction, they become furious. They speak highly of themselves—"I am beautiful and healthy. I have a beautiful house. I am great. My children are wonderful. I have good qualities. I am honest. No one is like me." The manifestations of arrogance can be summed up as ego and pride.

3. *Abhimanas:* pride and conceit

People of a demonic character are always thinking that they are superior to others; they expect constant attention and appreciation from others. They consider themselves to be very intelligent, handsome, and spiritual. Their boastful attitude is imbued with pride and vanity. Shri Chaitanya, the great fifteenth century spiritual master of Bengal, India said, *abhimana surapanam*—"Conceit is intoxicating like wine." Just as a drunkard or drug addict roams the self-created dreamland of his imagination, the proud man is always far from reality and truth. No one likes him and he feels alone and miserable.

4. *Krodhas:* anger

Anger is the manifestation of *rajoguna* (the quality of extroversion). At the slightest provocation, angry people chastise others. Anger is part of their status. Those who remain busy with extreme material activities, who are full of vanity and ego, who are overpowered by greediness due to extreme desire and ambition, become angry very quickly. If anything upsets their activities, they become extremely angry. Anger is very dangerous. Angry people cannot distinguish between what is right and what is wrong; they lose their common sense and as a result commit many mistakes.

5. *Parushyam:* harshness (cruelty, stiffness, insolence)

People endowed with demonic qualities are very harsh, rough, and unkind. Alienated from compassion and love, they are always cruel and violent. They use abusive language, misbehave and cause trouble.

6. *Ajñanam:* ignorance

Ignorance is to ignore God and truth, to love falsehood, duplicity, and immorality. It is the cause of all evil. The ignorant love darkness because their deeds are evil. They do not love good people or good action. They seek arrogance, not knowledge. They do not seek God. They may have great material intelligence, but they suffer due to the ignorance of spirit.

These are the demonic qualities of human beings. They are the product of the rajasic and tamasic modes of nature.

Verse 5

daivī sampad vimokṣāya
nibandhāyā 'surī matā
mā śucaḥ sampadam daivīm
abhijāto 'si pāṇḍava

Translation

It is said that the divine destiny leads to liberation, the demonic qualities to bondage. O Pandava (Arjuna)! Do not grieve! You are born with divine endowments.

Metaphorical Interpretation

Those who seek spirituality, seek the formless God. They want the truth; they are divine. When the sun rises, light spreads everywhere. The warmth of the sun enlivens and energizes everything; darkness disappears. When a person seeks God, his life radiates with truth, light, and knowledge. Ignorance and weakness disappear. This is liberation, being well established in truth. Liberation is called *moksha*, which is freedom from delusion, illusion, and error. Truth is God.

Those who are engrossed in extreme activity desire devilish qualities. Falsehood is the foundation of their life. They always tell lies. They want money, material prosperity, sex, food, alcohol, and harmful drugs. They love the demonic qualities.

Keeping one's awareness above the pituitary up to the fontanel and watching the divine is the foundation of spiritual life, the way to taste Truth. Above the pituitary is the realm of the good qualities and God-realization. To remain in the pituitary and beyond is to be engrossed in God consciousness. In this state, if one constantly watches the short breath, touches the imperishable soul, and gives love to the almighty God, one will quickly progress spiritually, and one will reach the state of God-realization. Those who remain in this state and maintain this divine mood are always endowed with divine qualities and are forever free.

On the other hand, rajasic people are so engrossed in their activities that they forget the indwelling self who is constantly breathing through them. They are extremely attached to money, sex, food, ego, falsehood, and so on, and as a result suffer from disease. Due to their poor physical condition they suffer much and may even meet with death prematurely. Extreme attachment brings bondage, which is a large obstacle on the path to spiritual progress.

Here the Lord calls Arjuna "Pandava." Those who remain in knowledge, consciousness, super-consciousness, and cosmic-consciousness are the Pandavas. The Pandavas are the friends of Krishna and the soul. They have divine qualities. This verse assures all seekers of truth because the Lord is saying, "O Arjuna! Your destiny is divine. You are after Me, the truth. Do not ponder. You will achieve liberation."

Man is born for God-realization. The marvelous power of God is dormant and hidden inside His entire creation. As the cloud covers the sun, the demonic qualities cover the soul sun. To be absorbed in the inner light of the Self and to be free from all negative qualities, everybody should nurture and protect their spiritual qualities. Spiritual food and lifestyle, and spiritual practice like Kriya meditation will quicken spiritual evolution. One can be free from sorrow, worry, anxiety, fear, and ups and downs. Dwelling above the pituitary and watching God, one can experience peace, bliss, and joy. Then surely one will proceed upward to the infinite north, to His presence, realizing the living presence of the formless God, godhood, and liberation—victory in everything.

Verse 6

dvau bhūtasargau loke 'smin
daiva āsura eva ca
daivo vistaraśaḥ prokta
āsuram pārtha me śṛṇu

Translation

There are two classes of created beings in this world, the divine and the demonic. The divine has been explained in detail. O Partha (Arjuna)! Now learn from me about the demonic.

Metaphorical Interpretation

Here Arjuna is called "Partha," which means, "one who is born of the finest conception of mother Pritha." Pritha concentrated her awareness in the navel center and then in the pituitary, watching God with a slow and short breath. By doing that she conceived an extremely spiritual child, endowed with strength, energy, and vitality. He is Partha—Arjuna.

The Lord is telling Arjuna, "In this world, there are two types of people: some are spiritual and some are devilish. Similarly, in every human being, both qualities exist. The spiritual quality comes from *sa* in the pituitary. It does not proceed from the body, but from *div*, the void, or inner sky. The demonic quality is born of the lower nature. People engrossed in the material world, eating, drinking, and merry-making, acquire only negative propensities."

Lord Krishna listed the twenty-six good qualities essential for spiritual life and God-realization. Then he briefly mentioned the six demonic qualities. Now in verses 7 through 24, Krishna will explain the demonic qualities of human beings , which make people live like animals.

One must be keenly aware that both animal and rational qualities exist inside and outside the body. Sometimes, due to troubles, sorrow, and destiny, people come under the influence of spiritual qualities. At other times, due to bad company, they succumb to demonic qualities. Spiritual qualities and evil qualities are present inside the body, as well as in the outside world.

As soon as people are in truth (*sattva*), they draw forth their spiritual quality, which remains inside the *sushumna* canal. But most people are extremely busy and engrossed in worldly activity (*rajas*), others in idleness (*tamas*); in both cases they can't discriminate between what is good and what is bad, so they remain engrossed in evil.

Verse 7

pravṛttim ca nivṛttim ca
janā na vidur āsurāḥ

na śaucam nā 'pi cā 'cāro
na satyam teṣu vidyate

Translation

Men possessing a demonic disposition know not when it is the time to act and when it is the time to refrain from action. Hence, they possess neither purity, good conduct, nor truthfulness.

Metaphorical Interpretation

Those who are overpowered by evil qualities are unaware of the real meaning and purpose of life. They do not clearly understand what is to be done and what should not be done. They are bewildered, unable to discriminate or judge. In this extreme delusion, they can't observe things in the proper way. Their judgment is far from rational. If people do not have intuitive force, if they do not search inside themselves, they cannot determine what is a good disposition or how to refrain from bad dispositions.

Worldly skill is often considered intelligence, but rationality and divinity are the true tests of intelligence. If people come to receive the touch of the realized master, they can obtain the real intelligence.

By practicing the scientific technique of Kriya Yoga, by which one can open the *sushumna* canal and remain in truth, one can remain in God-consciousness all the time, experiencing extreme calm. But most people are engaged in *ida* and *pingala* activities, which is why they are egotistical and engrossed in the delusive force of nature. Their deluded minds make them think that whatever they do is best, and this attitude creates many problems for them. They have no purity. They are ignorant. They are bewildered. They neither know the rules and regulations of spiritual life, nor how to approach the realized masters to follow in their footsteps. Although anyone can perceive inner purity by going above the pituitary, most people don't know how. Thus, they don't know the real art of living, which would enable them to perceive that the soul is the abode of God.

To perceive the Truth, one must rise to the fontanel at the top of the head where the formless divine father activates through the manifestation of life. People with a demonic nature cannot do this. Falsehood is truth to them. They will never know reality, purity, moderation, or divine life; instead they will know only falsehood, hypocrisy, and impurity.

Verse 8

asatyam apratiṣṭham te
jagad āhur anīśvaram
aparasparasambhūtam
kim anyat kāmahaitukam

Translation

They say that the universe is without truth, without a basis, and without a Lord, brought forth by the union (of male and female), hence conceived in lust—what is there besides this?

Metaphorical Interpretation

The thoughts, words, and deeds of those of a demonic nature are misconceived, erroneous, and based on falsehood. They say "There is no truth in the universe. No one can live by truth. Everyone tells lies." They do not believe in the existence of our creator, the Lord, the supreme almighty father. They do not have faith in God or His words as recorded in the scriptures and spiritual books. They hate talks on morality and God. They only know that they are born to eat, drink, and to be merry. They cannot discover a basis for the world. They are full of hypocrisy, engrossed in delusion, not believing in God's omnipresence, omniscience, and omnipotence.

Those of demonic nature have no desire for soul culture and truth. They declare the non-existence of God. To them, the cause of creation is only the passion between male and female—there is no other cause. Males and females enjoy sexually and engender children. The whole universe is just a by-product of this process, without any cosmic or eternal principle behind it. The five sense organs are meant only for enjoyment and nothing else. Demonic joy consists of mixing with the opposite sex, taking delicious and rich food, earning profuse wealth, and spending money for the gratification of the senses—this world is a playground of enjoyment.

This kind of life is based on disbelief. Unhealthy lifestyle and excessive sensual enjoyment make people prone to dreadful diseases, troubles, and premature death. These people are also dissatisfied, angry, proud, cruel, and insincere, without a higher purpose in life, with no supreme goal to achieve. They are just like insects—undergoing birth, growth, sexual enjoyment, and death.

Verse 9

etām dṛṣṭim avaṣṭabhya
naṣṭātmāno 'lpabuddhayaḥ
prabhavanty ugrakarmāṇaḥ
kṣayāya jagato 'hitāḥ

Translation

Holding to this false view, these lost souls of little talent or understanding and of cruel action rise up as the enemies of the world for its destruction.

Metaphorical Interpretation

In this text, "lost souls" refers to those who are far from truth and spiritual qualities (*sattva*), those who are engrossed in extreme material activity (*rajas*), and in idleness and doubt (*tamas*), busy in the activities of the lower centers. Their extreme state of delusion and their attachment to falsehood and darkness prevents the light of the soul from shining in them. "Lost souls" also refers those who are completely absorbed in body consciousness, thinking that they are the body, not the soul.

In the Bible (Matthew 10:28) it says, "Do not be afraid of those who kill the body, but cannot kill the soul. Rather, be afraid of the one who can destroy both soul and body in hell." The parable of the lost sheep in the Bible also refers indirectly to the lost souls.

The lost souls are full of demonic tendencies, always roaming through the *ida* and *pingala*. They do not believe in the realized masters and do not come to be touched by them so their *sushumna*s (spiritual canal) will open. Without education, they are uncultured and rough. Due to their ignorance, they are constantly engrossed in negative moods. Their brain power is used in a negative way, they commit many mistakes, and they indulge in mind-altering drugs and accomplish mostly negative works. They love falsehood, lies, and hypocrisy. They have a great passion for snatching money, and they commit numerous bad deeds to satisfy this urge—as thieves, robbers, pickpockets, adulterers. Being full of passion and seeking sense pleasure, they do not hesitate to commit cruel acts or to kill people to achieve their goals.

People with such narrow-minded understanding, who don't believe in God, are deviated from the truth, and they don't try to perceive truth. Their immoral, godless lives create chaos in the divine principle of the world. All their activities are self-centered, antisocial, and destructive to mankind. Constantly running towards death, they try to destroy the body world with negative, harmful actions.

Verse 10

kāmam āśritya duṣpūram
dambhamānamadānvitāḥ
mohād gṛhītvā 'sadgrāhān
pravartante 'śucivratāḥ

Translation

Cherishing insatiable desires, full of hypocrisy, arrogance, and pride, having accepted false notions through delusion, they act with tainted resolve.

Metaphorical Interpretation

People with demonic habits cherish their endless desires; they want to possess and to grab everything. But ambitions and desires are unlimited and insatiable, especially when it comes to material things. As soon as one desire is fulfilled, another arises. Satisfying desire is like pouring fuel onto a fire.

People with demonic habits are pregnant with ego, vanity, and hypocrisy. They devote their strength, energy, and their whole lives to fulfilling the evil desires that are barriers on the path of soul culture and spiritual progress. Such people do not hesitate to commit wrong acts to fulfill their petty material needs. They engage in various types of formal worship and even kill people. Their lives are undisciplined and impure.

In Sanskrit *vrata* is a vow to abide by a moral and spiritual discipline in thought, word, and deed, but those who are devilish by nature lead completely unrestricted lives. They eat all the harmful foods. Their misdeeds earn them constant restlessness and temptation, leading them to madness. Their egos overpower them; they cannot attempt to proceed on the path of truth. Their rajasic and tamasic foods, activities, and temperaments lead them in a downward spiral towards destruction, decay, disease, and death.

Verses 11 and 12

cintām aparimeyām ca
pralayāntām upāśritāḥ
kāmopabhogaparamā
etāvad iti niścitāḥ

āśāpāśaśatair baddhāḥ
kāmakrodhaparāyaṇāḥ
īhante kāmabhogārtham
anyāyenā 'rthasamcayān

Translation

Giving themselves to immeasurable anxieties ending only with death, they remain devoted to the gratification of desires as the highest aim, convinced that this is everything.

Tied in the bondage of a hundred expectations, devoted completely to lust and anger, they strive to amass hoards of wealth by unfair means to gratify themselves with sensuous pleasure.

Metaphorical Interpretation

People with evil motives keep these bad qualities until death. They are slaves to their passionate desires. Since passion has no end, life is turbulent and far from peace, bliss, and joy. To satisfy their paramount desires, they need great wealth. The sole aim of evil-minded people is money, sex, alcohol, and sensual pleasure. They are not free from sexual desire until death.

The highest objective of spiritual people is liberation. Self-disciplined, spiritual people of ancient times had four goals:

1. To lead a life based on morality *(dharma)*,
2. To earn wealth in a righteous way (*artha*),
3. To satisfy passion with moderation and discipline (*kama*),
4. To practice a technique of transcending the senses, to achieve liberation (*moksha*).

But people with a devilish nature forget the cardinal doctrines of morality and liberation, preferring to endlessly chase money, sex, food, and other material things. They are so rude, rough, cruel, and animal-like that they do not even think of morality. Their only concern is to satisfy their evil desires by any means. But one cannot satisfy desire. Passion and anger are twins, born from sense pleasure. Indulging any sense magnifies all the other desires. This is the burning flame of passion. When sensuous motives are not fulfilled, anger arises immediately.

These demonic people are extremely sexual and arrogant. Gratification of sexual desires requires a lot of money. Sexual desire is the cause of numerous wants: money, rich foods, fancy dress, and others. This ambition creates the habit of trying to earn and hoard vast amounts of money, even by unfair means. Skill and talent is devoted to earning and amassing wealth. Life becomes miserable. In the Bible (Matthew 6:19–20) it says, "Lay not up for yourselves treasures upon earth, where moth and rust doth corrupt, and where thieves break through and steal; but lay up for yourselves treasures in heaven, where neither moth nor rust does corrupt, and where thieves do not break through nor steal."

Extremely body-conscious, sensuous, and materialistic, leading an extroverted, sinful, and restless life, these deluded people cannot imagine a higher purpose.

Verses 13 to 16

idam adya mayā labdham
imam prāpsye manoratham
idam astī 'dam api me
bhaviṣyati punar dhanam

asau mayā hataḥ śatrur
haniṣye cā 'parān api
īśvaro 'ham aham bhogī
siddho 'ham balavān sukhī

āḍhyo 'bhijanavān asmi
ko 'nyo 'sti sadṛśo mayā
yakṣye dāsyāmi modiṣya
ity ajñānavimohitāḥ

anekacittavibhrāntā
mohajālasamāvṛtāḥ
prasaktāḥ kāmabhogeṣu
patanti narake 'śucau

Translation

This has been obtained by me today and I shall fulfill this ambition. This wealth is mine and again shall be mine.

That enemy has been slain by me, and I shall kill others too. I am the lord of all, the enjoyer of all power; I am endowed with all supernatural powers and am successful and happy.

I am wealthy and born in a highly esteemed family. Who else is like me? I shall sacrifice to God. I shall give to charity. I shall make merry. Thus, they are deluded by ignorance.

Led astray by many flights of fancy and enveloped in a net of delusions, attached to the gratification of sensuous desires, they fall into the foulest hell.

Metaphorical Interpretation

In this verse, the Lord recounts the egotistical words and ideas of evil-natured people. In the Bible (Luke 6:45) Jesus says, "The good man brings good things out of the good stored up in his heart and the evil man brings evil things out of the evil stored up in his heart. For out of the overflow of his heart, the mouth speaks."

The hearts of devilish people are filled with negative qualities like ego, arrogance, hypocrisy, passion, anger, and greed. They say, "Today I have earned much to fulfill my desires. I am happy. I have this much money. Yet I need more, and I will earn more in any way." These people do not hesitate to amass wealth through unfair means, such as corruption. "I have killed many of my enemies. I am very happy. No one can catch me—I will kill those who are against me." Robbery, murder, and immorality are not alien to such people. They play with human blood and life. Even if they have achieved a respectable position in society, their background activities are extremely corrupt and vicious. They think that they are very intelligent and wise, that no one is equal to them. Gentlemen by day, they are robbers by night.

These people think, "I am the king, I am the master, I am the lord, I am the most successful, I have fulfilled my life. I hail from a high and respectable family. Who is else in this world can compare with me?" This self-aggrandizement is arrogance. Extreme ego, arrogance, and stubbornness make them think they are great. People replete with these negative qualities can be seen worshipping and going to the temple and church with pomp and grandeur—but it is all hypocrisy and ostentation.

When these people go to temples and churches, it is for their own need and greed—to show others that they are highly spiritual. Or they entertain the idea, "I shall perform worship for my prosperity and also to bring harm to others who oppose me. I will perform many *yajñas*. I am pure. I am spiritual. By worshipping the gods, I shall become even more prosperous." They maintain a double standard—divine outside, devil inside. When they feel that they have enough material prosperity, they give to charity, but with great ostentation and vanity. They give only to draw attention and to receive praise. They constantly desire sense gratification. Although they speak high-sounding words, their minds roam below—like vultures flying high in the sky with their eyes searching for dead corpses on the ground. They talk about morality while being immoral. Consider Matthew 15:8, "These people honor me with their lips; but their hearts are far from me."

Delusion arises out of ignorance. In darkness, man stumbles and commits sins and mistakes. Darkness is ignorance, light is knowledge. Demonic people are always engrossed in delusion, illusion, and error. They perform many evil deeds and try to enjoy the world as much as possible. They do not think of how sinful their actions are because they are always right in their own eyes.

One who thinks, "I have killed many, and I will kill many more. What is wrong with that? Where is the fault?" dwells in hell in this very life.

People with demonic tendencies eat large quantities of rich food and lead irregular and undisciplined lives. They often cannot sleep at night due to their evil deeds. Their extremely unbalanced lifestyle causes them to suffer from disease and brings great distress to their families. Since their minds are completely deluded, they are bewildered by a multitude of restless and perturbed thoughts. Immorality makes life a living hell and will produce an afterlife of suffering.

Verse 17

ātmasambhāvitāḥ stabdhā
dhanamānamadānvitāḥ
yajante nāmayajñais te
dambhenā 'vidhipūrvakam

Translation

Self-conceited and stubborn, intoxicated by wealth and honor, they perform *yajñas* (sacrifices) only in name and with hypocrisy, without following the sacred rituals.

Metaphorical Interpretation

Spiritual people are extremely humble and free from ego and vanity, doing everything for the sake of God only. People with evil qualities are arrogant and egotistical. They never bow with love or honor. They think that they are very respectable and spiritual, while they behave in exactly the opposite way. Considering themselves to be extremely honorable and wealthy, they think, "No one with all my qualities and accomplishments can be found anywhere." Because of their arrogance and greed for money, they do not care for anyone.

Religious activities are done for the sake of name and fame only, without adhering to the rules and restrictions of the scriptures, as a masquerade of religious fervor. They dress piously to show people how religious they are. (See the Bible, Matthew 7:15–19 and Luke 11:39–47.) Their immense wealth is spent on religious activity to fan the flames of their ego, vanity, and hypocrisy. (See the Bhagavad Gita 9:12.) Praise is often given to these people out of selfish interest, but those who praise know very well that the objects of their praise are completely unworthy.

Verse 18

ahamkāram balam darpam
kāmam krodham ca samśritāḥ
mām ātmaparadeheṣu
pradviṣanto 'bhyasūyakāḥ

Translation

Given over to egotism, brute force, arrogance, lust, and anger, those malicious people hate Me dwelling in their own bodies as well as in the bodies of others.

Metaphorical Interpretation

Those who are demonic by habit are always egotistical, proud of their brute force and animal strength, arrogant, full of ambition, with their mind constantly dwelling in sex and anger. They defile their body and their life, while misbehaving and torturing others. They do not believe that God exists in man or in themselves. These people think that they are extremely intelligent—that is their self-conceit.

In the Shvetashvetara Upanishad (6:11), it says, *eko devaḥ sarva-bhūteṣu gūḍhaḥ sarva-vyāpī sarva-bhūtāntar-ātmā karmādhyakśaḥ sarva-bhūtādhivāsaḥ sākśī cetā kevalo nirguṇaśca:* "One God hides in all beings, all-pervading, the inner self of all beings, the ordainer of all deeds, who dwells in all beings as the witness, the knower, the only one, devoid of qualities." Similarly, the Bhagavad Gita (10:20) states, "I am the soul present in all living beings. I am in the beginning, in the middle, and in the end." The

Bible (1 Corinthians 3:16–17) also declares, "Do you not know that you yourselves are God's temple and that God's spirit lives in you? If anyone destroys God's temple, God will destroy him, for God's temple is sacred and you are that temple." (See also 1 Corinthians 6:19 and 2 Corinthians 6:16) And in 1 Corinthians (3:19) the Bible says, "For the wisdom of this world (material intelligence) is foolishness in God's sight."

Deluded people think, "I am the all-in-all." They are extremely proud and live according to their evil moods. They do not believe in the indwelling self. They think man is born only through sex. They hate spiritual people and do not hesitate to criticize and even torture them. They not only dishonor the indwelling self through their evil and immoral activities, but they also dishonor God present in others by torturing, insulting, abusing, coercing, and even attempting to kill them. They never realize that God is in all, that God is the all-in-all, all-pervading, the sole doer. The Lord made human beings in His own image; then He, being the multiplicity of the divine being, breathed in through the nostrils of every human being.

Verse 19

tān aham dviṣataḥ krūrān
samsāreṣu narādhamān
kṣipāmy ajasram aśubhān
āsurīṣv eva yoniṣu

Translation

Those haters, cruel and the worst of men, I constantly cast into the demonical wombs in this world.

Metaphorical Interpretation

In this verse, the Lord explains the unfortunate destiny of evil doers. Man is the maker of his own destiny. He reaps what he sows—

small seeds of action bring forth a big harvest. One is one's own best friend or one's own worst enemy (see the Bhagavad Gita 6:5–6).

Those with a demonic nature are selfish and extremely body-conscious. They are evil-minded and commit all kinds of sinful acts, thinking that no one will know. They don't know that God is the silent witness of all man's activities. In the Shvetashvetara Upanishad (6:11), *sakshi* is the witnessing consciousness. In the Bhagavad Gita (9:18), it says "God is the witness", as does the Bible, "I call God as my witness" (see 2 Corinthians 1:23). Hiding in man's pituitary and fontanel, God is the silent witness of the inner thoughts and outer words and activities. God gives to all the fruit of their deeds.

So the Lord is explaining, "The mind of demonic people remains below the pituitary, always engrossed in evil, wrong, debauchery, and immorality. I allow them to live only like animals. They remain constantly below the cervical center (neck) and lead extremely miserable, sorrowful lives." (See the Bible, Romans 1:28–32).

Verse 20

āsurīm yonim āpannā
mūḍhā janmani-janmani
mām aprāpyai 'va kaunteya
tato yānty adhamām gatim

Translation

Having entered the wombs of demons, those who are deluded, not attaining Me, birth after birth, O Son of Kunti (Arjuna)! From there they go to a condition lower still.

Metaphorical Interpretation

The Lord is declaring, "O Arjuna! You are the son of Kunti (sharp, divine intelligence). You are born from the pituitary, by the help of the soul. Your mother Kunti conceived you by fixing her attention on the food center while meditating in the pituitary. So your mind is constantly fixed in the pituitary and you always seek truth. Although you were born as a human being, your mind never dwells on demonic qualities. You are always in a divine mood and constantly asking Me how to be free from all human limitations and negative qualities.

"Because you keep good company and have the deepest desire to know Me, I am leading you from your lower centers to the higher centers, above the pituitary, up to the fontanel, and even beyond the physical universe. I am all-pervading, formless, and remain compassionately detached from everything.

"Arjuna! Be wary of the demonic qualities because they can be so tempting and alluring that one forgets everything and falls into the abyss of sin."

The indwelling self in the body breathes from the very moment of birth—that is why people are alive and active. Spiritual people seek the soul by ascending to the pituitary—the seat of the soul—and beyond. People with demonic natures are completely deluded: they are not attached to God; they are not seeking truth. They do not bring their awareness to the pituitary and the fontanel in an upward movement, but instead descend to ever lower centers, dwelling in ego, vanity, sex, money, and so on. These activities lead them from bad to worse.

"Arjuna! Remember that both attachment and detachment come from the breath. Will and woe, light and darkness—all arise from the breath. One who learns the technique of breath control for going beyond all negative, demonic qualities knows this secret and can perceive My presence constantly."

Those who remain constantly in demonic qualities, dwelling in these downward-pulling propensities during all their actions, will never achieve God-realization. Born as rational beings, they nevertheless sink to the lowest state of humanity, leading their lives like animals. The more they remain in the animal qualities, the more mistakes they make. This is the real hell; it is not an outside place.

Verse 21

trividham narakasye 'dam
dvāram nāśanam ātmanaḥ
kāmaḥ krodhas tathā lobhas
tasmād etat trayam tyajet

Translation

This is the threefold gate of hell, which destroys the self: passion, anger, and greed. Therefore one should avoid these three.

Metaphorical Interpretation

In the previous verse, the Lord said that people with demonic qualities go to hell. So the question inevitably arises, Where is hell? What does it look like? In almost all religions people believe in some form of hell. They also believe that one may go to hell after death. But in this verse the Lord states categorically that when a man lets passion, anger, and greed overpower him, he has already opened hell's door.

Kama (passion, desire, lust, ambition), *krodha* (anger, envy), and *lobha* (greed, possessiveness) are correlated and causally connected. These three rajasic qualities are discussed in detail in the Bhagavad Gita 2:62–63, 3:37, and in several other places. These three qualities are the seed, manure, and terrain for the growth of all negative qualities in a person's life. Ambition, fear, anger, and greed bring unlimited sorrow, conflict, disease, and death; as a result, there is always remorse, anxiety, and tension. The people of dark disposition roam in the lower realms of their being, from the heart center down to the bottom center. Remember, when one of these qualities comes to life, then one is entering the door of hell.

Until and unless they learn to control their lives and eliminate their negative propensities such as irrelevant talk, restless mind, and destructive intelligence, they cannot enter the state of purity. Their life is doomed, full of misery and suffering, hell in this very life.

To be free and to proceed towards God, one needs extreme calm. Calmness is the foundation of all religions and is essential for liberation. Serenity, peace, love, and calmness, are one and the same. But rajasic people, filled with passion, anger, and greed are extremely restless; tamasic people are lethargic and ignorant. In both, calm is absent. People with these negative qualities jump from one activity to another, committing one mistake after another, telling constant lies, thereby creating strain and trouble for their heart and brain. Spiraling down into the lower four centers of their being, demonic people develop anxiety, restlessness, bad health, and many kinds of disease. They are in hell.

Spiritual seekers must be extremely careful and vigilant. Negative qualities are born out of ignorance. When these propensities arise, one should immediately cut them away with the sword of knowledge. (See the Bhagavad Gita 4:42.)

Verse 22

etair vimuktaḥ kaunteya
tamodvārais tribhir naraḥ
ācaraty ātmanaḥ śreyas
tato yāti parām gatim

Translation

Released from these three gates to darkness, O son of Kunti (Arjuna), a man does what is best for himself and then goes to the highest goal (God).

Metaphorical Interpretation

Hell is called a place of darkness because people constantly roam in the darkness of ignorance, but one should release oneself from the so-called attraction and attachment of the three demonic qualities, and do what is the best. The Lord is saying "O Kaunteya (son of Kunti), you don't dwell in your lower centers, you fix your attention on the top, hearing the voice of the divine. You try your best to be completely free from ambition, anger, and greed. You are constantly searching for the indwelling self, and to reach the highest goal of life."

The Lord is now describing the path of spirituality—meditation. He gives two pieces of advice: first, do what is the best for oneself, and second, reach the highest goal. To seek one's own self by avoiding negative qualities and remaining in truth is the best for oneself; to realize God and *moksha* (liberation) is the highest goal. The goal is in the fontanel and meditation is the way to get there.

The pituitary and the fontanel are the place of calm; if one practices sincerely under the guidance of a realized master, one will be free from all negative qualities within a short time. Consider the story of Ratnakar, a renowned murderer, who in a moment's time with the help of a realized master left his bad qualities and sinful life behind and calmly searched for the almighty father hiding within. He became realized and subsequently was known as Valmiki, the great poet of ancient India and author of the great epic, the Ramayana. Everything depends upon one's desire.

If one practices going beyond the senses by perceiving the triple divine qualities of light, vibration, and sound within the whole body like Ratnakar did, one can go beyond the body sense and the world sense. Ratnakar became so calm and so extremely absorbed in God-consciousness that he didn't even notice when white ants built a hill over his whole body.

Everyone can discover this extreme calmness and can achieve God-realization. Everyone can go to the formless state and perceive the almighty father covering the whole body and the whole world during every breath. One can even attain the breathless state and can perceive and realize the Four Great Pronouncements of the Vedas:

1. *aham brahmasmi*: I am God.
2. *tattwamasi*: Thou art That.
3. *ayamatma brahma*: My imperishable soul is Brahma.
4. *prajñanam brahma*: Wisdom is God.

Entering into the atom point of the all-pervading consciousness in the fontanel is to perceive *samadhi*—the pulseless and breathless state. This is the highest liberation achieved through deep meditation. This is the best and most supreme work that one can do.

Verse 23

yaḥ śāstravidhim utsṛjya
vartate kāmakārataḥ
na sa siddhim avāpnoti
na sukham na parām gatim

Translation

He who acts arbitrarily under the impulse of desire, casting aside the injunctions of the scriptures, does not attain perfection, nor happiness, nor the highest goal.

Metaphorical Interpretation

In Sanskrit, the *shastras* are scriptures that make man disciplined. These scriptures lead man down the right path. All methods of spiritual practice must have a scriptural background. Following the techniques that are described in the scriptures and supported by the direct experience of a realized master is the true path to God-realization. Many hidden truths are in the Vedas, the Upanishads, the Bhagavad Gita, the Torah, the Bible, the Koran—in all the scriptures. Their real meaning is revealed to realized masters, and those who come to these teachers must listen to them politely and practice according to their instructions.

When people try to practice techniques according to their whims, they cannot get proper results. Those who do not follow the scriptural prescriptions, who are engrossed in the activities of the lower centers of the spine, who are restless, overwhelmed by anger, ego, and greed, cannot proceed forward on the path of God-realization.

In this verse, the Lord is explaining that everybody must follow the scriptures as explained by the realized masters and experience them directly. Spirituality is direct perception and experience of truth. If the scriptures are ignored, one cannot be successful in life—one won't attain God-realization (*siddhi*) or happiness (*sukha*), not even spiritual evolution.

Verse 24

tasmāc chāstram pramāṇam te
kāryākāryavyavasthitau
jñātvā śāstravidhānoktam
karma kartum ihā 'rhasi

Translation

Therefore, scripture alone is your guide in determining what is and what is not to be done. Knowing the scriptural injunctions, you should perform action in this world.

Metaphorical Interpretation

In the Bible it says, "All scripture is God-breathed and is useful for teaching, rebuking, correcting, and training in righteousness, so that the man of God may be thoroughly equipped for every good work." (See 2 Timothy 3:16–17.)

The scriptures are the ultimate guides. Realized masters are living scriptures, the practical guides. The scriptures are not mere words; they contain the spiritual truth that can be revealed only through deep meditation. All scriptures exhort us to lead a life of morality, truth, and righteousness. By leading such a life, by avoiding immoral, wrong, and passionate deeds while following in the footsteps of the realized master, one will taste reality and truth.

Everyone must read holy books, but reading books alone will not provide a real education. Reading the names of medicines does not cure diseases. Deadly diseases are eradicated by undergoing medical treatment and following the practical advice of a doctor. To cure the spiritual disease, one must read the authentic scriptures under the direct guidance of a realized master, practice meditation, and avoid all negative activity. The scriptures and the master's words free the disciple from confusion and from dilemmas about what course of action to take.

By right action, the mind is purified. With a pure mind, one perceives reality. Right action and meditation are two sides of a coin that foster quick spiritual evolution and God-realization.

Summary

Every human body, every human life, is a garden where fruit trees grow and flowers bloom, alongside many useless plants, weeds, and grass. One must remove the unnecessary weeds and take care of the flowering trees. The flowers and fruits will provide the satisfaction of peace, bliss, and joy. These flowers and fruits should be offered on the altar of God.

The altar of God is not outside, but inside the brain, from the pituitary up to the fontanel. Every thought, word, and action should be dedicated to God. If one watches the breath and perceives that the breath is inhaled and exhaled by the living power of God from the top, then one will achieve continuous God-consciousness and liberation.

Chapter 16 is entitled "The Yoga of Discrimination between the Divine and Demonic Qualities." In everyone's life, there are the Pandavas and the Kauravas, the *devas* and the *danavas*—the good and bad qualities. The Lord elaborately describes the divine and devilish qualities in the twenty-four verses of this chapter. The scriptures are the mirror that allows one to see one's image clearly. The scriptures are the lamps that light the path and show the goal. They tell the truth, however bitter it may be. After learning the difference between good and bad from the scriptures and from the mouth of the realized master, rational people must cultivate their virtues and eradicate their vices. No one offers rotten flowers or worm-eaten fruit to a beloved one. The worms of life are the negative qualities present in each human body.

In the first three verses, the Lord speaks to Arjuna, the devotee, about the twenty-six divine qualities. These divine qualities are the fruit of a sattvic spiritual nature.

In the fourth verse, the Lord briefly lists the six devilish qualities.

The fifth verse emphasizes how those with devilish qualities are attached to the world, and how this bondage leads them in a downward spiral.

In verses 6 to 20, the Lord describes in detail the psychology, character, behavior, habit, attitude, and way of life of the demonic person.

In verses 21and 22, the Lord warns that ambition (passion), anger, and greed as the three doors leading to hell.

The concluding two verses emphasize the importance of scriptures.

Divine qualities are the real assets, the only wealth of a spiritual person. Those qualities help the disciple proceed down the path of meditation and God-realization. On the other hand, the devilish qualities arise out of rajasic and tamasic nature. Everyone knows his own weaknesses, but man is a conscious devil who does not want to rectify his mistakes. But mistakes are not for the sake of mistakes, mistakes are for correction. One mistake becomes the cause of many mistakes if not corrected. A person who does not search for his own faults is his own enemy.

Every person should turn to the *shastras* (the holy scriptures) and a realized master for help. The master is the embodiment of the scriptures; he can help the disciple understand them and proceed accordingly. The scriptures are the textbooks of the science and art of spiritual life—the master teaches the real technique according to the capability of the disciple.

One should be careful when selecting a master. The scriptures not only proclaim what is right and wrong action, but they also describe the real guide, the master who is fit to impart knowledge. In the Bible (Matthew 7:15-18) it says, "Beware of false prophets, which come to you in sheep's clothing, but inwardly they are ravening wolves. Ye shall know them by their fruits. Do men gather grapes of thorns, or figs of thistles? Even so every good tree bringeth forth good fruit; but a corrupt tree bringeth forth evil fruit. A good tree cannot bring forth evil fruit, neither can a corrupt tree bring forth good fruit." In the same way, the Mundaka Upanishad (1:2:8) explains,

avidyāyām antare vartamānāḥ svayam dhīrāḥ paṇḍitam manyamānāḥ janghanymānāḥ pariyanti mūḍhāḥ, andhenaiva nīyamānā yathāndhāḥ—"Abiding in the midst of ignorance, wise in their own esteem, thinking themselves to be learned, fools afflicted with troubles go about like blind men led by one who is himself blind."

And in the Bible (Romans 2:19–22), it says, "[Thou] are confident that thou thyself are a guide of the blind, a light of them which are in darkness, an instructor of the foolish, a teacher of the babes, which hast the form of knowledge and of the truth in the law. Thou therefore which teachest another, teachest thou not thyself? Thou that preachest a man should not steal, dost thou steal? Thou that sayest a man should not commit adultery, dost thou commit adultery?"

If one reads the scriptures and meditates accordingly, one will achieve God-realization in a short period of time.

Divine and devilish qualities reside inside and outside of all human beings. Many people are sometimes very good and at other times extremely evil. Some people are constantly engrossed in demonic activities. Finally, a few people are extremely pure, free from negative, demonic qualities, and only seek truth. Every human being should try his utmost to eradicate his demonic qualities and lead a divine life, and thereby attain liberation, constant emancipation, and realization.

Chapter 17

Śraddhatraya vibhāga yoga

The Yoga of Classification of the Threefold Faith

Introduction

We love quality, because our comparative values are always taken into consideration in daily life. In a similar way, the quality of a person is very important from one's own personal viewpoint, as well as from another's. The quality of a person indicates the nature of that person, which is revealed through his thought, words, activity, habits and behavior.

The seventeenth chapter of the Gita is the indicator of one's own nature. Scriptures are the mirror which reflect our own threefold nature. These three qualities are called sattvic (pure, spiritual), rajasic (materialistic, restless) and tamasic (animalistic, primitive, slothfulness). Although a person has an amalgamation of these three qualities, one of these three qualities always predominates over the other two.

A person is not a slave of his own instincts or nature; he can change his own life through the use of his own willpower, disciplined life style, and meditative attitude. Sincerity in practice is the key factor for perfection. For example, in this chapter the Lord describes the eating habits of three types of people. Through eating habits, the nature of a person can easily be known. On the other hand, knowing the impact of food and drink in one's own life, one can change one's own eating habits, thereby bringing change in one's own life.

To lead a self-disciplined life, one can get great help from the scriptures and the assistance of teachers. Along with that, one's own self-effort is necessary.

In the previous chapter, the Lord explained the differences between divine nature and demonic nature. In this chapter He explains how the nature of a person is reflected through his own thoughts, words, and deeds.

The scriptures are the mirror to reflect one's own inner image. Knowing one's own weaknesses and vulnerability to temptation, one must try sincerely to eliminate the negative propensities and to become better every day. Man is not a puppet in the hand of unknown factors rather, he is the master of his own destiny and life.

By changing the negative quality through sincere effort, one will change one's own life with love and meditation.

This chapter discusses in detail how a person can reach the state of divinity by overcoming the demonic and devilish quality.

Verse 1

arjuna uvāca
ye śāstravidhim utsṛjya
yajante śraddhayānvitāḥ
teṣām niṣtha tu kā kṛṣṇa
sattvam āho rajas tamaḥ

Translation

Arjuna asked:
What is the position of those who, endowed with faith, neglect the injunctions of the scriptures and worship gods, O Krishna? Is it *sattva*, *rajas,* or *tamas*?

Metaphorical Interpretation

Arjuna is a spiritual seeker who wants to perceive the truth. He wants to hear how to practice spirituality and how to remove the doubt and confusion that bring downfall (Bhagavad Gita 4:40). So he (a disciple) is asking the master a question based on the advice and instruction the master gave him in the last two verses of the previous chapter.

The divine qualities lead to immortality, the demonic qualities to mortality. Depending on their actions, people will achieve either liberation or bondage, and the world is the theater where all this activity takes place. The scriptures define restrictions and ordinances for the thorough regulation of one's actions and explain how to avoid all negative actions. People can be known by their actions.

Some people are so weak-minded that they do not want to follow scriptures. Many people believe, "If we only pray to God, will He not respond?" Therefore Arjuna asks Krishna, "O master! There are many people who whimsically offer sacrifices and oblations to the fire. They do many rituals according to their own mind, and they do it with some sort of faith, but they ignore the rules and regulations of the scriptures. What is the result of such activity? I cannot really understand that type of worship. Is it truly spiritual (sattvic), or is it material (rajasic), or is it simply idleness or silliness—religious show (tamasic). I want to hear the answer from You."

Verse 2

śrībhagavān uvāca
trividhā bhavati śraddhā
dehinām sā svabhāvajā
sāttvikī rājasī cai 'va
tāmasī ce 'ti tām śṛṇu

Translation

The Lord answered:
The faith of embodied beings is of three kinds, born of their innate nature. It is sattvic (good), rajasic (passionate), and tamasic (dull). Hear of it from Me.

Metaphorical Interpretation

The Sanskrit word *shraddha* is translated as faith. *Shraddha* is always associated with *sat* (truth), and *dha* means to uphold. Faith is to live life in Truth and is developed from the impressions arising out of activity in practical life.

Depending upon destiny and past work, different types of dispositions arise in human beings. Due to these different dispositions, people have three different kinds of faith (*shraddha*): sattvic (good, spiritual), rajasic (passionate, restless), and tamasic (idle and slothful). Sattvic *shraddha* is unshakable faith in God, religious faith; rajasic *shraddha* is faith in egocentric activities; tamasic *shraddha* is little faith due to idleness, sloth, and inertia. So people work and worship according to their mood and inner nature.

The triple qualities of nature (*maya*) guide every action of man. People's faith changes according to change in these three qualities. In this verse the word *svabhava* means "innate nature." Destiny, the aggregated balance sheet of all activities, is this innate nature. It predisposes a person to be either religious, full of activity, or idle. Such differentiation can be seen in the behavior and activities of brothers and sisters born in the same family, raised by the same parents, and living in the same environment.

Verse 3

sattvānurūpā sarvasya
śraddhā bhavati bhārata
śraddhāmayo 'yam puruṣo
yo yacchraddhaḥ sa eva saḥ

Translation

The faith of all people is related to their mental condition (nature). O, Bharata (Arjuna), man is made of faith. Whatever faith he has, thus he is.

Metaphorical Interpretation

The Lord is saying, "Arjuna! Your name is Bharata; your mind is always engrossed in truth, in divine illumination. You have the deepest desire for God-realization. You always want to remain in a spiritual state, so you are always asking me questions.

"I am the imperishable almighty indwelling Self. I have created man and woman. I am breathing through the nostrils of every human being. Through breath the triple qualities of nature manifests in their life. According to heredity, environment, culture, family traditions, and even different dispositions, human beings do different types of work according to their faith. This faith depends upon their inner quality (*svabhava*)."

Some people perform spiritual work; others are extremely busy in material activities; still others are lazy and idle. According to their innate nature, they proceed in the material world either remaining in *ida* or in *pingala*. Those who are spiritual keep their mind in the *sushumna* canal through proper environment, the company of the master, and spiritual practice (sincere meditation). However, the minds of most are always engaged either in activity (*pingala*) or in idleness (*ida*). The almighty father hides in the body of every human being and leads them differently according to their faith and activity.

Think of a mirror. If one puts on clean and religious clothes and stands in front of the mirror, then one looks religious. If one stands in front of the same mirror with a expensive attire, tie, and shoes, one looks rajasic. If one stands with dirty, torn, and tattered clothes, the same mirror reflects the image of a tamasic, poor, and despicable being—simply because of appearance.

God is like a mirror. Each person's garb is their innate nature and faith. As is his faith, so is the man. Faith is the inner personality of man. This faith is created out of the qualities of nature, and these qualities (sattvic, rajasic, or tamasic) depend upon one's actions.

If a man becomes more introverted and looks inside a little, he can easily see that the body, senses, mind, and thoughts change constantly. But with faith, any person can increase his sattvic quality by keeping good company, living with the master, practicing deep meditation, and studying the scriptures.

Verse 4

yajante sāttvikā devān
yakṣarakṣāmsi rājasāḥ
pretān bhūtagaṇamś cā 'nye
yajante tāmasā janāḥ

Translation

People of a sattvic disposition worship the gods. Those of rajasic temperament worship *yakshas* and *rakshasas* (demigods) while others with a tamasic quality worship the spirits of the dead and ghosts.

Metaphorical Interpretation

In Sanskrit "gods" is *devas*, which comes from the root *div*. *Div* means ether, formless. Those who concentrate on the pituitary and the fontanel, the root of the body tree (see the Bhagavad Gita 15:1), will experience real love for God. There, the formless power of God dwells, but no one can see Him. He breathes from there. If one can keep his awareness there through deep concentration, meditation, and the help of a realized master, one can attain the formless state. This is an extremely spiritual state, which cannot be achieved by talking, chanting mantras, suggestion, magic, hallucinations, speculation, or imagination. This state is wisdom. The five sense organs cannot perceive wisdom; it can be perceived only by fixing one's concentration into the atom point, in the fontanel.

There are fifty types of breath out of which forty-nine are extroverted and restless. The quiet and tranquil introverted breath, *udana vayu*, is an extremely short breath. When one practices this *udana vayu* by the scientific technique of Kriya Yoga, one can feel the touch of the almighty father—pulsation, divine sound, the *aum* sound. There is no need to chant the *aum* sound with the mouth; one can perceive divine illumination by going above the fontanel, and by doing this, one will achieve breath control. Breath control is self-control, breath mastery is self-mastery, and the breathless state is the deathless state. This is the highest level of spirituality. At this stage, there is no sense of the material world. This is the state of extreme calm (godliness) that is described in the scriptures.

Nevertheless, there are people who worship gods (not the one God, but many gods or deities) for their personal benefit. People worship Shiva, Krishna, Surya, Ganesha, and Durga, which are the presiding deities of the different sense organs. Shiva is in the ear; Rama, Krishna, Narayana, or Vishnu, and so forth are in the skin; Surya is in the eye; Durga, Lakshmi, Kali, Jagaddhatri, or Shakti, and so on are in the tongue; and Ganesha is in the nose. Those who worship these gods do so with forms and formalities. They do not know how to perceive their divine power in the whole body.

Rajasic people busy themselves with a multitude of activities, always trying to earn and amass vast amounts of money through business, service, or allied activities. They worship *yakshas* and *rakshasas* (demigods). Yaksha is the lord of wealth, and Rakshasa is the lord of all sorts of protection. People worshiping these demigods hoard and save money in many ways. They also worship demigods for material satisfaction.

Tamasic people are always seeking personal gain without sincere effort. They worship ghosts, witches, and spirits by black magic. By such worship, they get power from evil spirits and try to fulfill evil desires. They have evil dispositions and are extremely furious at times. They are extremely restless and have deviated from the truth.

Verses 5-6

aśāstravihitam ghoram
tapyante ye tapo janāḥ
dambhāhamkārasamyuktāḥ
kāmarāgabalānvitāḥ

karśayantaḥ śarīrastham
bhūtagrāmam acetasaḥ
mām cai 'vā 'ntaḥśarīrastham
tān viddhy āsuraniścayān

Translation

Men who undergo terrible austerities and penance of an arbitrary nature not sanctioned by the scriptures are the vehicles of hypocrisy, egotism, desire, attachment, and pride of power,

and who, without thinking, emaciate and torture the elements constituting the body; they also torture Me, within the body. These men have demoniacal dispositions.

Metaphorical Interpretation

The Lord is giving Arjuna a clear answer to the question he asked in the first verse: "What is the faith of those who perform certain religious activities without following the injunctions of the scriptures?"

The Lord explains, "The scriptures make people disciplined and divine. The scriptures are a compilation of divine guidelines for regulating the activities of men."

There are people who try to achieve some gain through many different kinds of worship, imagination, hallucination, or magic, and so forth. These are not spiritual ways. Some of these people do not know the scriptures—nor do they want to know. They torture their bodies. They fast for a long time. They remain underwater or sit in a place surrounded by fire. They even cut out small portions of their body and offer their own blood to demons, ghosts, or spirits. Their bodies become emaciated. The terrible austerities torture the elements in the body, so the body revolts, which fosters numerous physical and mental ailments. Some of these people take unhealthy food: wine, fish, flesh, eggs, and so forth, and offer fish and flesh as oblation in the fire—which is not found in the scriptures. They think that they are extremely advanced in spirituality, but in fact, they are extremely primitive.

Undoubtedly, these qualities are anti-spiritual, creating many problems for the body and mind. People with evil power bring ultimate harm to themselves and others. Their so-called meditation is vain worship. Devoid of any true spiritual practice, they engage in multitudes of rigorous practices, stressful life, hardships, and fasting, only to fulfill their evil and material ambitions. All these are anti-spiritual and anti-scriptural.

By such practices, they do not experience the divine qualities described in the Bhagavad Gita (13:7–11 and 16:1–3). Instead, they experience vanity, ego, passion, lust, and desire, extreme attachment, and pride of power. Because of their inflated ego, vanity, and hypocrisy, they do not hear the words of the scriptures or the wise. Day and night, they chant and offer oblation—all in vain.

"I am the indwelling Self, but many are not seeking Me. They do not try to perceive me through real meditation. By ignoring Me, and worse by torturing the body, which is My temple, they lead the life of a blind person."

Verse 7

āhāras tv api sarvasya
trividho bhavati priyaḥ
yajñas tapas tathā dānam
teṣām bhedam imam śṛṇu

Translation

There are three kinds of food preferences, based on innate dispositions. There are also three kinds of sacrifices (*yajña*), austerities (*tapas*), and charity (*danam*). Hear now the distinction between them.

Metaphorical Interpretation

This is the mystery of God's creation. Each man is different according to his innate qualities. Behavior, taste, temperament, habit, food, clothing, education, and even worship are different and distinct.

As there are three qualities (*sattva*, *rajas*, *tamas*) in human beings, there are also different types of food. The food of a sattvic person is different from the food of a rajasic or a tamasic person. Those who are spiritual love healthy, divine, and easily digestible spiritual (sattvic) food. Rajasic people, due to their extreme material activities and egotistic life, enjoy rajasic food. Tamasic people, full of idleness, sloth and inertia, love tamasic food. One group does not appreciate the food of the others.

The fire ceremony, sacrifice, and oblation (*yajña*) are of three types as well. The austerities, penance, and charity are also practiced differently according to the qualities. All these differentiations and distinctions in food, oblation, austerities, and charity are explained elaborately in the following verses.

Verse 8

āyuḥsattvabalārogya-
sukhaprītivivardhanāḥ
rasyāḥ snigdhāḥ sthirā hṛdyā
āhārāḥ sāttvikapriyāḥ

Translation

Foods that promote life and longevity, vitality, virtue, intelligence, strength and vigor, health, happiness, and satisfaction are juicy, soft, firm, pleasant to the stomach and naturally agreeable. These foods are dear to the good and spiritual person.

Metaphorical Interpretation

There is a lot of debate and discussion about spiritual and healthy foods. In this verse the Lord explains spiritual food with a metaphor, so a literal explanation of the verse is not enough. Each word must be explained in detail, based on ayurvedic and hygienic considerations. This verse explains every aspect of healthy and spiritual food.

The Lord says that the food that gives long life, calmness of mind, vitality, vigor, strength, health, cheerfulness, and happiness and the food that is palatable, nutritious, substantial, and naturally agreeable is dear to spiritual people. Food should be wholesome and healthy.

1. *Ayuh* (long life): *ayur vai ghritam.* Food should have little fat (unlike *ghee* and butter). Fat should be taken moderately for long life.
2. *Sattva* (peace of mind, intelligence): *phale sattva.* Fruits have a lot of vitamins and minerals. A little fruit daily brings intelligence and peace of mind.
3. *Balam* (strength and vigor): *dugdhe balarn.* Milk is a complete food containing many necessary nutrients. Drink some milk everyday.
4. *Arogyam* (healthy, disease-free body): *tikte arogyam.* If one takes a little bitter food daily, one will enjoy good health.

5. *Sukha* (happiness): *madhurena sukham*. One should eat a few sweet dishes or desserts.
6. *Priti* (satisfaction). A little fermented food (rice water, called *kanji*)
7. *Rasya*: juicy
8. *Snigdha*: a little cream
9. *Sthira* (protein). Protein may be from animal or vegetable sources, and it should be in moderate quantity. Protein gives sound health, brain power, agility, and activity. It must be eaten with carbohydrates because they will be used to digest the protein.
10. *Hridya*. A little yogurt daily is good to pacify the stomach.

These are the spiritual foods, but one must remember the dictum of *ayurveda—jirnamanam prasamsriyat*: "The food that one can digest is the best food for that person."

The food of spiritual people is good and spiritual. It helps them meditate. Our mentality is affected by our food. When people achieve a spiritual mood through moderate good food, their *prana* and mind flow through the *sushumna* canal, which enables them to improve themselves.

Verse 9

kaṭvamlalavaṇātyuṣṇa-
tīkṣṇarūkṣavidāhinaḥ
āhārā rājasasye 'ṣṭā
duḥkhaśokāmayapradāḥ

Translation

Foods that are pungent (disagreeable), sour, salty, excessively hot, sharp, harsh, dry and burning, and cause pain, grief, and disease are loved by rajasic people.

Metaphorical Interpretation

As is the food, so is the health. Food brings all-around development.

Food is vitality, strength, and health. Food brings brain power and aids meditation and spiritual progress. Food is beauty and luster. Food gives long life and provides the proper conditions for God-realization. Sattvic, pure food creates calmness of mind and good concentration.

Rajasic food brings restlessness and worries. It is pungent. The first category of rajasic food is *katu*. Many translate it as "bitter," however, in the previous verse it was said that a little bitter food brings good health to the liver and ultimately to the entire body. So *katu* cannot mean "bitter." *Tikta* is "bitter." In *ayurveda*, there is an elaborate description of *rasa* (taste or juice). There are *sad rasas* (six types of taste) in which *katu* and *tikta* are categorically different. *Katu* is a pungent, disagreeable taste.

The second type of rajasic food is *amla* (acidic food and alcohol). These are extremely sour foods that are liked by many restless people.

Next, *lavana* means salty. Salt in excess is not good. It is the cause of many diseases.

Atyusna means very hot in temperature. Food should neither be very cold nor very hot. Very hot food and drink are not good for health. Hot food cannot be chewed properly in the mouth. If swallowed immediately, it causes many health problems.

Tiksna is the hot taste of chili or peppers. It is liked by rajasic people.

Ruksha is fried and roasted food with butter, oil, or *ghee*.

Vidahina is the food that creates a burning sensation, such as mustard, asafoetida, and so on.

Oily, rich, spicy, roasted, and fried foods are expensive, and difficult to digest and to assimilate. They damage the liver and colon. Many types of stones, cancer, spleen, and kidney troubles are the result of rajasic food, which also damages the eyesight. The extremely exciting rajasic foods create restlessness and passion and disturb one's peace of mind.

These foods cause pain, misery, and sickness. Little movement of the tongue while eating, as well as taking the wrong type of food at the wrong time in the wrong quantity brings physical ailments, pain, and mental unhappiness.

Verse 10

yātayāmam gatarasam
pūti paryuṣitam ca yat
ucchiṣṭam api cā 'medhyam
bhojanam tāmasapriyam

Translation

The food which is spoiled, tasteless, rotten (putrid), leftover (refuse) and impure is dear to the tamasic (the dull).

Metaphorical Interpretation

In this verse, the Lord describes the food liked by the tamasic person who is dull, idle, lethargic, always procrastinating, slothful, and who spends a lot of time in sleep, idle gossip, daydreaming, drowsiness, taking drugs and alcohol, and so forth. He therefore has less time to take care of himself. He takes any food available at any time. He is neither moderate nor considerate concerning his food.

First, the tamasic person may take cold and unhealthy food prepared a long time ago, even if cooked ten to twelve hours earlier. If this food was not kept in a proper hygienic place, it may have bred germs and bacteria. Second, he may eat half-ripe, overripe, or extremely dried foods lacking real nutritional value. This is tasteless and flavorless. The third category of tamasic food is rotten food with a foul smell.

Paryusitam means that there are people who cook the food only once, and then keep it in water, taking the same food for three days. This is unhealthy.

Uchista describes food that has been taken, touched, or leftover on a person's plate. Also, after putting a utensil in one's mouth, it should not be put back in the pot where food is kept for everyone. One should not take leftover food from one's plate and store it with the unused food. This is for hygienic purposes. A person may be diseased. There may be germs and bacteria. Many types of diseases are transmitted from one person to another due to contamination.

The food which is not clean, pure, and healthy is the food of the tamasic people.

Tamasic, idle people eat these foods with great relish because they do not want to work. They eat and then they sleep. Their health is extremely poor and they are emaciated. Also, they do not clean their bodies and clothes so they contract numerous diseases.

Verse 11

aphalākānkṣibhir yajño
vidhidṛṣṭo ta ijyate
yaṣṭavyam eve 'ti manaḥ
samādhāya sa sāttvikaḥ

Translation

The sacrifice (fire ceremony) that is offered as ordained by scriptural injunctions, by those who do not desire the fruit, and who concentrate their minds only on the thought "such sacrifices must be performed," is sattvic (spiritual) in character.

Metaphorical Interpretation

While sacrifice is usually thought of as an oblation offered to the ceremonial fire while chanting *mantras*, it also has a supreme and sublime metaphorical and spiritual meaning. In this verse, the Lord describes the real spiritual sacrifice, which is done only for God-realization.

In the Jñana Shankalini Tantra it says,
na homa noman ityahuḥ
samādhan tattu bhuyate
brahmāgnau huyate prānam
homakarma taducyate:

"The path to enter into *samadhi* is not by the *yajña* or *homa* where the oblation is offered in fire. Rather, it is the manner in which the life force or breath (*prana*) is given as oblation to Brahmagni, the God fire."

Those who are seeking spirituality should know that the breath of all living beings is the breath of God (see Genesis 1:27). God has been breathing life into every living being from their birth until now. Without breath, one will die. As long as there is breath, every person should try to realize the indwelling Self.

To do so, one must sit in a calm place and control the breath and mind with a very slow and feeble breath. Awareness must be concentrated in the pituitary and in the fontanel without any ambition or desire for the fruit of such supreme spiritual action. The breath must be of equal pressure in both nostrils. Inhalation and exhalation must be of equal counts. This must be learned directly from the master. With much practice, one will forget the sense of the world. One will be completely merged in God-consciousness. This is the real oblation, sacrifice, and fire ceremony—offering the breath to the God fire.

Everyone must understand the fire in the body. In the Mundaka Upanishad (2:1.8), it says,

sapta prāṇāḥ prabhavanti tasmāt
saptārciṣaḥ samidhaḥ sapta homāḥ
sapta ime lokā yeṣu caranti prāṇā
guhāśayā nihitāḥ sapta sapta:

"From Him came the seven *pranas* and the seven flames (fires). There are seven oblations (of firewood) and seven fire ceremonies. One can roam in these seven fires in the seven *lokas* (planes of life) through *prana* and can see the indwelling Self remaining in the cave (cranium)."

Of these seven fires in the seven centers (chakras) in the spine, the top fire is inside and even above the cranium. Every breath goes up and touches that fire, which is why the body is warm. The body heat is maintained, just like a candle burning with oxygen. When the candle is covered by a glass, the light will be extinguished within a few seconds. Breath, the life current, maintains the body. Oxygen is the oblation into the God fire. If one watches the ingoing and outcoming breath, and loves and thanks God, then each breath will be the real oblation to the fire.

This is the *yajña*, the sacrificial fire ceremony in all human beings. One will not become realized or liberated just by pouring *ghee* (clarified butter) into the fire while performing vedic fire ceremonies. People must learn the real fire ceremony, the correct way of practicing *prana karma* (*homa karma* or *yajña*), from a realized Kriya Yoga master. Accordingly, if one practices with love, then all restlessness will disappear. By magnetizing the spine and fixing the attention on the fontanel and above, in the superconscious state, one will perceive the constant fire ceremony that is going on in one's life. By this, one will enter into the state of *samadhi* (wisdom), which can be achieved by remaining in the atom point.

When one is breath-conscious and loving God in every breath without any expectation, only then will one be really free from the body sense and any sense of the world, free from mind, thought, intellect, and ego. This fire ceremony must be performed constantly and continuously. This is the spiritual oblation to the divine fire. It cannot be achieved by any external or extroverted rite or ritual, idol worship, or by chanting *mantras* (through the five sense organs).

Verse 12

abhisamdhāya tu phalam
dambhārtham api cai 'va yat
ijyate bharataśreṣṭha
tam yajñam viddhi rājasam

Translation

But the sacrifice that is offered in expectation of the fruit, for the sake of a show, with ego, O best of Bharatas (Arjuna), is passionate (rajasic).

Metaphorical Interpretation

In this verse, the Lord discusses the nature of the *yajña* (sacrifice, worship, fire ceremony, religious activities) of rajasic people. Rajasic people are busy with extreme activity, always aiming at name and fame.

People are religious. They go to the temple, church, or synagogue. They appear to be God-loving, but many put on their best clothes and go to the house of worship, not for God, but for their reputation. In the Bible (Luke, 11:43), it says, "Woe unto you, Pharisees! for ye love the uppermost seats in the synagogues, and greetings in the markets." People worship deities and offer *ghee* in the fire with much pomp and grandeur. They do many things for the fulfillment of their material desires.

Many also worship publicly, collecting huge sums of money from others. The whole locality is busy with all of this formal worship, done in a competitive spirit. There are many types of ostentation. Some even sing and cry in the temple only to draw public attraction, not God. This is done for the fulfillment of their ego. This is not real oblation—real oblation is sacrificing the ego and offering love to God in every breath. Worship and sacrifice for the fulfillment of ambition and ego, which is far from love, purity, and self-development, is rajasic.

Verse 13

vidhihīnam asṛṣṭānnam
mantrahīnam adakṣiṇam
śraddhāvirahitam yajñam
tāmasam paricakṣate

Translation

A sacrifice that has no respect for scriptural injunction, in which no food is offered (to the hungry and the poor), without *mantras* (sacred hymns) and without gifts (to the priests), which is empty of faith, is said to be tamasic.

Metaphorical Interpretation

In this verse, the Lord describes the sacrifices or worship of a tamasic nature. He points out the five characteristics of such *yajña*s:

1. These spiritual practices are not based on scriptural prescriptions. Real spiritual practice is the essence of all religious scriptures. It is not created out of whim; it is not a product of the human mind.
2. Sacrifice is always associated with charity. The real meaning of sacrifice is to give up one's own negative qualities and be free. Everyone should be very wary of their own mistakes and should correct themselves. But in tamasic worship, people neither give up their evils or immoral outlook, nor do they give charity to the poor and the needy.
3. *Mantra* is not just chanting unclear hymns and prayers like parrots. It means freedom from the propensities of the restless mind. In tamasic *yajña*, people have no control over their minds because they are slaves to the mind and are extremely idle.
4. In tamasic worship, people do not give fees to the priest.
5. Tamasic practices are faithless—truly speaking, tamasic people have neither faith in God, nor in themselves.

Tamasic people are dull, lethargic, and lazy. They perform some form of worship solely for the sake of appearance. They also worship deities in order to obtain favors and boons without any self-effort. Tamasic worship is truly a fruitless effort.

Verse 14

devadvijaguruprājña-
pūjanam śaucam ārjavam
brahmacaryam ahimsā ca
śārīram tapa ucyate

Translation

The worship of God, the twice-born, the teachers, and the wise; purity, virtue, celibacy, and non-violence; these are called austerities or the penance of the body.

Metaphorical Interpretation

In this and the next two verses, the Lord explains the basic requirements of spiritual life. In spiritual life, one should be very careful about one's activities. Inner purity and God consciousness are the foundation of spiritual progress and God-realization. One must worship and give love and regard to God (*deva*), the twice-born (*dvija*), the master (*guru*), and the wise (*prajña*). To understand this verse clearly, one must understand the meaning of these words.

What is *deva*? This word has two important meanings: vacuum and illumination (light). If one concentrates from the pituitary up to the fontanel and seeks God in every breath, then one will perceive a milk-white light covering the whole universe (See Matthew 6:22 and Luke 11:34) and hear the divine *aum* sound. Breath is formless. *Prana* is formless. *Mahaprana*, the supreme spirit hiding in each human being, is also formless. The supreme almighty father is in the fontanel. To love Him in every breath, in each human being, in all living creatures, in plants and everywhere, is the worship of God.

Dvija in English is twice-born. People think that *dvija* means the upper caste, but this is not correct. In the Bible (John 3:3) one finds, "Except a man be born again, he cannot see the kingdom of God." And in John 3:5, "Except a man be born of water and of the Spirit, he cannot enter into the kingdom of God." Being born again is the real baptism. Water means love for God, and spirit means the power of God. In this real baptism, one must give up old habits and start a new God-conscious, spiritual life. This is *dvija* (see Ephesians 4:22–24).

"Guru" is a beautiful concept. Gurus not only give *mantras*, they infuse divine power in the body of the disciple. The guru is the realized master. *Gu* means the indwelling spirit, and *ru* means this beautiful body, so someone who realizes the indwelling Self is a guru. The guru is the master of all the lower propensities and is established in truth.

Prajña is the man of wisdom who roams in the atom. He is not only learned in the scriptures, he also knows their inner meaning, their metaphorical interpretation.

With humility, every person should give love to God, the twice-born, the guru, and the wise.

Every spiritual seeker must try to be extremely pure, physically and mentally. External purity or cleanliness is the stepping stone; inner purity is also necessary. The mind must always remain above the eyebrows—this is real purity. Simply taking baths does not make one pure, but learning how to magnetize the spine from the master will produce a different circulation in the whole body and bring inner purity. Those who seek spirituality lead very simple, virtuous, noble lives without any material ambitions. They are always seeking the truth.

Those who seek God should also be free from carnal sex moods. Thus, they should be *brahmachari,* celibate (See Ephesians 5:3–5). The esoteric meaning of *brahmachari* is to roam (*chara*) in God-consciousness (*brahma*).

The true disciples are not malicious (*himsa*). Their lives are for the love and welfare of mankind. This is *ahimsa*.

Spiritual seekers do not torture the body; they are only searching for God, the indwelling soul. By practicing meditation in the company of the guru, they gradually move from the lower to the higher centers. During their everyday lives, during every activity, they give love to God. They are free from negativity and are well behaved. In every endeavor, they watch God.

This is the foundation of spiritual life.

Verse 15

anudvegakaram vākyam
satyam priyahitam ca yat
svādhyāyābhyasanam caiva
vāṅmayam tapa ucyate

Translation

Words that do not cause any distress (annoyance), that are truthful, agreeable, and beneficial, as well as regular study of scriptures (*svadhyaya*) are called austerities of speech.

Metaphorical Interpretation

In this verse, the Lord explains how people should worship God through speech.

God has given man sense organs so that he can make the best use of them. God has not given the senses for the destruction of man, yet most people, misuse, abuse, or do not use the sense organs. These sense organs, with regulated use, benefit us in many ways. It is through them that man acts, perceives, and realizes.

The most powerful organ is the tongue. The tongue is not made "to live by bread alone, but by every word that proceedeth out of the mouth of God" (Matthew 4:4 and Luke 4:4). Some monks do not speak. This is good because one must have thorough control over the tongue. But one must also realize that dumbness is not spirituality. Properly expressing spiritual truth enables people to taste the truth.

In the Bible (Proverbs 6:17–19), it says the Lord hates six things: "a haughty eye, a lying tongue, hands that shed innocent blood, a heart that devises wicked schemes, feet that are quick to rush into evil, a false witness who pours out lies." In Proverbs 8:13 it says, "To fear the Lord is to hate evil: I hate pride and arrogance, evil behavior, and perverse speech". One should thoroughly control the tongue while talking.

Those who practice Kriya Yoga have thorough control over the body's organs. They can easily avoid anger, pride, hypocrisy, and cruelty. Therefore, they can behave very sweetly, speaking the truth—their words are for the betterment of mankind. They never use offensive or harassing words. They read the holy books and explain them clearly to help people attain God-realization. This is *vanamaya tapasya*, worshiping the formless by words and speech, and giving oblation to the ears and hearts of the people—sweet, truthful, beneficial, and pleasant talk.

Any speech that comes out of the mouth for the betterment of human beings is truly spiritual. It is like medicine for the ear. It removes the darkness of ignorance (*karna rasayana*); it never creates any antagonism; it is sweet, humble, and divine. The talk of truth sets people free.

The marvelous power of God is dwelling in between the eyebrows and above. People who practice Kriya Yoga are constantly looking inside, not outside—they are free from extroversion. They always speak about truth, God-realization, and the benefit of mankind.

Through talk imbued with humility and God-consciousness, people receive inspiration, help, and ultimately, all-around development. They learn how to achieve success in the material world while remaining in the formless stage. Through this talk, people progress on the path of soul culture.

This is the talk of God.

Verse 16

manaḥprasādaḥ saumyatvam
maunam ātmavinigrahaḥ
bhāvasamśuddhir ity etat
tapo mānasam ucyate

Translation

Peace of mind, gentleness, silence, self-restraint and perfect purity of inner feelings—all these are called austerities of the mind.

Metaphorical Interpretation

People always try to control their minds without knowing how to go about it. Thoughts arise in the right side of the cerebrum, and one speaks from the left side. To thoroughly control speech and make it pure, one should be very careful about one's thoughts.

Through inner purity, one will achieve speech and mind control. Everyone should learn how to control the breath, practice, and lead a spiritual life. This will bring serenity of mind and inner peace.

One should be constantly content. Contentment is a state of peace and joy. Broadness of mind is contentment. One should, through deep meditation and a God-conscious life, try to be free from all negative qualities. One should lead a life of simplicity, silence, and self-control—and thereby proceed toward God.

The ordinary human mind always leads one toward restlessness. Instead of being a good and humble servant, the mind becomes a bad master, bringing many types of trouble. But when people learn that the way to control the mind is through breath control, they can achieve self control, self restraint, and ultimately, Self-realization. When restlessness comes, they will know how to regulate their breath and keep their tongue in the proper place to regulate thought and control speech.

In this state, they will be free from all crookedness. The five God-given sense organs can no longer disturb them. By the practice of the technique of Kriya Yoga, people can achieve an extremely introverted state, free from all dispositions. At this stage, people can meditate on God with peace, bliss, and ceaseless joy.

Inner purity of thought and mind, a gentle and divine mood, silence and self-control are called *manasa tapasya*—silent meditation with the tongue pointing to God.

Verse 17

śraddhayā parayā taptam
tapas tat trividham naraiḥ
aphalākānkṣibhir yuktaiḥ
sāttvikam paricakṣate

Translation

This threefold penance (of the body, speech, and mind), practiced with the highest faith by yogis who expect no fruit in return, this is called sattvic (spiritual, good).

Metaphorical Interpretation

In the previous three verses, the Lord discussed in detail the threefold austerity (worship): worship with the body, worship with speech, and worship with the mind. Each sincere seeker must try to maintain purity of the body, mind, speech, thought, and action by following the divine instructions given in the previous verses. In this verse, the Lord describes how to practice this penance: with supreme faith, with no expectation of result, in constant union with the Self.

If people meditate very deeply by controlling the body, speech, and mind, without expecting any fruit such as lower *siddhis* (material achievements), and if they fix their attention in the fontanel while breathing the extremely slow breath and follow in the master's steps, they will gradually become free from all worldly restlessness and enter into the real state of spiritual life—Godhood. They will become free from forms and formalities, and will remain absorbed in the formless state. Through deep meditation, they will perceive the milk-white light covering the whole world and will slowly enter into the stage of realization.

This is real, selfless, and spiritual meditation (sattvic *tapasya*).

Verse 18

satkāramānapūjārtham
tapo dambhena caiva yat
kriyate tad iha proktam
rājasam calam adhruvam

Translation

Penance that is practiced with hypocrisy, for the sake of honor, respect, and reverence and for show, is declared to be rajasic (passionate, extroverted). It yields uncertain and momentary fruit.

Metaphorical Interpretation

Rajasic people are extremely restless, materialistic, showy, extroverted, and hypocritical. In this verse, the Lord describes the rajasic *tapasya*—worship performed by rajasic people.

Although they know that they are dishonest, insincere, and corrupt in everyday life, they pretend to be honest and good. They hide all their negative qualities inside, and falsely advertise themselves to be highly advanced in spiritual life on the outside—by their appearance, speech, and activities. It is a show of spirituality.

Rajasic people also perform many rituals and worships with the expectation of gaining honor, respect, and reverence from people. They expect position and status in their community. Truly spiritual people are extremely humble, always thinking, "I am insignificant, I am not worthy of anything, except to love God and meditate." But rajasic people are the exact opposite.

Rajasic people spend huge amounts of money—not to serve God, but to earn respect and gratitude from others. Everything is done with an expectation of the fruit of their actions and worship. For prosperity, they pray to Lakshmi; for respect and strength, to Kartikeya; for success, to Ganesha; for freedom from trouble, to Durga.

Rajasic people are extremely busy with all kinds of religious activities, pomp, and grandeur, but they remain far from truth. They cannot achieve God-realization through all this show and pretense. Truly speaking, the mind of rajasic people is not seeking truth or God.

Verse 19

mūḍhagrāheṇā 'tmano yat
pīḍayā kriyate tapaḥ
parasyo 'tsādanārtham vā
tat tāmasam udāhṛtam

Translation

Austerity that is performed with deluded notions and self-mortification or to cause harm to others, is declared to be tamasic.

Metaphorical Interpretation

There are many idle, lazy, lethargic, procrastinating, and slothful people who do not work productively and properly. They maintain their livelihood by unfair means like theft, embezzling money, begging, and sometimes torturing people. They do not even hesitate to kill people. They are deluded. Their minds are full of chaos and confusion. They cannot decide what is good for them.

Tamasic people pray to and worship gods in an effort to hide their evil actions, so that even the police cannot trace their crimes. They do this out of ignorance. They worship not only to fulfill their evil motives, but also to bring harm to others through their so-called religious activities. They undertake long fasts and even perform very bad activities, such as animal sacrifice. They torture themselves and bring harm to others. Such religious activities, penance, and austerities are tamasic.

Tamasic people are filled with extreme pride, ego, anger, and cruelty. Their formal worship only serves to fool themselves as well as cheat others. Their minds are not seeking God at all; they are after the satisfaction of their inner, lower, evil aspirations. This is the lowest form of worship.

Verse 20

dātavyam iti yad dānam
dīyate 'nupakāriṇe
deśe kāle ca pātre ca
tad dānam sāttvikam smṛtam

Translation

The gift that is given at the proper place and time to the worthy person, from whom no return is expected (who has not done any favor), only with the thought "it is to be given," is spiritual (sattvic).

Metaphorical Interpretation

Charity, gift-giving, alms, and material help are part of the religious activities of all the world's religions, but *dana* (charity) is not just material aid. It has a deeper spiritual meaning.

Everyone must give to charity. "Charity begins at home," the saying goes. Many people give money for the welfare of mankind—providing education, food for the hungry, water to the thirsty, medicine for the diseased, help for those in distress, relief for natural calamities, and so on. Many people establish inns and rest homes in holy places and places of pilgrimage for religious people and pilgrims. Travelers are able to stay overnight for free and to receive many services.

There are many educated and highly advanced monks who also serve the sick and the needy. When there is any natural calamity like flood, drought, or epidemic, the monks help, serve, and nurse the people. The monks do not do these things expecting public appreciation or any reward. They feel that they are a part of God's creation and helping others is a noble and divine duty, at the proper time and place, to the proper people. This charity and service is, without doubt, spiritual.

This verse also has a very deep spiritual meaning. The real gift or donation is the gift of spiritual knowledge that the master gives to the disciple without any expectation. Material gifts, whatever good they may be, are only temporarily beneficial. Spiritual knowledge given to the disciple is the real eternal gift. If this gift of spiritual knowledge is given to the worthy disciple at the proper time and place, it constantly increases.

The sun gives light and heat without any expectation. The tree gives fruit, flowers, shade, and many other benefits—even if it is tortured in return. The river distributes water constantly and without rest. The realized master offers, with heart and soul, divine knowledge to the disciple. This is spiritual charity. This is the real divine work. The master selflessly helps the disciple's quick spiritual progress—the realization of his Self.

Verse 21

yat tu pratyupakārārtham
phalam uddiśya vā punaḥ
dīyate ca parikliṣṭam
tad dānam rājasam smṛtam

Translation

But that gift which is given with an unwilling spirit, with the aim of getting a service in return or in the hope of getting a reward, is called rajasic (passionate).

Metaphorical Interpretation

Here, the Lord explains rajasic people's gifts and charity. These people are usually rich and work hard for material success, but their minds are not as pure and broad as sattvic (spiritual) people's. Rajasic people's minds are always calculating. Undoubtedly, they give to charity, but with a lot of hesitation and deliberation. They decide what they will give based on the benefit they will get in return, and their charitable work is always done with a lot of self-advertisement and propaganda.

They think "I have earned money with much difficulty, why should I give it away unnecessarily? What do I gain?" This is the habit of miserly people. They do not realize that people come in this world empty-handed, and they are to leave it empty-handed.

In the Bible (Matthew 6:19–20), it says, "Lay not up for yourselves treasures upon the earth, where moth and rust consume, and where thieves break through and steal: but lay up for yourselves treasures in heaven, where neither moth nor rust doth consume, and where thieves do not break through nor steal. For where your treasure is, there your heart will be also."

Rajasic people who give to charity share three characteristics: they give unwillingly; they expect some return for their work, and they want some reward. All these things are due to their selfish motives and narrow-mindedness.

Verse 22

adeśakāle yad dānam
apātrebhyaśca dīyate
asatkṛtam avajñātam
tat tāmasam udāhṛtam

Translation

The gift that is given at the wrong place and time and to the undeserving person, without paying respect or with contempt, is said to be tamasic (dull).

Metaphorical Interpretation

People need help when they are in distress. To help such people is good, but there are some people who do not work due to wrong habits and a dull nature. They try to maintain their livelihood and finance their bad habits without success. Such people are unworthy of receiving help, but ordinary people cannot judge who deserves help.

Some people are wealthy enough to help others, but they are so hesitant that when a needy person approaches them for help that they do not behave appropriately. Afterwards, they give only a small token donation.

Many pretend to be worthy of receiving help. But when one gives money or a gift to such a person, it is a misuse of charity.

When a person approaches you to request some help, you should carefully determine the needs and worthiness of the person and should help him according to your capacity, with love and respect. Otherwise, any help given to the wrong people at the wrong time, without love and respect, with a lot of hesitation and after a lot harassment, is no doubt a tamasic gift.

Verse 23

om tat sad iti nirdeśo
brahmaṇas trividhaḥ smṛtaḥ
brāhmaṇās tena vedāśca
yajñāśca vihitāḥ purā

Translation

***Aum, tat, sat*—this has been declared the threefold symbol of Brahman. By this, the brahmins, the Vedas, and the *yajñas* (sacrifices) were created in ancient times.**

Metaphorical Interpretation

Aum tat sat is the *mantra*, the holy prayer, that people used in ancient times. *Aum tat sat* means that "*aum* alone is truth." In ancient times, people used these three words and realized their inner meaning. They achieved God-realization and perceived the divine force.

In this *mantra*, the three words are not really words. These three words independently as well as collectively represent the supreme almighty father. For example, in the Brihadaryanaka Upanishad it says, *sadeva soumya eva atma*: "O dear student, *sat* is the eternal, indwelling Self, who is none but the almighty father".

These three words not only symbolize the formless God and the indwelling Self, but also the *brahmins* (highly advanced spiritual persons), the Vedas (the holy scripture), and the *yajñas* (the ceremonial way of offering oblation to the sacred fire in sacrifices). These three are symbolically represented in these cosmic words, but they are nothing but the manifestation of the formless supreme almighty father.

Those who perceive *aum* in everything can easily understand its practical yogic meaning and are spiritual people in truth. They are the knowers of Brahman (*brahmins*). "*Brahmins*" does not mean the top caste of the degenerated Indian caste system. In the scriptures it explains, *brahma janati iti brahmana*: "The knower of the Brahman alone is a *brahmana* (or *brahmin*)." A realized person, a real lover of the formless God, is a *brahmana*.

The Vedas were originally known as the *triveda* or *trayi veda* (three Vedas), not the *chaturveda* (four Vedas). The three Vedas are Rik, Yajur, and Sama. The fourth Veda included as part of the *chaturveda* is the Atharva. The Vedas come from the root word *vid*—to know, to realize, to possess.

"Rik" means the "word" or the "object". Suppose a person is hungry and wants food. The speech coming out of the mouth with the feeling of hunger is Rik—"I am hungry".

"Yajur" comes from the root *yaj*, "to be united, to be associated". Yajur in this case is the word said to someone who can give or arrange food to be given. Yajur is the utterance of an inner feeling or experience to another person who can understand it and provide help—giving food, in this case.

That person gives the food with love because he felt the hunger of the person within himself—this is *sama* (harmony, equality). By taking the food, the hungry man receives strength throughout his whole body. This is also Sama Veda.

Thus, the creation of hunger up to the stage of its satisfaction is materialized in three stages: Rik, Yajur, and Sama. In this way, one gets complete satisfaction and joy. Food is matter. The matter is also Veda. If one chants the word "food, food, food!" any number of times, the belly will not be filled. When the food is put in the mouth, chewed nicely with love and appreciation for the food, swallowed slowly and offered in the *vaishvanara* fire as a sacrificial oblation, then one's appetite will disappear. This is the process of Sama Veda.

The satisfaction of enjoying food and becoming free from the problem of hunger is called Atharva Veda.

These three Vedas are known as *aum* (*om*). God absolute (Brahman) and the knower of Brahman (the brahmana and their spiritual experience as narrated in the Vedas and *yajñas*) are known as *aum tat sat.*

What is a *yajña*? Ordinarily, people think that offering oblation in the ceremonial fire is a *yajña*—fire ceremony sacrifice. But the real *yajña* is the breath. Oxygen is in the atmosphere, which is breathed in and out by the imperishable soul abiding in the body temple. With each breath oxygen travels to touch the real fire, which is the soul, the real God. In the Jñana Shankalini Tantra, it says, *brahmagnau huyate pranam*: "The oxygen touches the indwelling Self." Thus, *yajña* is life, all the activities of life, the fire ceremony of life—in man, animals, insects, plants, trees, and even in grain. It is the reason that everything is alive. This ceremony is the life of God. When one feels that every breath is an oblation to the fire in the fontanel for the love of God, this is the real fire ceremony. To know *aum tat sat* is real spirituality, the real oblation.

In the Isha Upanishad (Mantra 12), it says, *isavasyam idam sarvam*: "God is all-pervading". God abides and permeates everywhere. There is not a time nor a place to ignore the existence of God. Whatever one sees in the universe is nothing but the power of God. God Himself is remaining everywhere. God is *aum*. In the Yoga Sutras of Patañjali (1:27), it says, *tasya vācakaḥ praṇavaḥ*: "*Aum* represents Him, the formless, supreme imperishable soul." *Aum* is the integration of three aspects of God. Out of the many meanings of this mystical, eternal sound *aum*, one from the yogic approach is:
A—the imperishable soul, formless and omnipotent,
U—the conscious, super-conscious and cosmic-conscious state,
M—the gross physical body and the gross quality of anything.
These three aspects remain everywhere, including in the three bodies—causal (A), astral (U), and gross (M)—in a subtle way.

In every human body, the imperishable soul, the marvelous power of God, abides in the three bodies and is the life of each one. A *puja viddhi mantra* (sacred chant practiced in the *nitya karmani* or Hindu rituals) intones, *omkarasya brahma ṛṣi gāyatrī chhanda angirdevata sarvakarmā rambhe viniyogaḥ*: "In the beginning of every work, I perceive the divine fire, the *gayatri* vedic hymns, Brahma, and *omkara*, the formless God."

Any word said by any person is *aum*. First, the indwelling Self speaks from the top of the head in the form of thought. It is an inaudible word that comes from the almighty father to the indwelling Self. It is "A." The indwelling Self creates speech for the tongue, but the thought has not come out. It is inside the gross body—and that is "U." When the mouth opens, the word is expressed; this is "M". The mouth is covered by two sets of sharp teeth and a set of lips. If God, through the gross body, does not allow the mouth to open, the word can not come out. Every word is the word of God. Every word is *aum*.

In the Bible (Luke 6:45), it states, "A good man out of the good treasure of his heart bringeth forth that which is good; and an evil man out of the evil treasure of his heart bringeth forth that which is evil: for of the abundance of the heart his mouth speaketh."

In India, many Brahmins, out of ignorance, said that females cannot chant the *aum* sound. This is sinful. They do not know that God speaks through the mouth, that God gives His inaudible talk to all human beings with every thought. Everyone must feel that every word coming out of the mouth is *aum*.

Aum tat sat is revealed before one chants *aum*. The supreme almighty father, hiding in the body in the formless state, allows each person to speak through the mouth. If He does not allow speech, man will be deaf and dumb.

In Kriya Yoga, there is a technique by which people can learn how to gain control over the tongue and at the same time feel God's talk in every word and thought. God is A, breath is U, and the gross body is M. Anybody saying anything can feel that God is talking. This is also *aum*. This is the stage of knowing Brahma and the Veda. It is to become a *brahmana*.

These three words—*aum tat sat*—represent the supreme almighty father who exists in each body and in the whole universe. If people really understand this verse and practice Kriya, then they can feel that without His love, the gross body is dead. Although God is in the dead, as well as the stones, the sand, the hills, and everywhere, He is more manifest in the living. This is *aum tat sat.*

Verse 24

tasmād aum ity udāhṛtya
yajñadānatapaḥkriyāḥ
pravartante vidhānoktāḥ
satatam brahmavādinām

Translation

Therefore, acts of sacrifice and penance are always commenced uttering the syllable *aum* by the *brahmavadi* (the noble souls), as prescribed by the vedic injunctions.

Metaphorical Interpretation

In the Taittiriya Upanishad (2:1:1), it says, *etasmād ātmana ākāśaḥ sambhūtaḥ*: "From the supreme Self, the sky is created." This ether or sky symbolizes the sound—*shabda mulakah akasha.* The creation started from God and went to the ether, then air, fire, water, and earth. Ether being the first creation and the cause of sound, through that other elements came into existence.

In the Bible (John 1:1), it says, "In the beginning, there was the word. The word was with God. That word is God." This sound is the *aum* or *amen* or *amin*. This sound is God. It is therefore called *nada brahma* or *shabda brahma*. But everyone must clearly understand that *aum* cannot be uttered or chanted with the mouth. Only with deep concentration, when one introverts his awareness into the state of the vacuum, can one hear the continuous, nonstop *aum* or *amen* sound. This sound is all-pervading, but a restless mind cannot perceive this sound. The ether is full of sounds of different wavelengths that can be received with the help of electronic devices such as transistor radios, etc. Similarly, although this divine sound *nadabrahma* (*aum*) is everywhere, it cannot be perceived until the mind has been made pure by Kriya Yoga meditation.

By practicing Kriya Yoga, people can remain detached and can merge in God-consciousness, during every breath. They can feel the extreme divine love. They can know the indwelling Self. Then they are called *brahmavadi*, "those who are always after God, truth, and the soul in every thought, word, and deed."

Verse 25

tad ity anabhisamdhāya
phalam yajñatapaḥkriyāḥ
dānakriyaś ca vividhāḥ
kriyante mokṣakāṅkṣibhiḥ

Translation

Realizing *tat* (that) and without aiming at the fruits, acts of *yajña* (sacrifice), *tapas* (austerity), and *dana* (charity) are performed in various ways by those who desire liberation.

Metaphorical Interpretation

In the previous verse, details about *aum* were explained; now the Lord speaks about *tat*.

"What is *tat*?" *Tat* is "that" in English. Here, *tat* symbolizes God alone, the absolute, formless, all-pervading Brahman. In the Chhandogya Upanishad (6:8:7), it says, *tat twam asi*: "That thou art". Every living being is the presence of the living God in the form of the indwelling Self. In each moment, the seekers of salvation and liberation should feel *aham brahmasmi*: "I am God" (Brihadaranyaka Upanishad 1:4:10), and

"I am that I am" (Exodus 3:14). They should maintain this inner attitude of divineness, conscious of the living power of God in every ingoing and outgoing breath, practicing *yajña* in every activity and every thought and disposition. They must love God. That is *tat*.

Dana means to give. Every person should concentrate his mind in the pituitary and fontanel on the living presence of God so that their *dana* (giving) will be extremely spiritual.

Tapa means to be established in *tapa loka*. In the *gayatri mantra*, the seven *lokas* are described: *bhuh, bhuvah, svah, mahah, janah, tapah,* and *satyam*, corresponding to the seven centers. *Tapa loka* is in the pituitary.

So, this verse means that one must perceive God through the practice of Kriya Yoga by concentrating completely and absolutely in the pituitary and fontanel during every breath. Then, one can hear the non-stop *aum* sound without any deviation or distraction. One can perceive God as a moving sensation throughout the whole body and in every work, and one can realize that the soul is the sole doer.

Verse 26

sadbhāve sādhubhāve ca
sad ity etat prayujyate
praśaste karmaṇi tathā
sacchabdaḥ pārtha yujyate

Translation

The word *sat* is used in its meaning of "reality" and its meaning of "goodness." O Son of Pritha (Kunti's son Arjuna), the word *sat* is also used for an auspicious action.

Metaphorical Interpretation

The Lord is saying, O Partha! I spoke first about *aum* and then about *tat*, Who is unseen, unknown, formless, and remaining in the whole universe. Now I will explain the meaning of *sat*."

Sat means the truth, reality, the soul, the real, the essential, the best, the learned, the excellent, the good, and the virtuous man. In the Brihadaryanaka Upanishad it says, *sadeva soumya eva atma*: "O dear student, *sat* is the soul."

Sat is the indwelling, imperishable Self that exists in every human being. *Sat* is the supreme Self, the conductor of everything. The indwelling Self is *akshara brahma*, invisible yet activating the body by the help of the supreme Self. When people become aware that the indwelling Self is always compassionately detached within, they will become honest, truthful, real, and divine. *Sat* (honesty) is essential for realizing *sat* (God).

Just as the sun continuously shines in the solar system but is compassionately detached, similarly, the soul sun illuminating the body is ever free. God-conscious, divine people perceive themselves as the soul and enjoy freedom, remaining unattached, always feeling the almighty father's presence in the body.

In this verse there are two important words: *sadbhava* and *sadhubhava*. *Bhava* means mood, perception, attitude, outlook, realization, and so on. *Sadhubhava* is the attitude of a real monk or spiritual person. It is freedom from ego and any negative qualities. This is the divine mood.

Every person should lead the life of *sat* (truth), perceiving *sat* (soul) in every breath, and achieving God (*sat*), realization, and liberation.

Verse 27

yajñe tapasi dāne ca
sthitiḥ sad iti co 'cyate
karma cai 'va tadarthīyam
sad ity evā 'bhidhīyate

Translation

Being steadfast in sacrifice, austerity, and charity is also called *sat;* also actions for the sake of God are verily termed *sat.*

Metaphorical Interpretation

Every breath is a sacrifice, a fire ceremony. *Tapas* (penance or austerity) means to keep your awareness in the pituitary during every breath, perceiving the eternal fire. The real charity is giving divine knowledge, peace, and love. Keeping the mind in the fontanel is giving the mind to the almighty Lord. This is *dana* (charity).

Many people practice many spiritual techniques, but most are not well established in the state of truth. In this verse, the Lord says *sthitih*, meaning "steadfastness," being completely and firmly established. Everyone should try to be firmly established in the pituitary and fontanel. *Sthitih* also means freedom from restlessness. Restlessness brings all troubles in life, while calmness brings peace, bliss, and joy. Calmness is godliness. Restlessness is attachment and calmness is detachment. Those who practice Kriya Yoga sincerely and with love, will be free from restlessness through breath control. They are firmly established in God-consciousness: they never forget Him. Any activity performed in God-consciousness is *sat*. This is *kri* and *ya*—knowing that all work (*kri*) is done by the soul (*ya*) is *sat*.

All work is an offering to the fire of God. Avoid negative thoughts, words, and actions because these pollute human life and bring much suffering. All work done in God consciousness will bring liberation because work is worship. This is *sat*, the divine life.

Verse 28

aśraddhayā hutam dattam
tapas taptam kṛtam ca yat
asad ity ucyate pārtha
na ca tat pretya no iha

Translation

An oblation offered, a gift donated, an austerity practiced, and work performed without faith (love) is of no account hereafter or here, O Partha (Arjuna)!

Metaphorical Interpretation

Here the Lord explains, "O Arjuna! You have a beautiful body. Perceive that this body is made by God. This body is divine. Do not feel that it is your body; it belongs to God. In the material world, you have many things, but do not think that you possess anything. Everything belongs to God. If you do not feel this way, when you do *yajñas* (fire ceremonies), *dana* (charity), and *tapas* (penance), it is falsehood."

Throughout the world, there are many cults, monastic orders, traditions, and religions. People try to worship God by reading, singing, chanting, praying, even by observing fasts and doing many types of fire ceremonies, and on and on. God cannot be perceived by all of these things. What is really important is to know that God is in everything and that God is beyond that. In extreme silence, in the complete seclusion of the fontanel, in the atom, one can realize God.

Every activity should be done with faith in God and love. If one does anything in vanity, hypocrisy, arrogance, or without love and faith, it is known as *asad* (falsehood). Spiritual life is always free from falsehood and hypocrisy. Spiritual life should always be established in truth. With faith and love, one should proceed.

Activity devoid of faith and love is falsehood and delusion that brings bondage and suffering. It is rajasic and tamasic. Love and faith associated with divine work brings liberation and God-realization. This is the essence of spiritual life through the practice of Kriya Yoga.

Summary

The seventeenth chapter of the Holy Gita is entitled "Yoga of Classification of the Threefold Faith." This chapter dealt with the nature of human being, especially one's own nature that one can easily know through one's own self-realization; the goal is to know in essence that "I am the soul, immortal and perfect."

Food is necessary—not for appeasing the tongue, or filling the stomach— but for producing better health, balanced mind and spiritual progress. People eat with greed, few eat simply to fulfill the necessities of life.

This chapter was enriched with the divine gospel of the Lord for self control and spiritual evolution. This self-disciplining way of life should be based upon the scriptural prescription, not out of one's whims. Even in the path of meditation, sacrifice should aim at one's emancipation.

This chapter discussed not only *anna* (food), but also *yajña* (sacrifice), *dana* (charity) and *tapas* (self-disciple. meditation).

The twenty-eight verses of this chapter are distributed as follows:

Verse 1: Arjuna's question related to faith based upon one's own nature.

Verses 2-4: the Lord's answer to Arjuna's question on the threefold qualities.

Verses 5-6: prayer and meditation of evil-minded personalities.

Verses 7-10: highlight of three types of eating depending upon the nature of the person.

Verses 11-13: describe three types of *yajña* (sacrifice).

Verses 14-16: discussion about penance or self-discipline on a physical, verbal and mental plane.

Verses 17-19: elaborate discussion on *tapas* (meditation, penance, self discipline) based on three qualities *(sattvic, rajasic, and tamasic).*

Verses 20-22: three types of charity described.

Verse 23: description of *om tat sat*

Verse 24: explanation of *om*

Verse 25: explanation of *tat*

Verse 26-27: explanation of *sat*

Verse 28: anything done without faith and love is fruitless, declared the Lord

Change the life force, and then use this life—it will take care of the future. Strive to attain perfection now, then the future will be beautiful. Practice for perfection through faith, love and sincerity. This is key to success.

Chapter 18

Mokṣa sannyāsa yoga

The Yoga of Liberation through Renunciation

Introduction

Without devotion, and without faith in the words of the scriptures and the realized master, one cannot make progress in spiritual life. The scriptures cast their light on the spiritual path and the words of the teacher encourage the student to follow it. Through faith and love and the practice of meditation, the mind becomes settled and the intellect pure.

The holy Bhagavad Gita is the book of life; it is useful for leading a successful life in every way. To experience the truth and to realize it in its complete glory, there is no need for arguments or counterarguments. Breath is the necessity for life. Breath is God. Breath is the means to realization and the link to perfection. Perfection is the goal of life. This is the truth about life. The holy Bhagavad Gita is a guidebook for walking the spiritual path, for attaining emancipation, for finding perfection. If there is one single foundation for successful human life, it is breath control. Through breath control, purity and perfection can be reached.

The principal mistakes in life are attachment to the body and lack of control over the mind. To be aware of your mistakes and weaknesses is good. When you know your vulnerability to weakness, you can learn how to be free from imperfections. This body is a beautiful instrument for reaching the highest state of perfection, but to overcome all the limitations of life, you must be free from sloth, idleness, and doubt. By leading a moral life, you wash away the impurities of mind. Through meditation you can attain eternal union with the supreme self. Always remember, "I am not the body, I am the soul—beautiful, pure, and divine."

This chapter, "The Yoga of Liberation through Renunciation," is the summary of the Lord's teachings.

The lotus leaf lives on the water but is not attached to it. In the same way, we must maintain inner detachment while we live in the world. If a person is attached to the body and considers himself to be the body, the life stream cannot flow smoothly; it is obstructed. The body is a beautiful medium; use it in a moderate and healthy way.

The ultimate goal of life is to achieve perfection in thought, word, and deed. Everyone must attempt to achieve this end. Being established in the divine self in every breath, in every moment, is the key.

In this concluding chapter, the Lord discusses the meaning and purpose of life, the obstacles and weaknesses in human life, and finally the life of inner renunciation and perfection.

Verse 1

arjuna uvāca
saṃnyāsasya mahābāho
tattvam icchāmi veditum
tyāgasya ca hṛṣīkeśa
pṛthak keśiniṣūdana

Translation

Arjuna asked:
I wish to know the truth of *sannyasa* (renunciation), O Keshinishudana (Krishna), and also of *tyaga* (relinquishment or abandonment), and the difference between the two.

Metaphorical Interpretation

The Bhagavad Gita is a detailed and elaborate discussion of spiritual life and meditation. In it, Arjuna is extremely happy to learn about practical spirituality from his divine master, Shri Krishna. He is a sincere student: anxious to learn and ready to practice. When the disciple is really ready and fit, he can easily and quickly make spiritual progress and attain realization. In order to achieve more power and understanding, Arjuna questioned the Lord further and further. This verse is Arjuna's last question in this great scripture of the Bhagavad Gita.

Arjuna addresses the Lord by three names: Hrishikesha, Keshinishudana, and Mahabahu. These three names have beautiful spiritual connotations.

Hrishikesha comes from *hrishikanam isha. Hrishik* is the senses in the body. *Isha* is the Lord, the controller. So *hrishikesh* is the controller, the Lord, the master of the senses. The truly divine master is the master of the senses, not the slave of passion and sensation. The soul in the body controls the senses. The soul is Krishna. The soul is the guru, the master. "O Krishna, you are the master and controller of the senses."

Keshinishudana comes from *keshi*, meaning the delusive power or negative qualities, and *nishudana*, the complete destroyer. In this sense, Krishna is the divine incarnation who destroys all the negative demonic qualities. In every human being there are extremely negative qualities: delusion, illusion, and error. He who removes all the negative qualities and reaches the truth can lead all to truth, so all people can be free from delusion, illusion, and error.

Mahabahu means "the mighty armed"—full of strength, vigor, and vitality. The marvelous power of God is within every living being, providing strength and vigor. This is *mahabahu*.

"O Krishna," Arjuna is saying, "You told me everything. Every human being should try to shun all the negative qualities and avoid the tempting attraction of delusion, illusion, and error. From Your gospels I learned about two things, inner detachment and renunciation, but I am not completely clear about the difference between these two. I want to understand clearly and completely. Please explain it to me."

Although people consider these two words *sannyas* (renunciation) and *tyaga* (abandonment) to mean the same thing, there are subtle and metaphorical distinctions between the two. *Sannyas* (renunciation) and *tyaga* (abandonment) are always associated in yoga meditation and practical spiritual life.

Essentially, Arjuna is asking two questions:

1. How can I be detached from the material world (*maya*)?
2. How can I reach the state of *sannyas*?

Verse 2

ṣrībhagavān uvāca
kāmyānām karmaṇām nyāsam
samnyāsam kavayo viduḥ
sarvakarmaphalatyāgam
prāhustyāgam vicakṣaṇāḥ

Translation

The Lord said:

The sages understand that renunciation is giving up actions motivated by desire, and other intelligent thinkers declare that abandonment is relinquishing the fruits of action.

Metaphorical Interpretation

People have many kinds of ambition and desire. Motivated by all these propensities, they remain engrossed in material activity, which leads them to bondage. When actions motivated by desire are left behind and the seeker remains compassionately detached in the fontanel, this is *sannyasa*—renunciation of action prompted by desire. Those who are somewhat advanced search for their soul without expecting any fruit from their actions; they are *tyagi.*

Every action has its fruit, but ignorant are those who work to get a result. They do not know what renunciation and relinquishment are. People work in an office to earn money, but they should work for the sake of duty. They should realize that at any moment they may die, and if they do, they will not enjoy the remuneration for their labor. Their money will remain in the office or their heirs will receive the money.

Man is attached to children, relatives, and even his house, but the moment his breath quits, he cannot enjoy anything anymore. Therefore, he should cultivate this feeling: "According to my destiny, I am working. I have a family. For duty's sake, I work. But I will remain compassionately detached, because when I die, the family and the material possessions will not accompany me." When a person works with this understanding, he understands true detachment, and inner detachment will come.

Death may come at any time. A dead man cannot work. The indwelling soul activates man. The body is an instrument. The soul maintains life. The soul is working. Desireless work is called inaction: "God is doing the work. I am only watching Him. I am compassionately detached." This leads to renunciation.

Verse 3

tyājyam doṣavad ity eke
karma prāhur manīṣiṇaḥ
yajñadānatapaḥkarma
na tyājyam iti cāpare

Translation

Some wise men declare that action is to be abandoned and is full of evil, and others say that the acts of sacrifice, charity, and austerity are not to be abandoned.

Metaphorical Interpretation

In this verse the word *manishi* is used. He who has controlled the mind (*manas*) is *manishi*—learned, wise (see the Isha Upanishad, Mantra 8). There are many learned people in the world who say that work includes attachment and must be shunned, but others say that activities like *yajña* (sacrifice), *dana* (charity), and *tapas* (austerity) should not be abandoned (see Chapter 17).

What is real work? Real work is performed as an oblation to God. While working, one must watch the indwelling soul who is drawing the breath day and night. With every breath one is united with the almighty father.

One must also feel the presence of the marvelous power of God in every family member. When taking care of family members, the spiritual seeker must feel that he is serving the Lord. This service is *dana*—real charity. At the same time, one must also do charity for a noble cause.

Breath is life. Only with the breath can work be done. Without breath one cannot work. As the work changes, the breath also changes. The breath flows because of the soul inside. Every person must feel that the soul, through the breath, is activating his life. With every breath, if one perceives the presence of God, the creator of life in the body, then every breath will be oblation to God with love. This is *prana karma*, "action" of *prana*, the real worship of God.

Those who have not yet controlled their minds, who have not attained the state of *manisha*, should practice Kriya while working so they will realize, "The doer is He. He is working through this body from the fontanel through the pituitary." They will feel that they are serving God in every action. Service to human beings is service to God.

With this attitude, if you remain in the world and work, you will become compassionately detached and will attain realization. Through breath consciousness you can rise to the state of soul consciousness in *tapah loka*—the plane of meditation and penance. If you keep your mind on the Lord, and if in every breath while working you feel that every work is worship—"I am giving my love and life in work"—then this is the real fire ceremony.

Verse 4

niścayam śṛṇu me tatra
tyāge bharatasattama
tyāgo hi puruṣavyāghra
trividhaḥ samprakīrtitaḥ

Translation

O Best of Bharatas (Arjuna)! Please hear my conclusive remark on the topic of *tyaga*—renunciation. O Tiger among Men (Arjuna)! Renunciation is declared to be of three types.

Metaphorical Interpretation

Arjuna is addressed by Shri Krishna, the Lord and the divine preceptor, by two different names: Bharata sattama (best of the Bharatas) and Purusha-vyaghra (tiger among men). These two names stand for two important qualities of a sincere spiritual seeker. Bharata (*bhara* + *tana*) means the state of expansion attained by the life force (*prana*) when one practices Kriya, the supreme meditation technique in which brilliant divine light is perceived. Arjuna, following the teaching of his master, perceived that divine illumination.

The other name is Purushavyaghra (tiger among men). *Vyaghra* is explained in the Sanskrit scriptures as *vyajighrati ity vyaghra*: "One who has strong smelling power". This is the tiger, a most powerful animal whose power of nose (breath) is very strong. Arjuna, through the power of meditation, has thorough control over his animal qualities, and he devours all his ambitions. He also has a powerful ability to regulate his nose (he has breath control). Arjuna remains in the stage of superconsciousness, absorbed in the almighty father. He is the best of all seekers.

In Indian mythology Jagaddhatri, the divine mother, sits on a tiger, and Durga sits on a lion. The divine beings sit on the tiger and the lion, the kings of animals, symbolizing thorough control over the animal qualities of a person.

The Lord is saying, "O Arjuna! You desire God-realization. In your love to know more and more you repeatedly ask questions. I will explain the real meaning of renunciation. Please listen to me carefully".

Generally speaking, there are three types of renunciation: sattvic, the spiritual renunciation; rajasic, the renunciation of the extremely active; and tamasic, the renunciation of the idle. These three types of renunciation exist in every human being, but the true renunciant is free from all ambitions for present and future life.

Verse 5

yajñadānatapaḥkarma
na tyājyam kāryam eva tat
yajño dānam tapaścaiva
pāvanāni manīṣiṇām

Translation

Acts of sacrifice, charity, and penance (austerity) are not to be given up; rather, they must be performed. For sacrifice, charity, and penance sanctify the life of the wise men.

Metaphorical Interpretation

Renunciation does not mean to avoid all action, which is impossible. This describes the three actions that should not be shunned: *yajña* (sacrifice or fire ceremony), *dana* (acts of charity), and *tapas* (penance or austerity).

People usually take the meaning of these three types of action literally and perform fire ceremonies by offering oblations to the ceremonial fire, they do charity by giving some material help or a donation to the needy, and they undertake acts of austerity by which they torture the body. But the proper approach to these three spiritual practices is metaphorical. *Yajña* means *pranayajña*, offering oblation of breath to the soul fire in the pituitary and to the God fire in the fontanel. Those who want spiritual growth must be conscious of the indwelling Self in every breath so they will be free from all negative qualities.

Dana means to donate. Realization would be extremely easy if you could pass through its gateway by donating your belongings. Real *dana* is to donate the restless mind full of dirty ideas to God, so that every thought is divine and God-oriented.

Tapas is the breath (oxygen) that goes up and touches the God-fire in the fontanel, thereby maintaining body temperature. Another meaning of *tapas* is to remain in *tapah loka.* There are seven *lokas* (planes of consciousness)—*bhuh, bhuvah, svah, mahah, janah, tapah,* and *satyam*—corresponding to the seven centers in the spine and brain. *Tapah loka* is associated with the *ajña* chakra near the pituitary. *Tapas*, the real penance and austerity, is not allowing the mind to go below this point and keeping the attention above in the pituitary.

Through these activities the mind becomes pure. A person can be compassionately detached and God-conscious, a truly educated person. Those who perform these three types of work are perfect.

Verse 6

etāny api tu karmāṇi
saṅgam tyaktvā phalāni ca

kartavyānīti me pārtha
niścitam matam uttamam

Translation

Hence, these actions are to be performed without attachment or expectation of reward. This is My definite and highest verdict, O Arjuna!

Metaphorical Interpretation

The Lord is saying, "O Arjuna! Your attention is always in the pituitary. From your birth, you have always had the extreme power to shun evil dispositions. Repeatedly, I explain that a person who remains compassionately detached and does the works prescribed by Me, realizing that he is not the doer or enjoyer, is free. In every deed he feels that *ham* (the instrument, the gross body) and *sa* (the real doer, the soul) remain compassionately detached like the sun does when it lights the earth and helps others work".

In the ordinary spiritual practice of *yajña,* (a ritualistic fire ceremony), *dana* (charity), and *tapas* (penance), people are much too attached to the rewards. One should work, but should not expect any fruit from it. Keep the attention in the pituitary, from where the real work is originating. While meditating and practicing Kriya, do not harbor an expectation for a result or a reward. Be attached to meditation, but not to its fruit. Following the instructions of the realized master, meditate daily, regularly, and sincerely. Practicing Kriya with love and deep concentration will make the mind pure, so one can proceed on the path of realization.

"O Partha (Arjuna)! It is My supreme opinion that the breath is going in and out (*prana karma*) without any expectation. Please watch your breath, and in each breath love He who is breathing".

This is the highest verdict of the supreme Lord.

Verse 7

niyatasya tu samnyāsaḥ
karmaṇo nopapadyate
mohāt tasya parityāgas
tāmasaḥ parikīrtitaḥ

Translation

But renunciation of obligatory action is not proper. The abandonment of such acts through delusion is declared to be tamasic (idle).

Metaphorical Interpretation.

In the previous two verses the Lord said that *yajña* (sacrifice), *dana* (charity), and *tapas* (penance) should not be avoided because abandoning work brings idleness. Many people think that spiritual life is a life of inactivity. They think "I will not work. I will remain silently inactive." If someone has this type of disposition, then he is not *sannyasi*—a true renunciant monk.

All the work you accomplish or that God forces you to do is truly worship. God gives the motivation, but when the path of inactivity is adopted, God's motion is suppressed. Similarly, from a biological point of view, suppression of the motion of urine or of evacuation of stool leads to health disorders.

Deluded people want to avoid work. In this verse the Lord describes *niyata karma*, karma performed through the *indriyas*—activity of the senses. God has given us mouths for speaking and taking food. God has given us eyes to see good things. Many people however want to avoid natural exercise of the senses, which is not really divine action, to make themselves seem spiritually advanced. This is sheer idleness, *tamas.* Real spirituality requires the proper use of the mouth, eyes, ears, and so forth for good work. Above all, in every work, real spirituality means to be aware of the indwelling self. This approach to spiritual life is necessary.

Constantly keep your attention on the imperishable soul through breath consciousness. Do your work without negative or immoral activity. Realize that destiny plays a role and that you will experience antecedents and consequences. In every breath watch the almighty Lord. By remaining compassionately detached from the results and fruits of actions, by searching for Him in every breath, spiritual emancipation will be achieved. This is the work that everyone must accomplish well. This is the expression of love for the almighty Lord.

If you do not work and give love to the almighty Lord, then how can you grow spiritually? Work is the vehicle for spiritual growth. The soul is the cause of breathing and doing everything. If you do not change your attitude toward work, there is the danger of extreme delusion. Those who are inactive, lazy, or idle cannot love God in the true spirit.

Open your eyes and see the beauty of God. Walk and watch the living power of God walking. Do all the work given to you by the almighty father. Be free from negative activities. God has provided sense organs to be used in a positive way, for reaching the divine goal.

At times, due to a quarrel in a family, one leaves the family and takes *sannyas* in a faraway place. This is delusion, not *sannyas*. This is a tamasic (slothful) attitude toward life.

God has given you all the power. Search for Him. He is your life. Love Him.

Verse 8

duḥkham ityeva yat karma
kāyakleśabhayāt tyajet
sa kṛtvā rājasam tyāgam
naiva tyāgaphalam labhet

Translation

He who gives up a duty because it is difficult or painful or even because of fear or physical discomfort, performs rajasic

renunciation (material approach). He does not obtain the result of such renunciation.

Metaphorical Interpretation

God has endowed every person with three qualities—tamasic, rajasic, and sattvic—in different proportions. There are ups and downs in material life. Weal and woe come in turns. But people with negative understanding avoid activities that engender some physical discomfort, strain, and trouble. Avoiding such work is not renunciation; it is rajasic.

True renunciation is the state of desirelessness. Suppressing desire and spiritual posturing is not spirituality. If the internal instruments such as the mind and intellect are not properly purified, the suppressed mind will explode with a little experience of enjoyment. Suppression leads to explosions that ultimately bring downfall on the spiritual path.

So, by constant self-effort, fix the attention in the pituitary and then in the fontanel. In every breath, watch the living presence of God. Develop awareness of breath. Breath is your life. Your only real work is to watch your breath and love God. Remain constantly alert during every breath and thank Him; then you will proceed on the path of realization. If you are forgetful, it will create an unnecessary delay in accomplishing God-realization.

If you do not prepare your food with love and take proper food at the proper time, you will encounter trouble and difficulties, and you won't have good health. Food is one of the principal requirements of human life. Prepare food with love and offer it as an oblation in the *vaishvanara agni*—the digestive fire in the navel center. Do not think that you are taking food to satisfy your tongue, but rather as an offering to God. This type of attitude will accelerate your spiritual progress.

Many people try to leave their family and pose as renounced monks. They lead idle and inactive lives, afraid of the conflict in their family. This is negative renunciation, not true spiritual living.

If, as a result of deep meditation, a person achieves freedom from all worldly desires, material ambition, and craving of the sense organs, this person will reach *samadhi*. To attain this level and to experience constant liberation, one must labor hard and search for God constantly. This is the way. Otherwise, God-realization and liberation is a dream, too far away to be achieved. Avoid all types of idleness and lethargy. Be strong, bold, and active. Proceed steadily on the path of realization.

Verse 9

kāryam ityeva yat karma
niyatam kriyate 'rjuna
saṅgam tyaktvā phalam caiva
sa tyāgaḥ sāttviko mataḥ

Translation

O Arjuna! When action is performed constantly because it is a duty, and all attachment and expectation of fruit is given up, then this renunciation can be recognized as sattvic (spiritual).

Metaphorical Interpretation

The only purpose of human birth is for God-realization, which is the state of constant peace, bliss, and joy. To achieve such a state, you must strive sincerely and must be mindful to be always compassionately detached and free from expecting results.

A yogi is not attracted to or repelled by anything. The yogi's breath goes in and out day and night without any expectation; it is spontaneous and automatic. At the same time, the yogi constantly keeps his awareness in the fontanel without expectation through work. This is the practice of Kriya Yoga in everyday life.

"O Arjuna! Every day you must meditate and fix your attention in the fontanel. Watch and search for the Lord in the fontanel. Witness his presence in every breath. If you don't work, you cannot progress. To eat, you must work. You don't know the consequences of this work. There is no need for you to think about it. Remain compassionately detached from everything and work for duty's sake, then you will know Him. You were born for God-realization".

Through practice of a technique such as Kriya Yoga, you can learn to watch Him during the daily work that is given to you by God. The imperishable soul helps you do the work. In every work remember Him. This is how you live in the world and remain compassionately detached. In every work, perceive the living presence of God, remember Him, and love Him constantly.

Working with this attitude, approach, and understanding, applying Kriya meditation in daily life (*kri* and *ya*), and remaining constantly detached is undoubtedly spiritual renunciation (*sattvika tyaga.*) An outward display of renunciation only leads to spiritual corruption and hypocrisy.

Verse 10

na dveṣṭy akuśalam karma
kuśale nānuṣajjate
tyāgī sattvasamāviṣṭo
medhāvī chinnasamśayaḥ

Translation

The man of renunciation, the wise man, whose doubt is cut away, is full of goodness and neither hates disagreeable action, nor is he attached to auspicious action.

Metaphorical Interpretation

Every man in endowed with the triple qualities of nature: *sattva* (spiritual), *rajas* (material), and *tamas* (laziness), but in different proportions. To be active on the spiritual path, one must sincerely try to overcome the plurality of *rajas* and *tamas*—restlessness and idleness. When one becomes established in sattvic nature, life is full of illumination.

Those who are spiritual have steadiness of mind. They are free from all doubt and duality. They constantly search for God in every breath. They are liberated souls. If they encounter troubles when working, they are not disturbed, unhappy, or annoyed; they maintain equanimity.

Equanimity comes only through regulation of breath. By breath regulation one achieves self-regulation. While performing any action, a spiritual person is thinking of the almighty Lord, trying to be compassionately detached.

Rajas is the state of intense worldly activity that leads to anxiety, tension, and restlessness. *Tamas* is doubt, laziness, and a dwindling nature. Those who are free from *rajas* and *tamas,* who are proceeding toward *sattva*, calmness and spirituality, meditate sincerely and follow the teachings of their guru preceptor—their spiritual guide. They follow the master one hundred percent. They become more introverted and calmer. Restlessness disappears. Their minds are settled by breath control. Breath control is self-control.

True spiritual seekers develop strong determination and willpower through regular meditation and spiritual practice. They lead a life of extreme detachment, just like the soul. This is the sign of liberation. Free from desire and craving, in the state of constant God communion, they are ever free, liberated, and in *sa* (soul) consciousness.

To spiritual people, happiness and unhappiness are equal. They are steady in their dispositions and alert during every breath. They are free from duality and absorbed in the imperishable soul and the supreme almighty father. The ideal renunciant is established in God consciousness, free from doubt, delusion, and degeneration. Through regular practice of meditation they are more and more deeply absorbed into this divine state.

Verse 11

na hi dehabhṛtā śakyam
tyaktum karmāṇy aśeṣataḥ
yas tu karmaphalatyāgī
sa tyāgīty abhidhīyate

Translation

Since actions cannot be given up entirely by someone possessing a body, only he who renounces the fruit of actions is called a man of renunciation.

Metaphorical Interpretation

Most people are extremely attached to the body. They think that they are the body. They cannot realize that they are really the soul—living in the body. Body consciousness breeds many difficulties. Body-conscious people cannot perceive the importance of breath in their daily life. In this verse, these ignorant people are called *dehabhrit*, body-conscious, engrossed in activity, forgetful of the indwelling self. There are also those pseudo-spiritual individuals who present themselves as if they were renunciant monks, externally detached, but internally, in their minds, they are extremely attached to the material world. They always maintain a double standard, and that is not spirituality.

One must clearly understand the true principles of spiritual life. Every human being is the soul living in a body house. So long as the body is there, one must work. The body needs food. One must provide enough food for the nourishment, growth, and maintenance of the body. To obtain food, one must work and earn money, purchase foodstuffs, and cook. This type of work is unavoidable. If you do not eat regularly, disease, ill health, and ultimately suffering and death will come. Ordinarily, you cannot completely detach yourself from material work so long as the body exists.

So what should the spiritual aspirant do? He must reform his outlook. He must know the secret of work (*kri* and *ya*). Work must be worship.

While eating, be attached to the indwelling self, not the tempting tongue. While taking food, offer each taste of food as an oblation to the divine fire for the purpose of maintaining the body. This attitude will generate inner detachment and God-conscious higher living, making you free from the fruits of action, ultimately leading to liberation.

Most people are whimsical. They are afraid of work, but for the sake of the body, work must be done. Due to laziness, some people don't even cook their own food: they purchase and eat fast food, junk food. If they persist, they will acquire diseases (dis-eases) and ailments in their bodies. You must be careful about food. It should not be rich, spicy, and oily merely for the satisfaction of the tongue. Take food in moderation, only as required. In this way, during all work, with moderation and God-consciousness, you can avoid *karma-phala,* fruition of actions.

Inner detachment does not mean you work because of desire and ambition for achievement. Only for the sake of the body should material work be performed. When you constantly search for the indwelling self while performing action, you will perceive that you are not working, the soul is the cause of all activity. Through such inner awareness, all immoral and debauched attitudes can be avoided.

There is no need for pomp and grandeur in spiritual life. Spending a lot of money and spending day and night in extroverted religious exhibitionism will not yield the ultimate fruit. To be spiritual through calmness, only watch the Lord in the fontanel and silently search for Him in the breath. Then you can be free from attachment; then you can experience continuous God-realization and liberation.

Verse 12

aniṣṭam iṣṭam miśram ca
trividham karmaṇaḥ phalam
bhavaty atyāginām pretya
na tu samnyāsinām kvacit

Translation

Evil, good, and mixed—threefold indeed are the fruits of action accruing hereafter from the actions of those who don't renounce. But there is no fruit at all for those who have renounced.

Metaphorical Interpretation

Ordinarily, people are ambitious. The ambitious, who consider the fruit of their actions while undertaking any endeavor, enjoy the fruits of those actions. There are three types of fruits: evil, good, and the mixture of both. Every action generates results. A person who does bad works will receive bad fruit and will suffer. Those who do good work earn some temporary joy and satisfaction. Those who do mixed work will get mixed consequences. Those who work with ambition are always seeking passion, anger, attachment, and suffering. Ambition is the greatest enemy.

Man can be free from ambition and attachment and can reach the supreme state. Certainly, there are people with good destiny who are not ambitious, but anyone who properly understands the secret of work can make himself truly free from all material ambition.

Man must work; work brings the result. He who offers every work to the Lord works as a mode of worship (as prescribed in the Bhagavad Gita 9:27). He works to fulfill the divine will, free from material ambition. Ordinarily, when ambitions are not achieved, man suffers. But a spiritual person is free from all material ambitions. He has only one ambition: to be God realized. This ambition does not bring bondage; satisfying this ambition is liberation. God loves His creation. He is breathing in everyone as the imperishable soul.

A spiritual person should constantly seek and search for the power of God with every breath. Through this search, his awareness will rise up to the fontanel. Then love for God will flourish, and he will sincerely try to attain God-realization and liberation in this life.

A renunciant monk shuns all material ambition, but there is one expectation: self-realization and liberation. When he searches in the pituitary, he feels very strongly the presence of the imperishable soul residing in the body, compassionately detached. The soul is formless and is the cause of the inhalation from the cranium; that is why everyone is alive. When the sincere seeker searches deeper, he proceeds towards the almighty father, the Supreme One, who has given life to all. Thus, the seeker gets absorbed in the super-conscious and cosmic-conscious states, and then enters into wisdom, the realization of the absolute—*prajñanam brahma*— the externally pulseless and breathless state.

Wisdom cannot be perceived by the five sense organs, but only by bringing the awareness to the atom point in the fontanel. Those who are trying to penetrate into the atom point by the scientific technique of Kriya Yoga are free from all actions of the material world. Physical needs are secondary. In daily life, through the five sense organs, they perceive the almighty father. In the whole body, they feel the formless one. Through this they get liberation. They are extremely detached. They are truly God in the form of a human being.

Verse 13

pañcaitāni mahābāho
kāraṇāni nibodha me
sāmkhye kṛtānte proktāni
siddhaye sarvakarmaṇām

Translation

O mighty armed (Arjuna)! Learn from me these five factors, for the accomplishment of all actions as declared in the principles of Samkhya and Vedanta.

Metaphorical Interpretation

"O Mahabahu! Mighty armed! You are not an ordinary human; you are God in a human being. You have marvelous powers. You have the deepest desire for soul culture and God-realization." Mahabahu has many connotations. It literally means "mighty-armed." Arms and hands are the symbols of activity. He whose activity is always God-oriented is *mahabahu*.

"O Arjuna! I told you about Samkhya and Vedanta. What is Samkhya and what is Vedanta?" Samkhya is the knowledge that gives a person the power to carefully observe the truth in everything.

Vedanta consists of two words: *veda* (knowledge) and *anta* (end); it is the end of all knowledge.

Only through meditation and the practice of Kriya Yoga can one easily understand the play of this world and know that ego is the cause of all play and suffering. But when one practices Kriya sincerely and goes to the state of *paravastha* (the state of extreme tranquillity)—this is Vedanta.

Shri Lahiri Mahasaya said, "Kriya is the study of the Vedas; attaining the state of *paravastha* is the realization of the Vedas."

"O Arjuna! For soul culture and even for any material activity, an intelligent aspirant must know the five causes—the five instruments." These five instruments are explained in the next verse.

Verse 14

adhiṣṭhānam tathā kartā
karaṇam ca pṛthagvidham
vividhāśca pṛthakceṣṭā
daivam caivātra pañcamam

Translation

[The five causes or five instruments are] the seat of action (the body), the agent of action (the doer), the various organs, the various different activities, and destiny or providence.

Metaphorical Interpretation

Here the Lord continues His sermon on the causes of activity and the secret to success in any human endeavor or effort. He categorically classifies these factors to be only five:
1. *Adhishthana*: the seat of action—especially the human body.
2. *Karta*: the agent of action—the cause by which the body is activated. Ordinarily, due to ignorance, the egocentric personality thinks, "I am the doer."

3. *Karana*: the twelve instruments (*karanas)* or organs—five organs of action (speech, hands, arms, legs, and sex organ); five organs of perception (touch, taste, smell, sight, and hearing); and the mind and intellect.
4. *Vividha chesta*: efforts, endeavors, and activities.
5. *Daiva*: destiny or providence.

Here the Lord systematically lists the five factors responsible for carrying out any activity. The principal factor is the human body—the basic principle of all activities. If the body is kept in perfectly healthy condition, one can work and quickly achieve a goal. A healthy body is one of the basics for success in material as well as spiritual life. The body is the house in which the soul lives.

The second factor is the doer. In ordinary people, the ego thinks that it is the doer, not the body or the senses. This belief stems from ignorance.

The third factor is the instruments: the *indriyas* (the sense organs), with *manas* (the mental factor) and *buddhi* (the intellectual factor) as additional vital components. Pure mind and intellect in the regulated sense organs can work, enjoy, and reach any goal easily.

To achieve success in any area of life, effort is necessary. Without sufficient effort human endeavor cannot create the necessary result.

The last factor is human destiny, which is nothing but the accumulated effect of all past actions—*daiva* in Sanskrit. *Daiva* is derived from *div*, the state of emptiness, formlessness—in other aspects it is divine love. When you depend on God, love God, and perceive oneness with God, you will have success in life.

Suppose an artist wants to paint a picture on a piece of canvas. Canvas represents the first factor, the base of activity (*adhishthana.*) The artist is the actor (*karta*), the paints and brush are the material instruments (*karana.*) The process of painting is the human endeavor (*vividha chesta.*) The skill and knowledge of painting stored in the brain is the destiny (*daiva.)* These five factors are the basic requirements of painting, so also any action in the world.

Verse 15

śarīravāṅmanobhir yat
karma prārabhate naraḥ
nyāyyam vā viparītam vā
pañcai'te tasya hetavaḥ

Translation

These five factors contribute to whatever actions, right or wrong, that man undertakes with body, speech, or mind.

Metaphorical Interpretation

Man does work physically, vocally, and mentally. Any work accomplished with the body and sense organs is physical work. Every physical work can be classified as good or bad. A man's vocal expression, such as truthful or false talk, sweet, divine talk, or harsh words may also be good or bad. Yet man does not only work physically and express himself vocally—any thought arising in the mind, good or bad, will also cause either good or bad results. A divine and good thought can bring positive change in life, while a negative thought may bring mental suffering that leads to physical discomfort.

But every intelligent person should know that all activities—physical, vocal, and mental—are conditioned and influenced by the five factors: the human body, the ego, the organs of action and perception, mind, and intellect, human effort, and destiny. These five factors allow man to work physically, vocally, and mentally.

Verse 16

tatraivam sati kartāram
ātmānam kevalam tu yaḥ

paśyaty akṛtabuddhitvān
na sa paśyati durmatiḥ

Translation

This being so, however, one who sees himself or herself as the doer does not really see, because with perverted understanding one does not perceive truth.

Metaphorical Interpretation

In this material world, most people have misconceptions about doership. Many people think that they are the body, and that their body is doing all the work. Many other people think that work is done by the soul, *atma.* Both are wrong in their understanding.

The previous verses clearly delineate the five factors essential for any type of work. But without the presence of the soul, these five factors cannot function. The soul's presence energizes the five instruments and makes them active. Without the soul, they are inert and dead. On the other hand, many people with perverted understanding think that the soul is doing all activities, even bad work. They do not hesitate to say that the soul in the thief is stealing, or the soul in the murderer is killing. In which case, the result of the good or bad works would go to the soul, not to the person—sin would go to the soul. This is silliness and is completely wrong.

Consider the example of the sun. The sun is the source of light, energy, and activity. In the dead of night people cannot see anything and cannot work. When the sun rises, people are active. They can see everything. In the day, in sunlight, someone is meditating, somebody else is preparing food, and another is eating. Somebody else is taking a bath, and another is reading. They are all doing different work in the sun's light. Although the sun is the cause of all the activities, it is detached from everything. The sun can cause extensive activity while being detached.

Those who do not meditate or who do not know the nature of the almighty father and the imperishable soul cannot really perceive the truth. Those who seek truth meditate sincerely and remain compassionately detached like the sun. On the other hand, those who think that the soul is responsible for all work and is "guilty" are foolish and ignorant. They have scanty knowledge about the almighty father. And, as it is said, people with a little knowledge are dangerous.

Body conscious people who think that the body is the self, and that any work done by the body is done by the soul, are far from reality and the truth. They think that the soul is born with the body and dies with the body (see the Bhagavad Gita, 13: 31–32 and 14:19).

Verse 17

yasya nāhamkṛto bhāvo
buddhir yasya na lipyate
hatvāpi sa imāml lokān
na hanti na nibadhyate

Translation

He whose mind is free from the sense of doership and whose intellect is not tainted (by worldly objects and activities), even though he slays people, does not really slay and is not bound (by sins).

Metaphorical Interpretation

People engrossed in work become absorbed in the ego of doership. Because of this sense of doership, they suffer physically and mentally, enjoying the fruit of action. But spiritual people who are trying to cleanse their inner life with meditation inherit two vital qualities: *naham krita bhavah*, freedom from the sense of doership, and *buddhir na lipyate*, untainted, detached intellect. They are completely absorbed in soul, in God. Although they live in their bodies and the sense instruments work, they are inwardly detached.

Consider the example of the mother who has lost her child. She is so absorbed in sorrow that she is not aware of her surroundings.

When a large procession of loud musicians passes by the front of her house, she is unable to hear the melody of the music. Similarly, a mentally retarded man walking naked in the street does not feel his condition or any shame. If a lunatic, lacking all common sense, kills a boy with a sword—he will not realize what he has done. He has neither grief nor repentance for mistakes or crimes. He does not feel guilty and may not be punished.

Similarly, when a man is meditating very deeply and is completely absorbed in the soul, he doesn't know what he is doing. If he commits some mistake while in this state of detachment, he is not aware of his wrongdoing. His actions are not consciously motivated; his brain is different because of his detachment. An extremely spiritual person, completely God-intoxicated, perceives God's presence everywhere—and may even hug and kiss the trees. He is not attached to anything good or bad. When he eats, he doesn't know what he is eating. His mind is constantly fixed on God. He is without common sense and is not aware the world exists. Such was the condition of Shri Chaitanya Mahaprabhu, a realized master and God-intoxicated monk of fifteenth-century India.

Verse 18

jñānam jñeyam parijñātā
trividhā karmacodanā
karaṇam karma karte 'ti
trividhaḥ karmasamgrahaḥ

Translation

Knowledge, the object of knowledge, and the knower are the threefold motivation for action. The instrument, the action, and the doer are the threefold constituents of action.

Metaphorical Interpretation

In Verse 14, the five factors for action were discussed. Even with these five, work cannot be performed without motivation.

The Lord says that knowledge, the object of knowledge, and the knower are the threefold motivation for any type of action. The five factors with motivation can perform any action (*karma*). The threefold motivation can be described as *jñana,* the perception of necessity, *jñeya,* the object of fulfilling the necessity, and *jñata* or *parijñata,* the knower of these. In all circumstances, these aspects exist. So for a spiritual life, one should also consider them.

Everyone should have the desire for self-realization. Self-realization eradicates all suffering and gives you constant peace. The desire, the sincere yearning for God-realization is *jñana. Jñeya* is perceiving only God, perceiving God in everything at all times and in all places. God alone is to be known, perceived, and realized. *Jñata* or *parijñata* is someone who is truly willing to know God. This person is always sincerely striving to find God, thinking of Him continuously. His mind is extremely busy and joyful. He practices Kriya and meditates for hours at a time, even in the night. He has no sense of time. Busy in sincere contemplation and meditation, he is intensely engrossed in Brahman and has the deepest desire and love for God.

Such a person, busy with soul culture, questions his master over and over like Arjuna queried Shri Krishna. He is using all his *karanas,* his sense organs, his mind, his thoughts, everything, for self-inquiry. He is constantly trying to regulate his mind and be calm, sincerely trying to fix his mind in the pituitary. This is the real *karma—pranakarma*—the action of the vital air, the awareness that breathing is the manifestation of God's work.

The power of God pervades everything and is manifest everywhere. He is in every being. *Ayamatma brahma*: "This soul is Brahma." *Aham brahma 'smi*: "I am the living power of God." The marvelous power of God is always in me, inhaling and exhaling from above!

The mind is the other cause of action. When the mind is transformed into supreme consciousness, *sarva khalvidam brahma*, all-pervading God is perceived. One then goes to *prajñanam brahma,* the state of cosmic-consciousness and wisdom. By the spiritual work of breath control and self control, one becomes free and achieves *samadhi*—unity with the almighty father.

Verse 19

jñānam karma ca kartā ca
tridhāiva guṇabhedataḥ
procyate guṇasamkhyāne
yathāvac chṛṇu tāny api

Translation

It is declared in Samkhya that knowledge, action, and the doer are of three kinds, distinguished according to their quality. Hear these distinctions directly from Me as well.

Metaphorical Interpretation

Although the soul is always compassionately detached, still, due to the qualities of nature, the soul seems to be knowledge, action, and the doer—everything. Once again the Lord mentions the three aspects of nature: spiritual, material (restless), and inert (dormant or slothful) because knowledge can be either spiritual, material, or slothful, as can actions and the doer as well.

Classification according to the impact and the influence of nature's qualities is the subject matter of Samkhya. According to the qualities of a man, his mentality will be shaped. The sattvic quality makes one extremely spiritual, calm, quiet, introverted, and God-intoxicated. The rajasic quality motivates one to be restless, ambitious, extroverted, and possessive. The tamasic quality makes one lazy, idle, slothful, drowsy, and lacking an interest in anything.

In the subsequent verses, the Lord will explain three types of knowledge, three types of actions, and three types of actors in detail.

Verse 20

sarvabhūteṣu yenai 'kam
bhāvam avyayam ikṣate

avibhaktam vibhaktam vibhakteṣu
taj jñānam viddhi sāttvikam

Translation

The knowledge by which man perceives one imperishable divine being as undivided and equally present in all beings, know that to be sattvic knowledge (spiritual).

Metaphorical Interpretation

In this verse the Lord describes spiritual wisdom—the wisdom that every seeker must perceive.

God is supreme. He created sky, air, fire, water, and earth. Four fold creation: that which is born of moisture, such as fungus (*svedaja*), the vegetable kingdom (*udbhija*), creatures born of eggs (*andaja*), and mammals born of wombs (*jarayuja*). God created His supreme creation—man. Having created everything, He entered and permeated His creation. He is omnipresent. He is in males, females, and hermaphrodites. He is inside and outside. He is the supreme creator. He is abiding in all. He is in the air. He is the breath in all living beings: He is inhaling and exhaling that breath.

On the surface one can see God with many faces, many forms, a multiplicity of colors and many mentalities; however, there is a unity. Unity in multiplicity is the wonder of God's creation. The Vedas declare, *sarva khalvidam brahma:* "Everything is God", and *sarva brahma mayam jagat,* "The entire universe is God-pervaded, divine". A spiritual person endowed with divine wisdom perceives this unity. He feels the formless father in every name and form. He perceives God's presence in spite of differences in habit, attitude, and behavior. This mentality is sattvic knowledge—the spiritual outlook.

Every human being breathes by His power, as do plants, insects, and animals—every thing and every being is alive by His grace. The life breath (*prana*) of all living beings is the life breath of the One Supreme Father, who is formless. People who meditate and practice the authentic Kriya Yoga techniques based on breath control can feel that all perishable bodies are conducted and made alive by the imperishable supreme almighty father.

Only by calmly searching for Him, not with the five sense organs, but by going to the super-conscious, cosmic-conscious, and wisdom states—by going to the atom—can seekers easily realize the formless, all-pervading, imperishable soul within the whole universe. Although present in a multiplicity of divided and differentiated creation, He is unity. Perceiving this is truly spiritual knowledge.

Verse 21

pṛthaktvena tu yaj jñānam
nānābhāvān pṛthagvidhān
vetti sarveṣu bhūteṣu
taj jñānam viddhi rājasam

Translation

But that knowledge by which man cognizes many existences of various kinds as apart from one another in all beings, know that knowledge to be rajasic (passionate and material).

Metaphorical Interpretation

Now the Lord explains rajasic knowledge.

Those who live in the material world with strong ambitions for name, fame, and status—engrossed in many various activities with manifold dispositions—are rajasic people. They are busy with many kinds of enjoyment. They like rich food, costly beverages, and endless extroverted pleasures like the cinema, the theater, parties, and so on. When they perform religious activities, they do it with a sense of pride, glamour, and exhibitionism. They offer charity with the expectation of public applause and appreciation.

Rajasic people always differentiate mine from thine. They have a different vision. They cannot perceive the all-pervading God. This aspect of rajasic knowledge can be easily understood with the example of the rosary. Many beads are held together on a thread passing through small and narrow holes in all the beads. The thread is the cause of their unity. The spiritual person sees the thread hidden in the rosary; the rajasic person (material and passionate) sees the beads, not the thread.

Every human body is a bead in which the thread of the breath (*prana*, soul) is hiding. Extroverted, restless people are attracted to the external, material world and are active in it. They are body-conscious and can't see the truth present in every living being. These kinds of people forget God, spending their time in different moods, different dispositions, and different attitudes. Rajasic people have knowledge of external activity and restlessness.

Keeping worldly or material gain as the main objective in their minds, they cannot maintain peace of mind. They are not calm; they are far away from spiritual life and are devoid of peace, bliss, and joy. For them, God is very far away, maybe in heaven. Ignorant of their inner self, they cannot perceive the truth present within them. They lose their health, peace, and prosperity. Diversified knowledge cannot produce liberation; rather, it is the cause of bondage and suffering. In the Katha Upanishad (2:1:10), it says, *mṛtyoḥ sa mṛtyum āpnoti ya iha nānyeva paśyati*: "He who sees as though there is difference here, goes from death to death." Rajasic knowledge leads to impurity, doubt, confusion, and delusion.

Verse 22

yat tu kṛtsnavad ekasmin
kārye saktam ahaitukam
atattvārthavad alpam ca
tat tāmasam udāhṛtam

Translation

The (knowledge) that clings to one body as if it were the whole and which is irrational, has no real object, is small in significance, and is declared to be tamasic (dull).

Metaphorical Interpretation

Tamasic knowledge is always related to body or form. Tamasic people are extremely body-conscious. They are so idle and lethargic that they have no interest in working or studying. They are devoid of common sense. They are far from the truth. They experience great troubles as they engage in their livelihood. Many tamasic people are even drug addicts.

Their intellects are so dull that they cannot comprehend beyond the form. They think they are their bodies. Identifying with the body brings all sorts of complexities. They consider themselves very spiritual because of their religious activities and so-called spiritual practices. They think idols are God. They perform tamasic worship such as animal sacrifices to satisfy their material needs. Their ignorant methods of worship keep them busy, and they do not have any desire for God-realization or attaining real spiritual growth.

They think: "I am the body. I am male or female. Whatever I see is for my enjoyment." They are so firm in their wrong understanding that they accept falsehood as truth. They are devoid of spiritual goals and are narrow-minded. Tamasic knowledge is attached to the body, identifies with the body, and takes the body to be the self. Such knowledge cannot lead to self-realization and freedom from suffering.

Verse 23

niyatam saṅgarahitam
arāgadveṣatah kṛtam
aphalaprepsunā karma
yat tat sāttvikam ucyate

Translation

That action that is ordained (by the scriptures) and is free from attachment, performed without desire and hate, and with no wish to obtain the result, is said to be sattvic.

Metaphorical Interpretation

In this verse the Lord explains spiritual activity.

A person who is detached from useless company and who has a balanced mind is fit for sattvic activity. Any activity that helps you become free from attachment is spiritual. Spiritual actions cannot be desire-oriented; they must free you from affection and anger, and must help develop thorough control of the mind. When a person's mind is cleansed by spiritual actions, he is extremely calm during all activity, so extremely detached that the death of a near and dear one does not affect him. He loves seclusion, such as sitting in the corner of a room, and he is really wise—trying to perceive the Lord's presence constantly.

Man's breath is the cause of his restlessness as well as his calmness. Depending on the nature of the flow of breath through nostrils, human propensities change. When a person tries to make the flow of breath very calm, slow, and feeble, and equal in both nostrils, he develops a spiritual disposition. Meditation also frees one from the sense of duality. Free from all allurement, one can maintain pinpointed attention in the cave of the cranium. Meditation is the breath of life.

This verse on spiritual action mentions *niyata karma,* which is continuous action. Only *pranakarma*, the action of breath, is non-stop, continuous, and spontaneous. Because one does not consider the fruits of breathing, by watching this continuous action of breath, one can attain the divine stage. Maintain divine perception during every breath, and every action will be genuinely spiritual. Practice Kriya and remain in *paravastha,* and you will be spiritual.

Verse 24

yat tu kāmepsunā karma
sāhamkārena vā punaḥ
kriyate bahulāyāsam
tad rājasam udāhṛtam

Translation

The action, however, that involves a wish to fulfill desires, performed with (ego) selfishness or with much strain, is declared to be rajasic.

Metaphorical Interpretation

Work done with ambition for its fruits (results), which brings vanity and arrogance, is rajasic. Where there is ambition and ego, surely there is also extreme restlessness and apprehension. Extremely selfish attitudes also prevent people from taking the interests of others into account, which causes misunderstanding, friction, and extreme unhappiness.

People with selfish ambition engage in all kinds of hard work, so their lot is not easy. With expectation of prestige, status, public applause, and admiration, they may also do some charitable work—which ultimately works as a catalyst to increase the ego. They find neither peace nor truth. Restlessness is the cause of all human suffering. Pomp and grandeur, rich food, and enjoyment cause great harm to the body and mind. This is rajasic action, the work of arrogant people.

In spiritual life, without sincerity in meditation or Kriya practice, they spend their time in meditation thinking about what they should sit on and which rosary to use. Rajasic people always consider the way they appear to others; they are full of vanity.

Egotistical activities are endless, multifarious, and distracting. Ambition and attachment are the signs of rajasic activity.

Verse 25

anubandham kṣayam himsām
anapekṣya ca pauruṣam
mohād ārabhyate karma
yat tat tāmasam ucyate

Translation

The action undertaken out of sheer ignorance and delusion, disregarding the consequences, including loss to oneself or injury to others, as well as injury to one's own abilities, is said to be tamasic.

Metaphorical Interpretation

Ignorant people have no goal or purpose in life. With deluded minds, they cannot understand what is right and what is wrong. Due to their dull minds and clouded intellects, they undertake work that brings many troubles: loss of health, family disasters, and injury to others. They cannot foresee or analyze their own capacity and capability. Devoid of rationality, they cannot judge loss and gain—the two aspects associated with any work. They can't even think—to the point they cannot accomplish any work.

Man has an extreme tendency for deluded action. An idle mind is the devil's workshop for abusing and misusing the body, mind, and speech. Deluded people walk here and there without a purpose. They talk unnecessarily with friends, spending valuable time in a useless manner. People with less strength are more attached and more deluded, but often speak of dis-illusion. They are extremely passionate but pose as dispassionate. This is tamasic action.

In the above three verses, the three types of behavior are not only classified by specific kinds of activities, but rather by the attitude and outlook of the person doing the work. Activity may be sattvic (spiritual, leading to liberation), rajasic (material or passionate, leading to restlessness and attachment), or tamasic (dull and inert, leading to bondage and suffering). Sattvic action is devoid of expectation for the fruits of action. Rajasic action is full of ambition and expectation. The same work can be sattvic, rajasic, or tamasic depending on the nature of the person who undertakes the work and his approach.

The sattvic person is the symbol of harmony, equality, and equanimity. His life is full of love, purity, and truthfulness. His life is the symbol of sacrifice; selfless service is his motto. But a rajasic person, full of vanity, ego, arrogance, and self-aggrandizement, is always looking for appreciation, applause, and admiration from others. A tamasic person is devoid of the power of judgment, extremely dull and idle, often intoxicated and taking forbidden food, which often leads to bad health and suffering. His talent is misused. *Tamas* is the way to self-abuse and destruction. Tamasic minds are not seeking reality, but rather delusion, illusion, and error. Tamasic action is the work of the lazy and the idle who lead meaningless, animal lives.

Verse 26

muktasaṅgo 'nahamvādī
dhṛtyutsāhasamanvitaḥ
siddhyasiddhyor nirvikāraḥ
kartāsāttvika ucyate

Translation

Free from attachment and ego, endowed with firmness and zeal, undisturbed by success and failure—such a person is said to be sattvic.

Metaphorical Interpretation

After elaborate discussion of three types of action, the blessed Lord now explains about the characteristics of three types of doers.

Those who are spiritual are free from ego (*ahamkara:* "I am the doer"); instead, they perceive themselves as an instrument and God as the supreme doer. Arrogance and ego are dissolved. There is no attachment to work because of delusion. Spiritual people do not calculate or worry about the fruits of their actions. They accept work as duty. They are free from attachment and expectation.

Due to their divine qualities such as inner detachment, spiritual people are neither inactive nor impatient. They work with full strength, vigor, and patience. With strength, the battle of life can be faced with courage, with bravery. This is the spiritual life: Without attachment to the fruits of action, every moment is spent seeking divine emancipation.

The spiritual person maintains inner detachment while associating with all kinds of people. Free from ego and arrogance, patient and perseverant, he tolerates everything with forbearance, proceeding silently towards the goal of God-realization. His only goal is to perceive the presence of God in every breath, during every moment.

Because of his regulated life and regular spiritual practice, he is free from good and bad, success and failure, ups and downs, worries, emotions, pitfalls, and shortcomings. Slowly, he is detaching from everything. Always, his mind is absorbed in God. He is perceiving *sarvam brahma mayam jagat:* "Everything is permeated by God alone," and *ayamatma brahma:* "My soul is God." He is free from all negatives. His mind is free and pure. It is transformed in knowledge, consciousness, superconsciousness, and cosmic-consciousness. He is the real spiritual person.

Free from all extroverted states and thoughts, he roams the world as a brave soldier in the divine army, subduing all negative qualities. One cannot be spiritual with an outward show of spirituality. Inner transformation and constant God-consciousness are essential.

Virya (strength, vitality, vigor, and valor) and *dhairya* (patience and perseverance) are the two important qualities the real spiritual seeker will have.

Verse 27

rāgī karma phalaprepsur
lubdho himsātmako śuciḥ
harṣaśokānvitaḥ kartā
rājasaḥ parikīrtitaḥ

Translation

Full of attachment, seeking the fruit of actions, greedy, apprehensive (violent), impure, affected by joy or sorrow, such a person is said to be rajasic (materialistic and passionate).

Metaphorical Interpretation

People who are attached to the material world who seek name and fame are rajasic. The force motivating these rajasic workers is the desire for prosperity, material achievement, and success in the mundane. The more success they achieve, the more work they undertake. Human desire is insatiable.

Being greedy and aggressive, rajasic individuals will do anything for worldly achievement. They will lie without hesitation. They don't hesitate to oppress others in order to satisfy their own needs or ambitions. Moreover, the rajasic attachment to body, family, and the material world promotes greed. In the end, rajasic people find joy in prosperity and sorrow in adversity, but never experience real peace; they are always filled with apprehension and afraid of getting into trouble.

Even when they know full well that the marvelous power of God is hiding within, rajasic people will not seek this truth and have no desire for God-realization. They don't want to accept that God is the real doer, the sole doer. Those who don't seek God lead an animal life of sense gratification.

An extremely passionate life fills the heart with fear, anxiety, and tension. Rajasic people do not hesitate to obstruct others, are always violent and ferocious, and are always aggressive and intolerant, as they seek to fulfill their selfish desires. This selfishness leads to conflict, disease, and destruction, and covers the divine qualities with negative attitudes. Being self-centered is the only motivation for a rajasic person who must always calculate material loss and gain. Their every action is motivated by restlessness.

Those of rajasic temperament can never perceive the supreme divinity as the cosmic director of the mundane drama. Without hesitation, they will declare morality, religion, and spirituality as the rule of the weak and the timid. Restlessness and extreme material gain are the only activities that engage them.

Rajasic individuals can't sleep due to fear, tension, and anxiety. They have no peace, purity, or harmony. Their external, outer lives as well as their inner lives are devoid of love, calmness, and reality. This is life for rajasic people.

Verse 28

ayuktaḥ prākṛtaḥ stabdhaḥ
śaṭho naikṛtiko 'lasaḥ
viṣādī dīrghasūtrī ca
kartā tāmasa ucyate

Translation

Undisciplined, uncultured, obstinate, deceitful, inclined to rob others of their livelihood, slothful, depressed, procrastinating—such a person is proclaimed to be tamasic.

Metaphorical Interpretation

Devoid of sattvic or rajasic qualities, the human mind will automatically become tamasic (dull and lethargic). The Lord describes the eight qualities of the tamasic person:

1. *Ayukta* (undisciplined): A person who doesn't discipline his body, mind, and thoughts, and above all, who is not devoted to truth and God, is leading an animal life. A person with a weak mind and restless senses cannot make progress on the spiritual path.

2. *Prakrita* (uncultured, vulgar): People must strive to refine their actions and intellect. Truly intelligent people seek the truth during daily activity.

3. *Stabdha* (rigid, obstinate): A stubborn and obstinate person who does not make any effort to adjust and accommodate is not spiritual. A spiritual person is humble and sweet.

4. *Satha* (hypocrite): A tamasic person always maintains a double standard. Inwardly, he is filled with negative and devilish qualities, but outwardly he poses as a very advanced and spiritual person.

5. *Naiskritika* (insulting and torturing others): This is someone who exploits others physically, financially, and even morally with his work, words, and thoughts; someone who even insults others.

6. *Alasah* (dull): This person has a slothful nature lacking vigor, vitality, and strength.

7. *Visadi* (depressed): A spiritual aspirant will always be energetic and active with love and a divine mood, but a tamasic individual is always depressed and pessimistic.

8. *Dirghasutri* (procrastinating): A dull person always postpones work until tomorrow because he does not understand how valuable time is. Time does not wait. Wasting time is wasting your life.

In short, a tamasic person is lazy and idle, so he does not seek education and a cultured life. He is a dreamer. He follows the five sense organs and seeks a sensual life. He wants sense pleasure without work. His mind is always restless; his decisions are not clear; his mind is always fluctuating. He is arrogant and depressed most of the time, unlike an active man who is free from depression. Depression is a psychosomatic disorder that comes from idleness, unnecessary imaginary expectations, and lack of an enterprising nature. A tamasic person won't hesitate to earn something unfairly.

Even in spiritual life, tamasic people try to achieve power for material gain. In the tantric scriptures, there is a description of *panchamakara sadhana*—the five M's for lower spiritual practice by tamasic people: *madya* (wine), *matsya* (fishes), *mamsha* (flesh), *mudra* (fried food, money), and *mithuna* (sexual enjoyment). These people do not hesitate to eat, drink, and be merry even during religious activity. They also slay animals as part of their rituals.

This is life for the lethargic, tamasic people.

Verse 29

buddher bhedam dhṛteścaiva
guṇatas trividham śṛnu
procyamānam aśeṣeṇa
pṛthaktvena dhanamjaya

Translation

Now hear, O Arjuna (Dhanamjaya), the threefold distinctions of intellect, and also the firmness based on the predomi-

nance of the qualities of nature (*gunas*), taught completely and separately.

Metaphorical Interpretation

The Lord addresses Arjuna as Dhanamjaya. Dhanamjaya is derived from *dhanam jayati iti*—he who conquers six human qualities (*dhana*): birth, death, sorrow, happiness, appetite, and thirst. When a person goes beyond body consciousness after deep meditation and spiritual practice, he becomes endowed with supernatural powers and is then called *Dhanamjaya.* Fighting the battle of life with sincerity and concentration, he forgets his worldly propensities. He goes beyond human nature and the lower centers. Arjuna, a person of the finest intelligence with the deepest desire to achieve the super-conscious and cosmic-conscious states, is called *dhanamjaya.* He strives to overcome the triple qualities of *maya*: delusion, illusion, and error.

Shri Krishna is saying, "O Arjuna! Due to your deep desire and sincere spiritual practice you can overcome your lower nature. You can constantly remain in soul-consciousness during the battle of life. You have divine intelligence."

Every person is endowed with *manas* (mind) and *buddhi* (intellect). Ordinarily, the mind is restless; controlling it through breath regulation has been explained. *Buddhi* (divine intelligence) is impure because the triple qualities of nature can make it spiritual, material, or dull. But, ultimately *buddhi* is a divine quality that every person can develop. When the intellect becomes free from impurities, there is no attachment and aversion and extreme inner peace is experienced.

The spiritual aspirant must learn the secret of steadfastness—how to be firmly established in soul-consciousness without the slightest deviation. Often, people will ascend to higher levels of consciousness, but will not be able to maintain these states due to the play of the triple qualities of nature. The firm, steadfast concentration necessary for higher consciousness can be achieved through deep meditation and leading a spiritual life.

In the following verses the Lord describes the three levels of intelligence and steadfastness in detail. The Lord also explains how to develop your memory and make it sharp, which will free you from negative qualities and lead you to God-realization.

Verse 30

pravṛttim ca nivṛttim ca
kāryākārye bhayābhaye
bandham mokṣam ca yā vetti
buddhiḥ sā pārtha sāttvikī

Translation

The intellect that correctly determines the path of activity and renunciation, what ought to be done and should not be done, what is fear and what is fearlessness, what is bondage and what is liberation—that type of intellect is spiritual (sattvic).

Metaphorical Interpretation

In this verse the Lord describes spiritual intellect with four pairs of opposites:

1. *Pavritti* (the path of activity due to attachment): To be engrossed in some activity with expectation. Eating, sleeping, fearing, and sex are four activities common to man and animals.

1. *Nivritti* (the path of renunciation and detachment): A state of dispassion, which is the cause of liberation. In this condition, the mind becomes extremely pure and no thought waves are created in the intellect.

2. *Karya* (duty, real activity): The work that should be undertaken, in other words, the practice of Kriya—*pranakarma* is the real work to be done.

Akarya (unwanted work): The work by which life or *prana* is not in harmony or peace. The ordinary meaning of *akarya* is "the God-less state."

3. *Abhaya* (fearlessness): To perceive the state of immortality through control of the mind and the senses; to go beyond body consciousness.

Bhaya (fear): Fear of death and fear of losing happiness. Fear of following the spiritual path. The real causes of fear are wrong activity and attachment.

4. *Bandha* (one in bondage): People tied to body consciousness and bound to the fruits of their actions.

Moksha (liberation): The state of complete soul-awareness, emancipation, and *samadhi.* Freedom from the bondage and attachment that arise from delusion.

The spiritual intellect inspires one to do the work that leads to inner detachment, fearlessness, and liberation. Engaging in unwanted work (*akarya*) leads one to attachment, fear, and bondage.

In this verse, the Lord advises us to be completely detached during every disposition, which is possible only when we remain in the pituitary and the fontanel, because this allows the intellect to remain constantly focused on spirituality and truth. By using pure intellect and conscience, a person in this state can consider the positive and negative aspects of any action before undertaking it.

Searching for God during every breath and remaining compassionately detached from delusion, illusion, and error will make you calm and tranquil within. You will continuously hear the divine sound, you will feel the sensation of God moving in the whole body, you will perceive divine light, and you will experience extreme love. This is the result of the real work of life.

Try your utmost to be free from bad deeds; be terrified of negative work; shun the pitfalls of life; then you will become established in the pure intellect. At first it may be difficult to climb up from the lower centers to the upper center, but with regular practice, it is easy to overcome attachment to money, the sex mood, tempting food, and the propensities of the heart (freedom from bad company). One can be free from addiction to wine, smoking, and even narcotic drugs that cause heart and lung diseases.

A man with spiritual intellect loves seclusion. He meditates without show in the jungle or in a cave; in the inner chamber of the cranium, he contemplates sincerely. A man free from attraction and attachment to the lower centers gets the taste of liberation.

Verse 31

yayā dharmam adharmam ca
kāryam cākāryam eva ca
ayathāvat prajānāti
buddhiḥ sā pārtha rājasī

Translation

The intellect that cannot correctly perceive what is *dharma* and what is *adharma,* what ought to be done and what should not be done, is rajasic (material, passionate), O Arjuna (Partha).

Metaphorical Interpretation

In this verse, the Lord explains the rajasic intellect by addressing Arjuna as Partha, which means the son of Pritha. Arjuna was not born as a result of sexual pleasure. His mother was Kunti, who is also called Pritha. Kunti means of the finest conception—attitude remaining in the pituitary. She meditated very deeply; then by concentrating from the navel to the pituitary, she conceived Arjuna. Arjuna has the deepest desire to bring his awareness up from the navel to the pituitary where the imperishable soul dwells.

So Krishna is saying, "O Partha, O Arjuna! He whose intellect is not steady, who cannot understand what is good and what is bad, is a passionate person. Everything good and bad can be perceived by the imperishable soul in the pituitary. Until a person brings his awareness there instead of remaining below, he cannot really understand what is real and what is unreal, what is *dharma* (religion) and what is *adharma* (devoid of religion).

The word *dharma* is from *dhri* (root) and *man* (suffix), meaning that which upholds. The breath upholds life in man. The power of breath upholds life in every human being and is the cause of life and activity. To be breath-conscious and to offer love with every breath is *dharma* (religion); to forget the breath and the soul and to be engrossed only in pleasure is *adharma* (non-religion). When someone does not understand the real work of life, he lives restlessly and bewildered.

Those who do not understand the real meaning of *dharma* merely move from one cult to another, from one tradition to another, from one set of beliefs to another. They waste their life. Rajasic people do not know what to do and what to avoid, and so remain busy with material activities and worldly glamour in the clutch of the five sense organs. Using the sense organs, they chant and sing, revere idols and statues, and engage in prayer and worship, but they are not spiritually advanced. They lack the essential qualities of conscience and rationality. They lack the faculty of the pure intellect.

Verse 32

adharmam dharmam iti yā
manyate tamasāvṛtā
sarvārthān viparītāmśca
buddhiḥ sā pārtha tāmasī

Translation

The intellect enveloped in darkness (ignorance) that imagines *adharma* to be *dharma* and sees everything upside down (perverted and contrary to the truth) is tamasic (dull), O Partha (Arjuna).

Metaphorical Interpretation

A person of a tamasic (dull) intellect lacks vision and understanding. With perverted ideas, he perceives everything in a negative way. He sees, thinks, and understands incorrectly.

The soul is the cause of the breath. The indwelling self is the essence of human life. By the practice of meditation one can realize this. But a tamasic man of dull intellect cannot perceive it. To a man with jaundice, everything looks to be yellow; similarly, to an idle man of impure intellect, good work appears to be bad and vice versa.

In the first chapter of the Bhagavad Gita, Arjuna mistook every good work to be bad. In his deluded compassion, he did not want to control the restless senses, and this is not spiritual. All human beings must control their negative and bad qualities; they must choose to be rational and spiritual. But tamasic people cannot find the way and always proceed toward activities that lead to bondage and suffering. With restless minds, and through the delusive power of the five sense organs, they remain constantly engrossed in the material world, inactive and uncultured. Their lives are full of misdeeds. They are engrossed in addiction. Their intellects are misused and abused. They are sluggish and bewildered.

Verse 33

dhṛtyā yayā dhārayate
manaḥprāṇendriyakriyāh
yogenāvyabhicāriṇyā
dhṛtiḥ sā pārtha sāttvikī

Translation

The unwavering firmness attained through the yoga of meditation by which man can control the functions (activities) of the mind, the vital breath, and the senses—that firmness, O Partha (Arjuna) is sattvic.

Metaphorical Interpretation

The word *dhriti* in Sanskrit describes the power of beholding, unifying, and deciding. When knowledge manifests in a human life, it is revealed in two ways: One is the intellect, and the other is firmness, the power to behold. This firmness is of three types, corresponding to the three qualities of nature. In the following three verses, the Lord explains the sattvic *dhriti,* spiritual firmness.

Even though the mind is restless and confused by nature, it can be well regulated and controlled with regular meditation. Moreover, the mind, the vital breath, and the senses are correlated and causally associated.

Anybody who receives the touch of the a realized master and learns the yoga of meditation will develop discrimination and rationality. Thus, he will also learn the art of successful living—remaining compassionately detached from the attraction of sense objects.

Those of the finest conception who remain in the pituitary can be free. When the yoga of meditation is practiced regularly, the capacity to perceive the truth increases. So, by the power of the master and with sincere practice, thorough control over the turbulent senses and restless mind is achieved. A well-developed discriminating faculty is the result, which can easily decide what must be done and what should be avoided. Meditation brings balance in body and mind. Life is ever new and harmonized. The cultivated body land leads to a disease-free, peaceful life.

As a result of regular Kriya practice, you gradually rise from the lower centers to the upper center. Then a sharp intellect, prompt understanding, and a ready wit will make your life divine.

Verse 34

yayā tu dharmakāmārthān
dhṛtyā dhārayate 'rjuna
prasangena phalākānkṣī
dhṛtiḥ sā pārtha rājasī

Translation

But the firmness by which one holds onto worldly duties, pleasure, and wealth, and by which one seeks the rewards for action with attachment—that firmness, O Partha (Arjuna) is rajasic.

Metaphorical Interpretation

In the scriptures it says that everyone must try to achieve success in life. Real success is the achievement of perfection, God-realization, and liberation. This is the true goal in life. But there are three other secondary goals. These four together are called the fourfold objectives—*dharma* (righteousness), *artha* (material prosperity), *kama* (sense pleasure, fulfillment of desires), and *moksha* (liberation). While a spiritual person keeps *moksha* as the primary objective; the rajasic—the material-minded, worldly people—regard the other three as the target.

The ordinary human being is always roaming in the material world wanting to enjoy the fruits of *dharma, artha,* and *kama.* To a worldly or passionate person, the real *dharma* does not exist. Instead, *dharma* is thought of as religion in the ordinary sense, a play of forms and formalities—an outward show of worship, ceremonies, and festivities. The *kama* (desire) of the spiritual person is to know his indwelling self, while the *kama* of the passionate individual is fulfillment of the desires of the senses and the lower centers.

A rajasic person has intense desire focused on amassing huge wealth, good buildings, and delicious and rich food, as well as enjoying sex, food, wine, television, radio, cinema, theater, and so forth. He cherishes these worldly desires. But to perform extravagant religious rites and to fulfill sensual desires, he must have material accomplishments. So, the rajasic person works with special skill and worldly knowledge in the material world, earning a great deal of money. He also needs public appreciation.

This kind of determination is not the sign of someone established in truth; this is merely a worldly life of sense enjoyment. To be steadfast in this limited understanding of action is a lower grade of *dhriti.*

Verse 35

yayā svapnam bhayam śokam
viṣādam madam eva ca
na vimuñcati durmedhā
dhṛtiḥ sā pārtha tāmasī

Translation

The firmness by which a stupid man does not refuse sleep, fear, grief, depression, and vanity—that firmness is tamasic.

Metaphorical Interpretation

In this verse the Lord describes the lowest quality of *dhriti* (firmness), the tamasic. The idle person's brain is the devil's workshop, always creating more and more delusion.

Most people are engrossed in the material world. Their minds, vital breath, and senses are tempted by religious practices, monetary pursuits, passions, sleep, fear, sorrows, delusion, depression, and attachment to the objects of the senses. These ordinary kinds of firmness are the rajasic and tamasic forms of *dhriti.*

The Lord calls stupid or foolish those people whose minds are always engrossed in sleep, fear, grief, depression, and vanity. They are the people without common sense, devoid of study, and always lazy. They are not active in life. They are busy in falsehood, far away from the truth. They spend their precious time in idleness and sleeping. It is foolishness.

Man is not an animal born to die. Man is endowed with hidden spiritual power. Man is born to experience the divine. Although humans can change their destiny, those with a tamasic nature cannot cherish high ideals such as God-realization and soul culture. Instead, they are extremely fearful. Fear is a sign of a weak personality. Fear and anxiety are the by-products of mental laziness, which leads to depression.

Tamasic people are not free from ego. They are extremely rough and whimsical. Theirs is the lowest type of *dhriti* (firmness). The simplest meaning of *dhriti* is the manifestation of intellect, by which one gets prompt understanding. But tamasic people are far from understanding. Living in a lower center, they lead animal lives.

Dhriti is the strength of a person. You can change your life and activity with self-effort, by living in the company of good people and a realized master, and by sincerely practicing the techniques that will help you reach the divine goal hidden within.

Verse 36

sukham tv idānīm trividham
śṛṇu me bharatarṣabha
abhyāsād ramate yatra
duḥkhāntam ca nigacchati

Translation

Now, hear from me, O Best of Bharatas (Arjuna), of the threefold happiness that one enjoys through practice and by which one reaches the end of suffering.

Metaphorical Interpretation

In this verse the Lord calls Arjuna "Bharatarsabha." He is saying, "O Arjuna! You are born in the dynasty of Bharata. You are the best of your race and family. All your ancestors sought the truth, the light (*bha-rata*). You have a great desire to realize your self, so you are the best kind of person.

Everyone desires happiness. No one wants sorrow. Although finding happiness is the supreme desire in all people, most don't know what happiness is. "O Arjuna! Although happiness is the state of inner tranquility and joy, it is of three types depending on the nature of the person: spiritual happiness (*sattvika sukha*), material or passionate happiness (*rajasika sukha*), and idle happiness (*tamasika sukha*). O Arjuna! True happiness is the result of *abhyasa*—regular practice of meditation (see Chapter 6)."

Every human being must know what *abhyasa* (practice) is! In the Yoga Sutras of Patañjali (1:13) it says, *tatra sthitan yatno-bhyasah*: "The sincere effort to remain in inner tranquility through meditation is practice (*abhyasa*)." When one achieves freedom from desire and thought, one finds happiness.

Most people try to achieve happiness by amassing material goods because they don't know that real happiness is possible only by realizing the absolute. In the Brihadaryanaka Upanishad, it says, *yo vai bhuma tat sukham, na alpe sukham asti*: "Happiness is only in the infinite, not in the finite." Another definition of happiness is provided here by the Lord: *duhkhanta*—the end of suffering.

If you practice the supreme technique of soul culture and lead a life in truth, you can find real peace, joy, and happiness.

"O Arjuna! Please listen to me as I detail the three types of happiness that people may enjoy depending upon their inner nature."

Verse 37

yat tad agre viṣam iva
pariṇāme 'mṛtopamam
tat sukham sāttvikam proktam
ātmabuddhiprasādajam

Translation

The happiness that is like poison in the beginning, but like nectar in the end, born from the tranquility of mind in the divine self (clear understanding) is declared to be sattvic (spiritual).

Metaphorical Interpretation

In this verse, the Lord describes spiritual happiness. In Sanskrit happiness is *sukha,* which consists of two parts: *su* and *kha. Su* (*sundara*) means beautiful, and *kha* means sky or vacuum. *Sukha* or real happiness is keeping your conciousness in the pituitary and above, in the state of vacuum and nothingness. This is the formless stage. *Duhkhas* (unhappiness) is when you cannot remain in the formless stage and you descend, becoming engrossed in the body and the world. That is a deviation from the formless state or vacuum.

Now you may ask, how is the vacuum or calm state attained? It can only be reached after receiving the touch of a realized master and practicing a technique such as Kriya Yoga, not by using of the five sense organs or worshiping with them. Through deep meditation you can go beyond the domain of the mind, body attachment, and worldly ideas.

By practicing Kriya Yoga meditation very deeply and rising above the eyebrows, you can touch the imperishable soul and remain in the formless vacuum state. You will hear the divine sound, perceive the God-movement sensation in the whole body, and visualize snow-white light everywhere. You will be free from all unhappiness and unpleasantness. It is impossible to describe with words.

Reaching this state is no doubt difficult and troublesome at first because the human mind is engrossed in the five lower centers, and lower center thoughts may occasionally pop into the mind. But by the practice of deep meditation and by constantly following the guru's advice, this initial difficulty will disappear.

When you bring your awareness above the eyebrows, you can experience extreme joy and emancipation. With a little effort in the beginning, the divine joy perceived, and ultimately it is like nectar. Nectar is *amrita,* which gives immortality. Meditation alone grants God-realization and the taste of immortality. In this state there is liberation from all worldly liabilities. There is no delusion or attachment.

Deep meditation enables the devotee to constantly maintain awareness on the top, in the brain and even above that. His gratitude toward God multiplies. His life becomes more pleasant, loving, and divine than the nectar itself. It is a heavenly life. Although the seeker may have a family and lead an ordinary life, his inner peace will be extraordinary.

During every breath, this extraordinary person will feel the presence of God. In all speech and with every word, he will perceive the power of God. He will spend every moment of his life immersed in God. In fact, not even the five sense organs will be inimical to realization. Instead, the devotee will feel the beauty of God and divine joy through every sense organ. Spiritual happiness is peace, bliss, and joy.

Verse 38

viṣayendriyasamyogād
yat tad agre 'mṛtopamam

pariṇāme viṣam iva
tat sukhkam rājasam smṛtam

Translation

The delight that follows when the senses contact their objects is like nectar in the beginning, but like poison in the end; hence it is rajasic (passionate).

Metaphorical Interpretation

There are five senses and five objects of the senses. When the sense organs and their objects are associated, temporary pleasure is created in the senses. People pass the night without sleep to enjoy sense pleasure. The pleasure due to sense gratification is often associated with pain.

Sense pleasures are very tempting and attractive. But in reality, a little sense joy brings a lot of trouble. A sweet or palatable food may give some happiness while it is eaten, but without proper consideration, taking a lot of rich food creates problems with digestion, gripping pain, vomiting, and diarrhea, and in the long run too much rich food can lead to fatal disease.

Drinking wine or smoking may be very pleasant to some people, but they are at the root of many problems that can cause an early death. There are also people who eat green chilies, black pepper, and a hefty quantity of spices—tastes the tongue relishes—but too much of these is not good for one's health.

Every person knows the apparent beauty of sense pleasures. In the beginning they are enjoyable, but too much sense joy to appease the lower nature causes a loss of vitality, beauty, intelligence, brainpower, memory, talent, wealth, and health.

God created the sense organs for self-unfolding and spiritual evolution, but foolish people, those of rajasic nature, do not understand their significance. These sense organs function only because of the breath and the indwelling self. Joy and happiness conditioned upon sense gratification and enjoyment is rajasic, material happiness. Because it is conditional, this joy is limited and temporary. At the moment of enjoyment it appears pleasurable, but after that, it brings only pain.

Spiritual happiness is infinite and unlimited, while material happiness is temporary. While spiritual happiness arises from regular meditation and leading a life of self-discipline, material happiness is the result of the association between a sense organ and its object, which leads to enjoyment. Although it may be somewhat difficult to practice meditation and inner detachment, ultimately spontaneous and continuous divine joy will flourish. Rajasic happiness is apparently beautiful, but ultimately painful.

In spiritual happiness there is complete cessation of sorrow, but in material happiness there is a mixture of pleasure and pain. Spiritual happiness is born out of purity of mind and thought, but material happiness causes the mind to be restless and dirty.

Verse 39

yad agre cānubandhe ca
sukham mohanam ātmanaḥ
nidrālasyapramādottham
tat tāmasam udāhṛtam

Translation

The happiness that deludes the soul during its enjoyment as well as in the end—derived from sleep, sloth, and negligence—such happiness is tamasic (idle nature).

Metaphorical Interpretation

In this verse the Lord explains the happiness of idle and lazy people. He is saying, "O Arjuna, when a person sleeps, at that time he has no sorrow. Sleep is a temporary forgetfulness of one's own state, but it is not cessation of sorrow or suffering. Too much sleep causes more lethargy. People who try to sleep in order to forget sorrow are in error. This is not the way to overcome sorrow. Some tamasic people take wine, drugs, or other intoxicants to forget sorrow, to sleep, or to dream for a short time, but this neither removes the cause of sorrow nor produces strength and energy. When the intoxicated state passes, there is only drowsiness, laziness, and sloth, with a concomitant loss of stability, joy, and happiness.

In this state, a person is extremely deluded. In the tamasic stage, the illumination of the soul cannot be revealed by sheer ignorance and sloth. Tamasic happiness is not only illusory and temporary, but it also has a veiling power. It covers the intellect, and the tamasic individual lives far away from the soul, the true source of happiness.

Rajasic happiness is enjoyable in the beginning and painful in the end, but tamasic joy is no good in the beginning or in the end. Because of its tempting nature, tamasic happiness is like being bound in chains. It makes a person so weak and idle that he loses the strength to stand up and proceed under his own power.

Those who want to be educated in truth shun laziness and spend every moment of time with care and caution. But a lazy person only sleeps. He is a dreamer; he is not realistic; he puts everything off until tomorrow. He does not know the value of time. Laziness makes people like animals, even inferior to animals. They maintain neither themselves nor their family.

The tamasic quality makes the body, mind, and intellect weak; knowledge is covered. Tamasic happiness is not happiness at all; truly, it is nothing but sorrow.

Verse 40

na tad asti pṛthivyām vā
divi deveṣu vā punaḥ
sattvam prakṛtijair muktam
yad ebhiḥ syāt tribhir guṇaiḥ

Translation

There is no being on earth or in the ether (heaven), or even among the gods or elsewhere, who is really free from these three qualities (*gunas*) born of nature (*prakriti*).

Metaphorical Interpretation

God created everything by His nature, which has three qualities: *sattva* (spiritual), *rajas* (material) and *tamas* (darkness, ignorance, or dullness). In this world and even in the vacuum state, nature's three qualities are at play. That which exists throughout the universe also exists in the human body, so the three qualities of nature are found in every human body.

In this body, there are seven centers, of which the *muladhara* chakra (coccyx) is the earth and the *visuddha* chakra (neck) is the vacuum. Whatever thoughts, ideas, or activities are born in between these centers—from the earth center to the etheral center—is influenced by the three qualities of nature.

In the human spine, *prana* (the vital breath) flows through three *nadis* (pranic-channels): *ida, pingala,* and *sushumna*. These are also found in every other living being. These three *nadis* correspond to the three qualities of nature. *Ida* is tamasic, *pingala* is rajasic, and *sushumna* is sattvic. *Ida prana* flows in the left nostril, *pingala* in the right, and *sushumna* in both. Everyone is entangled in these three qualities.

Human activities are influenced and regulated by these triple qualities, but human beings have rational powers. Therefore, they can control their body nature and strive to bring their awareness up to the pituitary where they can perceive the divine calm and become liberated. Nature's threefold play exists only up to the pituitary. Beyond this point is the *brahma loka,* that which is beyond the *deva loka* (vacuum), where one can remain compassionately detached. Complete freedom from nature's three *gunas* is *samadhi*.

Exercising the power of rationality, discrimination, and deep meditation, sincere seekers become extremely detached, filled with tranquillity, far away from both happiness and sorrow. During the most severe failure and the most exalted success, they are not affected and without repentance, watching their own lives as a witnessing consciousness.

Verse 41

brāhmaṇakṣatriyavaśām
śūdrāṇām ca paramtapa
karmāṇi pravibhaktāni
svabhāvaprabhavair guṇaiḥ

Translation

The duties of the *brahmins,* the *kshatriyas,* the *vaishyas,* and the *sudras*, O Conqueror of Enemies (Arjuna), are distributed according to the inborn qualities.

Metaphorical Interpretation

Action causes bondage and liberation. Action reflects the three qualities of nature. Action determines the quality of the person. According to the quality and activity of human beings in this world, there are four categories of people.

Those who are on the spiritual path, who keep their attention constantly above the pituitary, meditating very deeply, are called *brahmin*, the knower of Brahma, the absolute. They keep their minds on the top where the breath is continuously activated. Through this spiritual practice, they realize *sarvam khalvidam brahma*: "The whole universe is Brahma", and *aham brahmanasmi:* "I am Brahma". These realizations make the seeker *brahmin*.

Other people have a deep desire to know Brahman. They sincerely try to meditate, and through the company of the guru preceptor they try to bring their consciousness up to the pituitary. They are fighting with their own negative qualities. They are *kshatriyas,* the warrior class.

The life of one such warrior (*kshatriya*), a king named Vishvamitra, is known to us from mythology. He wanted to meditate because he thought God-realization would give him more power. He tried his utmost to remain in the fontanel. He went to Vasishtha and asked him to make him a *brahmin*, but Vasishtha declined, as the *brahmin* state cannot be achieved by begging, but only by willpower and meditation. Vishvamitra threatened to kill Vasishtha if he was not declared a *brahmin.* But a *brahmin* such as Vasishtha, who is always merged in God-consciousness, is never afraid of death. So Vasishtha said no.

Vishvamitra decided to celebrate a fire ceremony that would cause Vasishtha's death, and he invited Vasishtha to be the chief priest on this occasion. A *brahmin* will never refuse to accept an invitation to conduct a ritual, even at the cost of his life. So Vasishtha accepted the invitation without hesitation. Upon seeing this, Vishvamitra was transformed. He bowed at the feet of Vasishtha, acknowledging his greatness and his brahmanic quality. Vishvamitra cried out of repentance. Vasishtha told Vishvamitra that he had now cultivated the values like love and compassion in his heart and was fit to be a *brahmin.*

The *vaishyas* cultivate, do business, and serve society externally. In the spiritual sense, one who cultivates the body land and thinks carefully how to use precious time for making the most profit is a *vaishya.* The *shudras* serve all with love.

Anyone can make spiritual progress and reach God-realization by following the master's teachings and practicing the principles of spiritual life. In Indian mythology there is the story of Ratnakar, a murderer and robber who committed many crimes. Through the love and compassion of his guru, he was completely transformed. He meditated in the shade of a tree. His meditation was so deep that he didn't realize that his whole body had been covered by an anthill. His meditation gave him God-realization. Spiritual life can cause a complete transformation in a human life.

In the Purushasukta in the Vedas, the categories of people are described as follows:

1. *Brahmanaḥ asya mukha āsīt:* "Any person who always keeps

his attention above, free from lower propensities, is *brahmin*" (the priest and teacher class).

2. *Vāhu rājanya smṛtah:* "Arms are to fight and remove evils". Those who constantly fight with lower qualities to reach the divine goal are *kshatriya* (the warrior class).

3. *Uru tadasya yad vaiśya:* "People who do extreme work are *vaishya*" (the merchant class).

4. *Padbhyām śudro ajāyata:* "Those whose attention is below are *shudras*" (the unskilled labor class).

So not by birth, but by quality and activity one can be known as *shudra, vaishya, kshatriya,* or *brahmin.* Every spiritual practice aims at attaining Brahman. A spiritual person is a leader of society.

Verse 42

śamo damas tapaḥ śaucam
kṣāntir ārjavam eva ca
jñānam vijñānam āstikyam
brahmakarma svabhāvajam

Translation

Serenity, self-restraint, austerity, purity, forgiveness; uprightness of mind, senses, and behavior; knowledge, superconsciousness and cosmic-consciousness; and love for God are the natural duty (inborn qualities) of the *brahmins*.

Metaphorical Interpretation

In the following verses the Lord explains the qualities of the four kinds of spiritual seekers: *brahmin, kshatriya, vaishya,* and *shudra.*

The *brahmin* is considered the highest of all because of his spiritual attainment. A tree is known by its fruits and a person is known by his quality as revealed by his behavior and actions. According to the Lord, a *brahmin* must possess the following nine qualities:

1. *Shama* (serenity): This is thorough control over the internal instruments such as the mind, thought, intellect, and ego. Ordinarily a person's heart gives rise to anger, pride, ego, hypocrisy, and so forth; so the precise meaning of *shama* is to have thorough control over the heart, making one serene and divine.

2. *Dama* (self-restraint): By the practice of Kriya, people gain control over the sense organs. They then reach the super-conscious and cosmic-conscious states, and can therefore easily avoid negativity.

3. *Tapas* (penance): Ordinarily this means doing penance and austerities, but the metaphorical meaning is to watch the breath as an oblation in the holy fire that maintains the heat in the body. *Tapas* means that in every breath one loves God and remains alert.

4. *Saucha* (purity): Lead a clean and pure life both externally and internally. You don't become pure just by washing the outside of your body, you must also purify your life with regular meditation. When you can maintain keen attention on the fontanel and love God, you are truly pure.

5. *Kshanti* (forgiveness): Ordinarily people are intolerant, but meditation brings tolerance and patience. Forgiveness is the ability to forgive others in spite of harm done.

6. *Arjavam* (simplicity): Literally, this is uprightness of the body, mind, senses, and behavior. Meditation makes a person pure and loving, simple and divine.

7. *Jñana* (knowledge): Knowledge is the study of the scriptures and understanding the essence, secret, and significance of all the holy books. Spiritual knowledge is also obtained from personally listening to the words of a realized master.

8. *Vijñana* (spiritual experience): Knowledge translated into practice brings transformation. Then the devotee can enter the super-conscious and cosmic-conscious states.

9. *Astikyam* (living in the presence of God): Perceive the power of God in every breath and love Him and thank Him.

The *brahmin* is endowed with these nine qualities. Through thorough control of senses and mind, a balanced life ensues—a life absorbed in God-consciousness. To be in God (Brahman) is to be *brahmin.* It is not a caste, but a state of spiritual attainment. Maintenance of *paravastha* in Kriya practice will produce this state.

Verse 43

śauryam tejo dhṛtir dākṣyam
yuddhe cāpy apalāyanam
dānam īśvarabhāvaśca
kṣātram karma svabhāvajam

Translation

Heroism, fearlessness, firmness, cleverness (efficiency), not fleeing from battle, generosity, and lordliness are the duties of *kshatriyas* (warriors) born of their innate nature.

Metaphorical Interpretation

In this verse the Lord describes the seven duties or qualities of a *kshatriya,* a warrior:

1. *Shaurya* (heroism): The hero is not someone who fights enemies without, but he who is able to maintain his inner strength so he can destroy the enemies within—the weaknesses experienced in human life. To get success in this divine battle requires regular Kriya practice with love. To remain in *paravastha* constitutes victory in this battle.

2. *Tejas* (fearlessness, valor): The mind of the ordinary human being goes downward (see the Bhagavad Gita 15:2), but through the power of regular meditation the advanced student develops mental strength and can easily remain in the upper center for a longer periods of time. This powerful quality is called *tejas.* Inner strength brings charm and beauty, glory and glamour.

3. *Dhriti* (firmness): Meditation and right action make a person strong. Deep meditation brings inner calmness, then a sharp memory and heightened mental receptivity. As a result, one can work with firmness, determination, and full conviction.

4. *Dakshyam* (efficiency): This is skill in action, alertness, and success through cleverness. Meditation creates tact in the practical life, skill, and proficiency.

5. *Yuddhe ca apalayanam* (not fleeing from battle): With firm determination the spiritual seeker strives to maintain complete God awareness at any cost—do or die. "I am to proceed in my work. Any way I can, I am to complete and to succeed. I am to destroy evil". This is the attitude of a true spiritual seeker.

6. *Danam* (generosity): Material charity is good, but real charity is dedicating the mind to God, offering every breath to God with love. Every breath must be spent for God-realization. Breath is the spiritual wealth of man.

7. *Ishvarabhava* (lordliness): Ordinarily this means administrative ability. But metaphorically this describes your relationship with God and the soul—to love God and accept His sovereignty in every aspect of life.

With these qualities a spiritual seeker can fight the negative tendencies and proceed toward the divine goal.

Verse 44

kṛṣigaurakṣyavāṇijyam
vāiśyakarma svabhāvajam
paricaryātmakam karma
śūdrasyā 'pi svabhāvajam

Translation

Agriculture, raising cattle, and trade are the natural duties of the *vaishyas* (trading people). Service is the duty of the *shudras*, born of their innate nature.

Metaphorical Interpretation

In this verse the Lord narrates the natural duties of the *vaishyas* and the *shudras.*

Superficially speaking, the *vaishyas* are businessmen or traders. They work with the profit motive. They cultivate the land and engage in the dairy and poultry business and other allied trades. In the same way, the *shudras* are those who help *brahmins, kshatriyas,* and the *vaishyas* in their work. They coordinate in their works and cooperate with others.

But the Lord is not teaching us about ordinary, mundane activities. In the beginning every spiritual seeker is a *shudra* and a *vaishya*. The *vaishyas* do three types of work: *krishi* (cultivation), *goraksha* (cattle-rearing), and *vanijya* (trade or business).

What is *krishi,* cultivation? In the Bhagavad Gita, Chapter 13, it states that every human being is a land to be cultivated, and every spiritual person must cultivate the body land to achieve the maximum spiritual harvest. As a farmer takes care of the land, removing stones, pebbles, and weeds, the seeker must remove the negative qualities and obstacles to spiritual life.

Goraksha consists of two parts: *go* and *raksha. Go* in Sanskrit means the world, that is, the body world. *Raksha* means the maintenance of the body land. How is the body land maintained? When the senses and the mind are well regulated and trained, the body is maintained and protected. This is *goraksha.* Another meaning of *go* is "tongue," so *goraksha* also refers to the control of the tongue that a student of Kriya Yoga practices.

Vanijya means to do business, to work with expectation of profit or reward. Each person, in the beginning of the spiritual life prays or meditates with the expectation of good health, prosperity, or other gain. To undertake any activity with expectation of reward is to work with desire, and thus is *vanijya*—business.

These are the three innate qualities of the *vaishyas.*

The *shudras* are the primary school students in spiritual life. In this verse, the Lord explains that these people should try to learn spiritual life by serving advanced spiritual seekers and the realized master with love (see the Bhagavad Gita 4:34). With this service and by practicing the technique, they will slowly proceed along the spiritual path and reach the divine goal.

Verse 45

sve sve karmaṇy abhirataḥ
samsiddhim labhate naraḥ

svakarmaniratah̤ siddhim
yathā vindati tac chr̤n̤u

Translation

The man who is keenly devoted to his own natural duty attains the highest perfection. Hear then, how one who is devoted to his own duty reaches this highest communion.

Metaphorical Interpretation

In the preceding three verses the Lord described the inborn qualities of four categories of people in detail. First, each spiritual seeker must correctly perceive his nature, attitude, aptitude, and inner quality. What is his mind like? To what extent is it pure and calm? Accordingly, he can know his own level of consciousness. This is the beginning of self-inquiry. The realized master can also know the state of the student—what he is and where he is.

After becoming aware of his own condition, the student must work with great efficiency, earnest desire, and zeal. The human body is the field of activity. Action brings perfection. Spiritual attainment is not the result of dreaming, but rather is achieved through sincere effort, by which people can have success in their life. Ultimately, the only real work is spiritual practice and leading a God-conscious life.

God made man and woman in His image and breathed into their nostrils the breath of life, so they became living beings. All human beings are the children of God. Caste or social position is unimportant. Instead, one should only perceive that every human being is the living power of God, the marvelous power of God breathing through the nostrils, the reason we are all alive.

With the guidance of a master, people of all the different castes and categories can succeed in life—both in the material world and in the spiritual kingdom. It depends on the students' sincerity in following a master and practicing the techniques—in doing their homework, so to speak. According to their effort, skill, and earnest desire, aspirants will proceed on the spiritual path and will attain God-realization. One will perceive God as earth, water, fire, air, and sky—working, dreaming, and sleeping, in every stage and in every moment.

Verse 46

yataḥ pravṛttir bhūtānām
yena sarvam idam tatam
svakarmaṇā tam abhyarcya
siddhim vindati mānavaḥ

Translation

Man attains the highest perfection by worshipping through his natural duty, Him, from whom all beings have their origin, Him by whom this universe is pervaded.

Metaphorical Interpretation

God is one without a second. God is all-pervading. God has created everything from Himself. He is also the indwelling self, the inner being of everything. From Him, all work is created. Every action of every person comes from Him. Man's action is controlled and regulated by the breath that is inhaled and exhaled by the soul. Every living being is full of activity, but few realize that every action (*kri*) is possible only by the breath, only by the soul that is *ya*. *Kri* and *ya* make the world, the universe.

Yena sarvam idam tatam: "Man must know Him who is all-pervading." God is omnipresent. There is neither place nor time where there is no God. The Isha Upanishad (Mantra 1) says, *isha vasyam idam sarvam:* "God is everywhere."

Svakarmana tam abhyarchya: "Worship Him during all activity." Work is worship. Every work should be performed with the sense of worshipping God. During every action one must perceive *kri* and *ya*. Ordinarily people don't perceive that every thought, every word, and every action is from God, for His worship. As every action is worship, every result is the grace of God.

Sva-karma: "The action of the breath." Worship the all-pervading God through the action of the breath. Perceive His presence—He Who is everywhere. By doing this, you will have success in life. If people of different levels of mentality and spiritual ability do their own natural work with the greatest efficiency and earnest desire, following the instructions of the teacher, they will have prompt understanding, ready wit, and ultimately, God-realization.

People will succeed depending on heredity, environment, and culture, but by the power of soul culture, every person will achieve God-realization. If the desire is great, and one lives in seclusion and meditates with absolute sincerity, immediate success will follow. Deep meditation is the cause of divine perception, the ability to perceive God everywhere. During every breath one must touch the supreme almighty father with love. This is the essential cause of quick spiritual progress.

Verse 47

śreyān svadharmo viguṇaḥ
paradharmāt svanuṣṭhitāt
svabhāvaniyatam karma
kurvan nāpnoti kilbiṣam

Translation

Better is one's own duty (*dharma*), though imperfect, than the duty of another well performed. Performing the duty prescribed by one's own nature, one does not incur evil (sin).

Metaphorical Interpretation

In this verse the Lord explains spiritual life.

Svadharma is one's own duty. The duty of every person is to search for God. Soul culture is *svadharma.* Ordinarily, people understand *dharma* as religion. But *dharma* is truly that which upholds. The upholding principle that keeps the body and soul together in each living being is *dharma*—the breath. The breath links the body and the soul. Thus, *svadharma* means to watch one's own breath—to become aware of the indwelling self.

The almighty father hides in every living being, everywhere. He is the cause of breath, and ultimately, the cause of life. Although there are fifty kinds of breath, only one breath out of the fifty leads to genuine calmness and gives the taste of reality. The other forty-nine breaths are extroverted, restless, and deluded. In his gross body man engages in many types of activities in an extroverted state. All these activities are the result of the forty-nine extroverted breaths. Only with breath control can you have self control. With breath control you will reach realization, which is wisdom.

Wisdom cannot be perceived with the five sense organs, by emotion, hallucination, speculation, miracles, or magic. It is possible only by going to the atom point in deep meditation. Without merging into the atom point, you are constantly busy with the many "externals," a condition called *paradharma*. In *paradharma* there is attachment to the sense organs and the external world, which brings restlessness. *Paradharma* is the religion of many. It is dreadful. No matter what someone is doing, if proper attention is not given to the breath and the soul, it is *paradharma*.

Paradharma is attachment to the senses and is therefore extroverted. It may be somewhat pleasing and attractive in the beginning, but ultimately it is dangerous. *Svadharma* is breath control through meditation. It may be a little difficult in the beginning, but it must be practiced. Those who receive the touch of a realized master, who try to practice Kriya sincerely, will perceive God's presence in every center of the spine.

Leading a spiritual life according to the instructions of the master, perceiving *ham* and *sa*, the unity of body and soul, in every breath, and rising to the awareness of the formless state, you will discover moderation in daily life, and inner detachment. You will experience divine joy while doing everyday activities in the material world.

All of man's activities depend on his stage of life, his environment, and the company he keeps. In childhood there is one kind of work, in the youthful stage work takes another form, and in old age yet another. God continuously changes the body, so the nature of work changes with the stages of life: infancy, childhood, youth, adulthood, and old age. These changes are due to *svabhava*, the changes in the body nature and mother nature.

Work is worship of the formless God when it is done by a person who maintains a relationship (*bhava*) with the soul (*sva*) during every breath and every moment, who perceives the formless power of God through meditation and self-control. Such a seeker will not develop evil propensities or sins. Deviation from the soul causes sin; awareness of the soul causes liberation (see the Bhagavad Gita 3:35).

Verse 48

sahajam karma kaunteya
sadoṣam api na tyajet
sarvārambhā hi doṣeṇa
dhūmenāgnir ivāvṛtāḥ

Translation

Therefore, O son of Kunti (Arjuna), one should not abandon the duty to which one is born, even though it may be tainted with blemish, for even as fire is enveloped with smoke, all beginnings of undertakings are clouded with demerit.

Metaphorical Interpretation

When the child is in the mother's womb, the child cannot inhale by itself. The head is below and the body is above. The mother is responsible for the circulation and respiration in the child. The very moment the child is born, the marvelous power of God inhales through the nostrils of the baby. Breathing is *sahaja karma,* the action born with birth. *Sahaja* means *saha jayate iti*—with birth comes the breath.

The Lord addresses Arjuna as Kaunteya, the son of Kunti, he who is born of the finest conception, the one who always seeks truth, who strives to keep his awareness in the pituitary. The baby does not know that breath is his life. The child growing up does not know it either; he believes that by the power of nature alone the breath goes in and out. But in truth, living beings survive by the marvelous power of God.

Every man and woman is made in the image of God. The marvelous power of God hides in all of them, but most don't realize it. They don't understand that the breath is their life. From infancy they are not taught the spiritual truth. Ignorant, they do not know the value of breath. But the age-old divine wisdom of the realized masters teaches that every living being has two aspects—*ham* (the body) and *sa* (the soul). The soul, the imperishable power of God, hides in every body.

Humans breathe fifty kinds of breath, forty-nine of which cause delusion. *Sadosham api na tyajet*: "Even when the breath is the cause of delusion, do not be disgusted; instead, love God with every breath." In this verse, the Lord uses the imagery of someone trying to ignite some wood, which initially becomes covered by smoke. But with a little puff of air, the fire is able to burst through. Similarly, out of ignorance, people think that there is no God. Their mind dwells on many different things, like the sun covered in a cloud. But with a little puff of air the smoke disappears and the fire appears—with a little practice of meditation such as the Kriya Yoga technique, one can perceive God.

Breath is the principal manifestation of life. At first, people may not believe it, but the more they practice meditation according to the instructions of the realized master, the more they will automatically perceive the living presence of God through the breath. With breath consciousness, there is freedom from evil, immorality, and negative qualities. The spiritual breath is the only breath where no warm breath comes out of the nostrils. Breathe this breath and you will perceive extreme calm and love. This is divine.

Many people worship idols. Although these rituals are done only by the power of the breath, these people don't understand that in order to worship properly, they must first remove negative thoughts and feelings by practicing *pranayama* (breathing techniques).

In the practice of Kriya Yoga, there is no hardship. Through the practice of *kevala kumbhaka* (to be learned from the master), divine illumination is perceived inside the body, in the seven centers. With earnest effort to control the breath, the marvelous power of God hiding in the body will be experienced, day and night.

Verse 49

asaktabuddhiḥ sarvatra
jitātmā vigataspṛhaḥ
naiṣkarmyasiddhim paramām
samnyāsenādhigacchati

Translation

He whose intellect is unattached everywhere, who has self-mastery, whose thirst for enjoyment has altogether disappeared by renunciation, attains the supreme state of freedom from action.

Metaphorical Interpretation

Every person is active in the world; it is human nature—one cannot be idle while engaged in material life. But man must not forget that the real purpose of all action is to realize God. Keeping the divine goal always in mind while working, the aspirant will slowly make progress.

In this verse, the Lord describes three important qualities: *sarvatra asakta buddhi* (intellect unattached everywhere); *jitatma* (self-mastery); and *vigata spriha* (no thirst for enjoyment).

Ordinarily, man is passionate, constantly busy in material activity, forever attended by temptation and greed. But those on the spiritual path realize that material wealth is nothing, that breath is the only real wealth. So, they practice breath control. During every breath they are attached to the almighty father.

A life of God-consciousness brings inner detachment. God's

presence is perceived everywhere. In earth, fire, water, air, sky, in all the elements, in all activities, the seeker perceives God and loves God. His intellect is pure and he is compassionately detached like a lotus leaf floating on water.

The breath activates the sense organs and the mind. Restless breath leads to a restless mind and then a restless life. This is the secret of breath control. Breath control is self control and breath mastery is self mastery. With it, God can be experienced through every portal of the senses.

Spiritual life is complete freedom. Passion becomes compassion. Expectation disappears. There is no attraction to money, sex, or food. This is *nispriha* (desirelessness). The spiritual person also perceives that everybody is himself. His heart is open to all. He takes food as medicine, without being attached to taste or desirability. He has no expectation of reward for his actions. His life is an example for everyone. He is extremely engrossed in God-consciousness. This is the true meaning of renunciation. This state can be attained while living a life of activity and family in the world.

Far beyond all action (*naiskarmya*) is the breathless, pulseless state.

Verse 50

siddhim prāpto yathā brahma
tathāpnoti nibodha me
samāsenaiva kaunteya
miṣṭhā jñānasya yā parā

Translation

O son of Kunti (Arjuna), learn from me briefly how one who has attained perfection also attains Brahman, which is the highest state of knowledge.

Metaphorical Interpretation

Up to this point and in this verse as well, the Lord explains the qualifications for attaining the supreme stage of self-realization. This is the ever-compassionate God, the divine mother, teaching the supreme secret with extreme love to the able disciple and obedient child, Arjuna.

Self mastery, self control, and self analysis are the foundations of higher spiritual life. Through practice of meditation and with inner transformation, the seeker constantly touches the indwelling self, which leads to knowledge, consciousness, super-consciousness, and cosmic-consciousness. There is no world sense; the world becomes God. In this state, the mind is so pure it cannot produce a single thought. This is wisdom, constant God-awareness.

Every human body is a house of nine doors. But in a state of extreme tranquility—the ocean without waves, breathless living, complete communion with God—even when the sense organs, the nine doors are open, no thoughts can enter. This is *naiskarmya siddhi*—the supreme state of freedom from action. In this stage one perceives himself as one with the almighty Lord. In the Mundaka Upanishad (3:2:9), it says, *brahmaveda brahmaiva bhavati:* "One who knows that supreme Brahman becomes Brahman." Just as electric current flows through the whole body when a live electric wire is touched, so the whole system of a God-conscious person becomes divine.

Verse 51

buddhyā viśuddhayā yukto
dhṛtyāmānam niyamya ca
śabdādīn viṣayāms tyaktvā
rāgadveṣau vyudasya ca

Translation

Endowed with pure intellect and understanding, controlling oneself with firmness, abandoning sound and other objects of the senses, cutting off all attraction and hatred,

Metaphorical Interpretation

Every spiritual seeker must cultivate seventeen divine virtues (as described in these verses) and must sincerely meditate to reach the divine goal of God-realization.

1. *Pure intellect.* Intellect is the deciding faculty of man. Good decisions are made when one is calm. With deep concentration, one can penetrate into the midbrain and go to the pineal gland. When the attention is fixed there, the intellect is rendered pure and divine; God is perceived everywhere.

2. *Self control.* Through repeated contemplation one can become highly receptive. One achieves self control through breath control. Restlessness disappears.

3. *Abandoning sense objects.* God created the senses and sense objects for spiritual progress and God-realization, not to create danger and difficulty. In deep meditation, merged in God-consciousness, one forgets words. While breathing the very feeble and slow breath (*see the Bhagavad Gita 5:27–28*), one can remain compassionately detached from tempting sense objects and turbulent sense organs. By virtue of a technique such as *jyoti mudra,* one can develop deep friendship with the sense organs and lower centers. Deep meditation also causes the spiritual seeker to perceive God's presence in the objects of the senses. At this point, God's omnipresence produces continuous God awareness.

4. *Freedom from raga (attachment) and dvesha (hatred).* Lacking attachment or maliciousness, the spiritual seeker is free; his conciousness is always in and above the fontanel, in the super-conscious state above the perishable body. This is *paravastha.* Those who practice Kriya regularly know this state and can remain there for long periods, even during the activities of daily life. They have no attachment and no aversion.

Verse 52

viviktasevī laghvāśī
yatavākkāyamānasaḥ

dhyānayogaparo nityam
vairāgyam samupāśritaḥ

Translation

Dwelling in solitude, eating lightly, controlling speech, body, and mind, constantly devoted to yoga meditation, taking refuge in dispassion.

Metaphorical Interpretation

5. *Living in seclusion.* Meditation in a secluded place allows more concentration. External seclusion is good, but real seclusion occurs in the cave of the cranium (see the Bhagavad Gita 13:10).

6. *Light food.* The ordinary meaning is to take moderate food. Overeating brings drowsiness. Undereating makes one weak. But more important, moderating food intake and maintaining attention on the Lord while eating is essential. One who meditates while eating cannot be attached to what he is eating. He avoids harmful food. He seeks God, not flavor.

Breath is another food. While taking this food, while breathing, one should be very careful. Through scientific breathing (slow breathing—to be learned directly from the teacher), one gets the "light food" that one really needs.

7. *Control over speech, mind, and body.* Ordinary people are so engrossed in the body and the mind that they don't take care of themselves well. Meditation requires thorough control over speech, mind, and body. While meditating, the body is still. Through breath control one achieves control over the mind and speech. The five sense organs and the twenty-four gross elements become merged in God. The eyes, while open, do not blink. There is no restlessness of the body. The Bible says, "Be still and know that I am God" (Psalm 46:10). The man of meditation easily attains this state.

8. *Constant meditation.* The mind must be constantly absorbed in God-consciousness. People think that meditation is for a limited period of time. But in reality, meditation is a continuous process of keeping the mind focused in God-consciousness and love.

9. *Dispassion (detachment).* This develops from regular meditation and a spiritual life. It makes the seeker free from objects, people, and even thoughts. A detached person knows that nothing is more important than God-realization.

Verse 53

ahamkāram balam darpam
kāmam krodham parigraham
vimucya nirmamaḥ śānto
brahmabhūyāya kalpate

Translation

Having given up ego, violence, arrogance, lust, anger, possession of properties, unselfish and tranquil, he is qualified to be one with Brahman (the absolute).

Metaphorical Interpretation

10. *Egolessness.* "I am the doer"—this sense of doership is ego. A man of meditation perceives that he is merely an instrument, that soul is the sole doer in man. The soul is the cause of all activity: *kri* and *ya*.

11. *Non-violence.* The Sanskrit word used here is *bala,* which means the strength used for violence. This is an animal quality. The spiritual person loves everything. He uses his physical, mental, and intellectual strength for spiritual progress, to help others, for God-realization. The true strength is inner spiritual strength.

12. *No arrogance.* People who meditate a little, who develop a little spiritual power, think that they are highly advanced and divine. But a truly spiritual person is filled with humility and love. He has no vanity. He thinks he is insignificant. He knows that without God he has nothing.

13. *Non-possessiveness.* The child is born into this world empty-handed, but with the passage of time, because of poor environment and culture, he becomes possessive, thinking that he owns his body,

family, wealth, and status. But he does not own his possessions, his possessions own him. Through proper understanding, the spiritual person realizes that he will leave this world alone and empty-handed. Whatever he thinks he possessed in this life will not go with him, except the merits and demerits he acquired.

14. *No lust.* Passion is a great obstacle. A man who is always seeking God and leading a divine life is free from unnecessary desire. His only desire is to merge with God.

15. *No anger.* When desires are not fulfilled, anger arises. Lust and anger are twins. A spiritual person is free from narrowness and is always in a God-like mood, far from anger. Anger is the indication of a weak mind. (*see the Bhagavad Gita 2:62–63*)

16. Unselfish. The spiritual person has no sense of mine and thine. He is always soul-oriented. His life is full of love. His love is divine and is manifested in daily activity.

17. Tranquil. Through deep meditation, the spiritual person stays in the formless state in the vacuum. Extreme tranquillity of mind makes him God-conscious at all times.

These are the qualities of a highly spiritual person who maintains constant godhood (*Brahma-bhava*). Even while remaining in the mortal, physical frame, a spiritual person is extremely absorbed in the superconscious state. This is the divine state that everyone should try to achieve.

Verse 54

brahmabhūtaḥ prasannātmā
na śocati na kāṅkṣati
samaḥ sarveṣu bhūteṣu
madbhaktim labhate parām

Translation

Absorbed in Brahman, he who is serene and cheerful neither grieves nor desires. He is the same to all beings. Such a yogi attains supreme devotion to Me.

Metaphorical Interpretation

Now the Lord is describing about liberation. In the Vedas, it says that a person who controls his life and meditates deeply is absorbed in God consciousness. He perceives:

tat tvam asi: Thou art That (Sama Veda, Chhandogya Upanishad 6:8:7)

aham brahmasmi: I am Brahman (Yajur Veda, Brihadaranyaka Upanishad 1:4:10)

ayamatma brahma: This soul is Brahman (Atharva Veda, Mandukya Upanishad 2)

prajñanam brahma: Wisdom is Brahman (Rig Veda, Aitareya Upanishad 3:1:3)

sarvam khalvidam brahma: Everything is Brahman (Sama Veda, Chhandogya Upanishad 3:14:1)

sarvam brahma mayam jagat: The entire universe is God

The person who attains *prajñan* (wisdom) has no narrow-mindedness, no worldly mood. He is constantly engrossed in that which is all-pervading. His inner and outer life is full of tranquillity and peace. He is free from agitation and irritation. He is not disturbed or perturbed by any loss or gain. He is free from all repentance and remorse.

Consider the business attitude of a banker. When people deposit and withdraw money, the banker is neither happy with deposits nor unhappy with withdrawals. He profits from the flow of all the money. In the same way, a spiritual person does not forfeit inner peace with material loss nor rejoices with gain. He is not expecting anything. He is free from agitation. In truth, nothing can be lost in the universe except character. When character is lost, everything is lost.

By regular practice of Kriya, deeply, sincerely, and faithfully, you can be compassionately detached, free from ambition, and constantly aware that you are God in a human being and a human being in God. Constantly seeing God in everything and everywhere, your life will be ever divine, without attraction or attachment. *Parabhakti*, supreme devotion to God, is reached by merging with the supreme self through self-inquiry and soul culture. Such devotion and continuous God communion cannot be achieved in a state of duality.

Where there is no wind, no storm, the lake is tranquil and free from waves. In the same way the life of a spiritual seeker is filled with peace, bliss, and joy. The spiritual person is God-intoxicated and divine.

Verse 55

bhaktyā mām abhijānāti
yāvān yaścāsmi tattvataḥ
tato mām tattvato jñātvā
viśate tadanantaram

Translation

Through that supreme devotion, he comes to know Me in reality: what and how great I am; and then having known Me in essence, he enters into My being.

Metaphorical Interpretation

When a devotee practices Kriya with implicit faith, love for the master, and loyalty to him, his mental impurities are slowly removed. With a pure mind and intellect, he perceives his inner divine nature and the divinity all around him. To know God is to realize Him in two ways: to know who God is, in essence, and to know what God is, his glory.

A person who correctly practices *karma* (action) comes to receive the touch of a realized master and practices the techniques taught by him. Through regular practice, the student becomes free from the body sense and sensitivity to the world. As a result, he receives divine knowledge. As he goes deeper and deeper in practice with the help of knowledge, he goes beyond consciousness into super consciousness, cosmic consciousness, and wisdom. He develops real love for God. From *karma* (action) he develops *jñana* (knowledge). Finally, knowledge leads to *bhakti* (real love for God). These three are correlated and causally connected.

The real lover of God searches for Him sincerely. God is beyond the reach of body, mind, speech, and thought. Through deep meditation the seeker becomes free from body consciousness and the worldly sense, perceiving himself in the state of "I Am That I Am" (see the Bible, *Exodus* 3:14). This is the knowledge of Brahman, God the absolute. This knowledge is attained not by hearing exposition of the scriptures or by study or by intellectual inquiry, but by meditation through devotion.

To realize God and to know His divine glory brings liberation and godhood. God is all-pervading. His glory is boundless. In every aspect of life, in pleasure and pain, the devotee loves and perceives the glory of God. Even extreme pain and trouble will carry a sincere devotee to more divine joy.

The spiritual person does not go anywhere, except to the north of the body, to God's abode. He practices meditation and Kriya and feels the formless father hiding everywhere. He is above the jurisdiction of the body world, in the state of infinite consciousness, silently witnessing. He sees that God is the light of the body and the world, the life of everyone.

Absorbed, merged and saturated in absolute God consciousness, there is no duality, only complete unity.

Verse 56

sarvakarmāṇy api sadā
kurvāṇo madvyapāśrayaḥ
matprasādād avāpnoti
śāśvatam padam avyayam

Translation

Performing all actions, he whose reliance is always upon Me, attains by My grace the eternal and imperishable abode.

Metaphorical Interpretation

In every being, in every object, in every action, and in all states of restlessness, God is the hidden principle. Everything is sustained by Him, the creator, sustainer, and destroyer of everything.

When the devotee performs every action feeling the almighty father, the cause of all actions, the imperishable soul in all—he becomes an instrument of the will of God. While ordinary people work with ego, a spiritual person is without ego and aware of the cosmic principle of God. Every work is God-oriented and divine.

With every action he perceives the almighty father; he perceives *kri* and *ya*. His mind is always in God, in constant union with God. He loves God in every breath and in every moment. He continuously experiences divine joy.

With the grace of the almighty father and the divine mother, he realizes that the formless power of God is activating his life from the top of the head. His mind is never below in the lower objects of the senses in the mundane world. He is always watching *sa*, the formless one, in the body form, *ham,* and becomes fit to obtain divine grace. By God's grace, he obtains such an ecstatic state that he feels God's love continuously. God's abode is on the top, in the cave of the cranium. The pure devotee, by divine grace, enters the divine abode without deviation and finds eternal peace, bliss, and joy.

Verse 57

cetasā sarvakarmāṇi
mayi samnyasya matparaḥ
buddhiyogam upāśritya
maccittaḥ satatam bhava

Translation

Mentally surrendering all actions to Me, remaining devoted to Me as the supreme, taking refuge in the yoga of discrimination, constantly think of Me,

Metaphorical Interpretation

In every human body two things are operating—*ham* and *sa*. In *sa* there is no restlessness. *Sa* is formless, free from attachment. Just as people go to work because the sun rises in the sky, the body, *ham*, is active and works because of *sa*. People are ambitious and attached, engrossed in body consciousness (*ham*), but people can remove restlessness and bring their awareness up to the pituitary by the practice of Kriya Yoga. Then they will feel the imperishable soul (*sa*). This is real detachment.

People work and are busy in the world, not realizing that without the soul (*ya*) the body cannot work (*kri*). Those who meditate perceive that every work is an offering to the Lord so they surrender all their work to the Lord. Watching and searching for the imperishable soul and remaining in knowledge, consciousness, super consciousness, and cosmic consciousness, they are free from extroverted tendencies. Although they remain in the world and work, their consciousness is absorbed in God with extreme devotion to Him. They are free from anger, pride, hypocrisy, and cruelty. They take recourse in *buddhi yoga*, the yoga of discrimination, perceiving God's presence everywhere, free from the secular mood.

So the Lord is telling Arjuna: "My dear, constantly give your mind to Me. This is the key to success and will lead to a real divine life. I am your best friend and guide."

Verse 58

maccittaḥ sarvadurgāṇi
matprasādāt tariṣyasi
atha cet tvam ahamkārān
na śroṣyasi vinankṣyasi

Translation

Fixing your mind on Me, you shall pass over all difficulties through My grace. But if, through ego, you will not listen, then you will perish.

Metaphorical Interpretation

When the living presence of God is perceived everywhere, always, the ego will disappear. As long as you have ego, you cannot give your mind to God. The only way to overcome this critical obstacle is to perceive *kri* and *ya*, the presence of the soul in every action. This is the divine link to soul culture and God-realization. When meditation is sincere and the presence of God is perceived in every action, there is freedom from conflict, worry, anxiety, and tension.

The Lord says, "O Arjuna! If you constantly feel Me in every breath, you will never have any bad thoughts." In human life, there are sorrows, sufferings, conflicts, obstacles, and ups and downs to be sure. But the God-oriented disciple has sufficient inner strength to overcome.

All the sons of Vasishtha were killed by Vishvamitra (in the Ramayana). But Vasishtha was highly realized, so he said, "O Lord! Nothing dies. How can my sons die? All is Your play!" He was not heartbroken; he was not unhappy; he had no hatred for Vishvamitra. He did not even once think to take revenge against him. Because of his meditation and love for God, he was free from sorrow. There are many saints, sages, *munis,* and *rishis* who were imperturbable in the face of extreme sorrow and suffering. Because of their constant attachment to the indwelling self and the almighty father, they were not affected.

In this verse there is the word *durga*, which ordinarily means difficulty. But the real meaning is fort. Every person lives in the fort of the body and mind, the fort of memories and experiences. Those who practice meditation sincerely free themselves from all attachments to the body, mind, and experiences. If people do not meditate and live like animals, they will surely endure many difficulties in the body fort, which is full of negative qualities. They will suffer and face death. Happiness is joined to unhappiness. So ordinary people, remaining in vanity and pride, are engrossed in the material world. They eat, drink, and make merry. And they suffer. They cannot go north to His presence (in the fontanel); instead they live with degradation and degeneration. They are like animals; they are subhuman.

Many people think they are rational, but in truth, rationality is the ability to discriminate the real from the unreal, to perceive truth and God. With true rationality, one can search for God during times of pleasure and pain and attain God-realization.

With these words, the Lord has described His grace, which grace can easily be realized through meditation and divine love.

Verse 59

yad ahamkāram āśritya
na yotsya iti manyase
mithyaiṣa vyavasāyas te
prakṛtis tvām niyokṣyati

Translation

If, filled with egoism, you think, "I will not fight," your resolve will be in vain. Your inner nature will compel you to act.

Metaphorical Interpretation

"O Arjuna! You and all the people in the world are on the battlefield of life, filled with evil propensities, temptation, and negative qualities. Fight these enemies that are hiding within you even now. They hinder your spiritual progress.

In the previous verses, I described in detail the qualities of *brahmins, kshatriyas, vaishyas,* and *shudras*. All these types of individuals must struggle to proceed toward the state of God-realization. You must not to remain in delusion, illusion, and error.

"O Arjuna! Due to your illusory compassion, you are not willing to fight with evil." Those who are attached to the lower centers of the body insist that in killing the evils they would be killing their dear relatives. But who are these relatives? They are the qualities related to your body nature, the cause of all negative propensities. Delusion, illusion, error, ego, selfishness, and more exist in the body.

When you refuse to kill the evil within today, you will have to do it tomorrow. This is the law of nature. Everyone will realize God; it is the birthright of every person. But people rarely want to ascend to the pituitary and the fontanel. They totally forget God's presence. If the Lord does not inhale for them, they have nothing. Their material efforts and determination are false. Their decisions are in error.

"I am the supreme father in you. You are so attached to the body and its propensities that you didn't want to fight. But Arjuna! Your destiny is great. You are a *kshatriya* (warrior). Your nature is to fight. If you don't fight with your negatives today, you will be forced to fight them tomorrow."

Verse 60

svabhāvajena kaunteya
nibaddhaḥ svena karmaṇā
kartum necchasi yan mohāt
kariṣyasy avaśo 'pi tat

Translation

Also, action that you are not willing to undertake out of delusion; bound by your own duty, born of your own innate nature, you will helplessly do it, O Kaunteya (Arjuna, son of Kunti).

Metaphorical Interpretation

"O Arjuna! Your destiny is great. Your mother is divine. You were born from her divine power and meditation. But your ego and ignorance make you not want to fight with evil."

People are ignorant and deluded; their intellects cannot direct them rightly. Ego and ignorance deflect people from their goals in life. Delusion, illusion, and error arise in the spinal centers from the money center up to the neck center.

"Arjuna! You are a strong and brave warrior. You have great noble qualities. You are constantly in My company. I know your nature, but you do not know My nature completely.

"Arjuna! You must be attached to your natural work, which is your breath. You must always be aware of your breath, and you must know who is inhaling from the top. The soul is breathing. The soul is beyond everything, even the mind. So, do not regret anything. Every person who is born must die. Until the time of death, every person must fight the negative qualities and the evils. So fight the enemies within you! Your nature is to fight and destroy the enemies."

Like Arjuna, everyone in the world is constantly engrossed in ignorance, prey to conflicts, temptations, and difficulties. Be very careful; temptation, a law of nature, is the greatest enemy.

If you practice Kriya and remain in the pituitary and fontanel, you will be free from evil and will experience extreme calm and divinity. You will develop the power to discriminate between right and wrong. Through more and more practice of Kriya, you will become highly realized. So, be compassionately detached and fight—by practicing Kriya.

Verse 61

īśvaraḥ sarvabhūtānām
hṛddeśe 'rjuna tiṣṭhati
bhrāmayan sarvabhūtāni
yantrārūḍhāni māyayā

Translation

O Arjuna! The Lord abides in the hearts of all beings, causing them to revolve (according to their karma) by His illusive power, as if fixed in a machine.

Metaphorical Interpretation

God has created the entire universe. God has made man and woman in His image. Having created everything, He is hiding in all. The formless God is hidden in all names and forms.

But people do not realize the presence of God within themselves and in everything else. They are deluded, seeking money, sex, and food. Sex prevails. It makes people restless and mad. But people also have extreme attachment in the heart center where delusion is born. The heart center is a colorful drawing room where people sit, gossip, and mix in the five sense organs. As a result, they are automatically engrossed in *maya*, bewildered, without the ability to make clear judgements.

The delusive power of *maya* is a veiling power. People associate with evil and while hearing, seeing, talking, touching, and smelling, they develop strong attachments—in both male and female. People engrossed in the five sense organs are filled with temptation. Like fish who look at a bait but do not see the dreadful hook inside, people succumb to temptation. To swallow the bait is death. Even a big fish can be pulled from the water in a moment's time. Similarly, people who yield to temptation commit many errors and mistakes that bring misfortune. When people are overcome with *maya*, their hearing is affected, good things taste bitter, and their material needs multiply.

But you can be free from *maya* if you learn how to go to the top of the body house where the imperishable soul sits compassionately detached in the pituitary. The Lord is in the center and *maya* is on the periphery. The periphery is born from the center. If you go to the center where Ishihara (the Lord) is hiding and creating delusion, you can become divine, free from the temptations of *maya*.

Verse 62

tam eva śaraṇam gaccha
sarvabhāvena bhārata
tatprasādāt parām śāntim
sthānam prāpsyasi śāśvatam

Translation

Take shelter in Him alone, with all your being. O Arjuna, by His grace you will attain supreme peace and the eternal abode.

Metaphorical Interpretation

Here the Lord addresses Arjuna as "the man of divine illumination" (*bha-rata.*) Arjuna is sitting inside the cranium, near the *kutastha* (the center of Krishna consciousness). His third eye is open, and he is continuously perceiving super consciousness and cosmic consciousness. He is constantly listening to the divine voice of the Lord.

The Lord states that every person should take shelter in Him alone. People naturally take shelter in someone superior who can rescue them from difficulties and who can free them from fear. God is the creator, protector, and destroyer of everything. Through the breath, He maintains every living being. Many people think spirituality is completely dependent on destiny, so they do not attempt to reach the ultimate goal during their life. But the Lord says, "O Arjuna, please take shelter in Me." The Lord, being the Divine parent, urges all human beings to strive for soul consciousness.

Sarva bhavena means that the divine life consists of perceiving God's presence in every way, in every thought, in every activity, and in every moment. Every thought must be God-directed. Without God there is no thought. Practice breath awareness all day and all night. Immediately shun any bad thought that arises. Think of Him. Love Him. Remain alert. In every action perceive the divine presence. When all action is worship of Him, the work will create *prasada*—that which comes from God as His grace, gift, and greetings. *Prasada,* the fruit, will bring *prasannata,* inner peace and equanimity.

Distinguish good from bad, lovingly avoid all bad desire, and work to keep your awareness in the fontanel, and you will receive the divine grace. The result of divine grace is *parashanti,* supreme peace, bliss, and joy. Constantly keeping your attention on the top, on the source of His breath, you will discover continuous peace and freedom from restlessness, worry, pitfalls, and difficulties. You will reach the divine abode, eternal God consciousness. This is the ultimate goal, the expanded plane of life, free from limitations.

Verse 63

iti te jñānam ākhyātam
guhyād guhyataram mayā
vimṛśyaitad aśeṣeṇa
yathecchasi tathā kuru

Translation

Thus the knowledge, more secret than secrecy itself, has been imparted to you by Me. Having reflected on this completely, do as you like.

Metaphorical Interpretation

"O Arjuna! I have told you the supreme secret doctrine." Why is this teaching secret? In the Katha Upanishad (1:2:23), it says, *nāyam ātmā pravacanena labhyo na medhayā, na bahunā śrutena*: "The self cannot be known through much study, nor through the intellect, nor through much hearing." The secret is that the divine self, hidden within, whom cannot be realized with the sense organs, can be realized only by self-effort, by self-discovery. You cannot be a doctor just by reading books and hearing the words of the teacher, it requires inner experience.

Every person knows what is good and what is bad. When someone fails to avoid what is bad and makes no attempt to be free from the clutches of delusion, illusion, and error, it is foolishness. In this verse, the Lord expresses His love by granting the greatest freedom to man, saying, "Do as you like."

"O Arjuna! In detail I told you about practical spirituality, the secret spiritual doctrine, the key to success for a divine life. I answered all your questions and doubts. The secret of success lies within the reach of every person. Sincerely strive for the experience of the truth. You can be your own best friend or your own worst enemy. Be careful of what you do."

Verse 64

sarvaguhyatamam bhūyaḥ
śṛṇu me paramam vacaḥ
iṣṭo 'si me dṛḍam iti
tato vakṣyāmi te hitam

Translation

Hear again, My supreme word, the most secret of all. You are extremely dear to Me, therefore I shall speak to you.

Metaphorical Interpretation

Arjuna surrendered himself to the Lord. In the Bhagavad Gita (2:7), Arjuna said, "I am your disciple. I take refuge near You. Please make me disciplined and self-realized. Arjuna is the ideal disciple. His love for the master is manifest, so the Lord says, "You are extremely dear to Me." Although the Lord tells Arjuna that he is His extremely dear one, remember that Arjuna represents all mankind. All people are the children of God. God loves all His children, even though many suffer from delusion, illusion, and error. Man enjoys the fruit of his actions. God creates the result of those actions.

"O Arjuna! For your spiritual progress, for your benefit, I am telling you My supreme word, the most secret of all. Please listen to Me." God is calling all His children, from the fontanel, as would a loving mother. People whose eyes are always looking below are extremely engrossed in money, sex, food, and ego. They don't hear the divine call; they don't look up with concentrated attention, with love and eagerness. This is the foolishness of man.

The Lord told the secret doctrine to Vivaswan. It was also revealed by Babaji to Lahiri Mahasaya. This secret technique is taught directly from the able master to the worthy disciple.

Verse 65

manmanā bhava madbhakto
madyājī mām namaskuru
mām evaiṣyasi satyam te
pratijāne priyo 'si me

Translation

Give your mind to Me, be devoted to Me. Worship Me, bow down to Me. Doing so, you will attain Me alone. I truly promise this, because you are so extremely dear to Me.

Metaphorical Interpretation

In the previous verses, the Lord said, *tamabh yarcha,* "Worship Him," and *tameva sharanam gachha,* "Take shelter in Him." In this verse the Lord says, *manmana bhava:* "Give your mind to Me." The Lord makes a simple equation of He and I: "He is I and I am He," *soham, aham sah,* "I and He are one."

The human mind is ever restless, constantly moving in the lower centers of the body world. It is never calm and quiet. The mind does not know that God is all-pervading. It does not know that sense objects the power of God. But when you enter into the company of a realized master and learn a technique of meditation such as Kriya, your mind slowly comes up until the power of God is perceived in every thought and disposition.

The mind is restless because *prana*, the life force, is restless. A mind devoted to the world is restless and turbulent, but the mind devoted to God is calm and peaceful. The realized master teaches breath control techniques, and breath control brings self-control. As the mind is slowly stilled, man becomes a true lover of God. A spiritual person practicing a technique such as Kriya perceives that every action is worship of God. In every action he feels the living presence of God. His karma (action) is *dharma* (true spirituality).

Such a person is humble and in effect is bowing down to the

Lord physically, mentally, and intellectually, in thought, word, and deed. In every breath he bows to the formless God. This leads to emancipation.

"O Arjuna! It is my sincere promise that if you follow this secret spiritual doctrine and transform your life, you will perceive Me constantly. You are extremely dear to Me. O Arjuna! You have beheld My universal form. Please follow Me. Realize that *ham* (body) and *sa* (soul) are one".

These four steps are the four Vedas, the four steps to realize God:

1. *manmana bhava:* Give your mind to Me (mind)
2. *madbhakta bhava:* Be devoted to Me (*prana*, vital breath)
3. *madyaji bhava:* Worship Me (karma, all actions)
4. *mam namaskuru:* Bow down to Me (be one with Me)

This is *upasana*—to sit near the soul. This is the promise of God to all human beings, because all are dear to Him.

Verse 66

sarvadharmān parityajya
mām ekam śaraṇam vraja
aham tvā sarvapāpebhyo
mokṣayiṣyāmi mā śucaḥ

Translation

Resigning all your duties (dharma), take refuge in Me alone. I shall liberate you from all evils. Do not worry.

Metaphorical Interpretation

There are many sects, cults, traditions, and monastic orders in this world. They teach and preach many types of techniques. But whatever they teach, it is usually to effect the worship of God by the five sense organs. People sing, chant, read, worship, and so on: It is their religious practice.

Suppose a person is extremely thirsty. If he chants "water...water...water" one thousand times, will his thirst disappear? Or suppose a person is hungry. If he gazes at delicious food in a restaurant, will his hunger be satisfied? One must eat and drink to satisfy hunger and thirst. Using the five sense organs one can make a little progress on the spiritual path, but it is difficult to reach liberation.

Wisdom is beyond the perception of the five sense organs. Emotion, hallucination, suggestion, or magic cannot take you to wisdom. Wisdom is perceived only by entering into the atom point in the fontanel. So eschew extroverted techniques and practice a scientific technique. Magnetize your spine for only two minutes and you can experience deep calm. You can perceive the all-enveloping snow-white light. This is formless meditation. One ounce of such practice is worth tons of theories.

By abandoning all the extroverted tendencies of the senses and the restlessness of the mind, one can touch the atom point, completely annihilating negative qualities. Body consciousness and forgetting the soul are sins. Perceiving the imperishable soul via breath control, one becomes free from sin, error, debauchery, and immorality.

"O Arjuna! If you practice this, from Me you will receive liberation during every breath. Do not forget Me. If you touch Me and become one with Me, this is your salvation."

Practice Kriya meditation with implicit faith, love, and loyalty. Do not regret anything. God-realization is at hand.

Verse 67

idam te nātapaskāya
nābhaktāya kadācana
na cāśuśrūṣave vācyam
na ca māṃ yo 'bhyasūyati

Translation

This (divine gospel) should never be imparted to a man who lacks patience, nor to he who is without devotion, nor to one who

does not render service (obedience), nor to one who does not desire to listen, nor to one who speaks evil of Me.

Metaphorical Interpretation

This is an extremely secret technique, extremely hidden. Those who remain engrossed in the material world—like being absorbed in wine, drugs, drowsiness, and sleep—are not qualified to learn and practice this secret spiritual science.

One who is not devoted to the preceptor and God is not human, but merely subhuman. Those who are devoid of love for God and faith in Him are not worthy of the divine path. Devotion to the guru and God is essential. The disciple should touch the feet of the guru, which causes immense divine power to flow from the body of the guru to the disciple. The marvelous power of God is in the realized master. When people love and serve their master, their ego and vanity disappear and they become divine.

Those who lack rationality and discrimination, who live like animals (eating, drinking, enjoying sexually, engaged in the lower centers) should not be taught this hidden technique. Those who hate God, who do not believe in He who is all pervading, omniscient, and omnipotent, who believe that this creation is accidental or are not fit for this divine knowledge.

A properly cultivated field produces the best harvest. Thus, the human body and life should be cultivated and cultured to produce the divine harvest of self-knowledge.

Verse 68

ya idam paramam guhyam
madbhakteṣv abhidhāsyati
bhaktim mayi parām kṛtvā
mām evaiṣyaty asamśayaḥ

Translation

He who teaches this supreme secret to My devotees,

having performed the highest devotion to Me, shall come to Me, without a doubt.

Metaphorical Interpretation

The Bhagavad Gita is the most sacred scripture for soul culture and God-realization. It is a dialogue between the master and the disciple on the most secret and sacred spiritual science. The real meaning of holy scriptures is difficult to understand and to realize.

The exposition and explanation of the Bhagavad Gita must be heard from the mouth of a spiritually advanced person and should be delivered only to sincere devotees. Who is a sincere devotee of God? A devotee wants self-development, spiritual progress, and self-realization. The real devotee wants to be one with the almighty father. He is worthy of hearing the secret and sacred spiritual doctrine.

But spiritual progress is not achieved by merely reading and hearing the scriptures. If you swallow a small piece of sugar cane, you cannot really enjoy it. It must be chewed to enjoy the taste and its nourishing quality. A person who does not meditate deeply cannot understand the deeper import of sacred scripture. Those who are advanced in meditation or who are realized consider the Bhagavad Gita the most useful and practical scripture. It addresses questions that arise in spiritual life, questions that arise for sincere seekers treading the spiritual path. It contains the answers to these questions from the mouth of the Lord Himself. Human life is explained in detail.

In Indian spiritual traditions, there are three books known as *prasthana trayi*—three scriptures for God-realization, to return back to the source (God). They are the Upanishads, the Brahma Sutras, and the Bhagavad Gita. People who understand the deep meaning of the scriptures and lead life accordingly will surely attain liberation.

The divine knowledge in the Bhagavad Gita enables a person to develop supreme devotion to the almighty Lord. Divine knowledge makes one free from doubt. In the Bhagavad Gita (4:40), it says, *samshayatma vinashyati:* "The man with doubt is destroyed." Conversely, a man free from doubt finds immortality.

He who explains this sacred scripture to seekers and who helps them lead a life on the divine path acquires all-round development, peace, bliss, and joy. He is God's best devotee. There is no doubt that he will be liberated.

Verse 69

na ca tasmān manuṣyeṣu
kaścin me priyakṛttamaḥ
bhavitā na ca me tasmād
anyaḥ priyataro bhuvi

Translation

Among men, no one does Me a more loving service than he, nor shall anyone be dearer to Me on the earth than he.

Metaphorical Interpretation

This verse is an extension of the previous one. The Lord is emphasizing the importance of doing His work. Of all the people in the world, the Lord's favorite are those who explain the Bhagavad Gita, Bible, Koran, and other authentic scriptures. Human life is very short, full of complexities and intricacies. People are far away from truth, busy with money, sex, food, emotion, friendship, and religious formalities. Sense gratification never extinguishes desire, but only creates more passion. Endless desire fills human life with trouble, worry, anxiety, and tension. The fire gallops with more fuel thrown on it.

He who explains the scriptures to true seekers loves God the best. He is dearest person to God. Constantly perceiving God's presence, he helps other people to do the same. He is in truth and helps others to be in truth.

Verse 70

adhyeṣyate ca ya imam
dharmyam samvādam āvayoḥ
jñānayajñena tenāham
iṣṭaḥ syām iti me matiḥ

Translation

And he who studies this sacred dialogue of ours, by him too shall I be worshipped through the sacrifice of divine knowledge. Such is My opinion.

Metaphorical Interpretation

Knowledge is fire. Ignorance is darkness, the cause of all suffering. The fire of knowledge burns ignorance and frees one from the bondage of action (see the Bhagavad Gita 4:19, 37 and 41). Knowledge eliminates doubt. By destroying ignorance, the knot of action and doubt, one becomes free, liberated, united with God.

Below the eyebrows there is ignorance, and above them there is knowledge. When the seeker brings his awareness up into the cranium where Shri Krishna and Arjuna are seated, when he listens to and understands the divine dialogue, he is engaged in *jñana yajña*—the sacrifice of knowledge. To study the sacred dialogue is to meditate on the holy scriptures and understand them. Ultimately, God is worshipped with the flowering of knowledge.

Verse 71

śraddhāvān anasūyaśca
śṛṇuyād api yo naraḥ
so 'pi muktaḥ śubhānl lokān
prāpnuyāt puṇyakarmaṇām

Translation

Even he who hears with faith and frees himself from malice is liberated and shall attain the happy world of those whose actions are pure.

Metaphorical Interpretation

Those who hear an exposition of the Bhagavad Gita must listen with belief and faith, with implicit love and loyalty, with their minds free of doubt, and with a clear conscience. They must be free from malice; they must not have a faultfinding nature. They must seek to discover and remove their own faults, defects, and negatives, and must try to be free. The true listener is faithful and lives a fault-free life.

Those who perceive the whole universe as the universal form of the Lord, who can accept that the Lord Himself speaks the divine gospel from the mouth of Shri Krishna, can be free from malice. Their love will flourish. Gradually, those who hear the Bhagavad Gita daily, regularly, with love and faith, will desire spiritual progress and meditation. They will move forward, becoming free from birth and death, sin, wrongdoing, and immorality. Their lives become pure and divine.

Verse 72

kaccid etac chrutam pārtha
tvayaikāgreṇa cetasā
kaccid ajñānasammohaḥ
praṇaṣṭas te dhanamjaya

Translation

Has this been heard with a concentrated (pinpointed) mind, Arjuna? O Dhanamjaya (winner of riches, Arjuna), has your delusion born of ignorance been destroyed?

Metaphorical Interpretation

Shri Krishna, the Lord, is the most efficient master, and Arjuna is the true disciple. Arjuna repeatedly poses questions to the Lord about life and self-discovery. With patience and love, the Lord explains everything to dispel Arjuna's doubts. After completing His teaching, the Lord then poses two questions to Arjuna, addressing him by his two names.

"O Partha (son of Kunti, Pritha), have you listened to Me with concentration?" Kunti means the finest conception or intelligence. Arjuna is the son of Kunti. Arjuna has deep desire for soul culture and God-realization. Even though the human mind is restless and distracted, a sincere seeker tries to achieve concentration and deep intuitive attention.

Krishna also addresses Arjuna as Dhanamjaya, the conqueror of wealth. Dhanamjaya signifies someone who has conquered birth, death, happiness and unhappiness, hunger, and thirst. As each must try to act in a manner that befits his name, the Lord is asking Arjuna: "Are you free from the cloud of delusion born of ignorance?"

The Bhagavad Gita starts with the yoga of dejection (delusion). Arjuna, forgetting his divine self, is temporarily deluded. His divine master, the Lord, tries His utmost to liberate Arjuna by teaching Arjuna the secret of spiritual life and self-unfoldment.

Arjuna is a warrior—ready to fight with all his inner enemies. He is also extremely dear to the Lord. So now the Lord wants to see Arjuna's spiritual achievement. After completing the teaching, the master asks Arjuna, "Have all your delusions disappeared or not?"

Verse 73

naṣṭo mohaḥ smṛtir labdhā
tvatprasādān mayācyuta
sthito 'smi gatasamdehaḥ
kariṣye vacanam tava

Translation

Arjuna said:

My delusion is destroyed and I have gained my memory through Your grace. O Achyuta (unchanging one, Krishna), I stand firm with all my doubts dispelled. I shall do as you say.

Metaphorical Interpretation

This is the best answer of the able student to his divine master. This verse is a statement of confirmation, realization, and complete surrender to the Lord.

In the beginning Arjuna was full of sorrow, unhappiness, and dejection. But the master, through His divine sermons, worked to dispel Arjuna's ignorance and delusion. Having listened to the Lord carefully with a fully contemplative attitude, Arjuna now says, "O Achyuta! Thank You for Your love and grace." Achyuta means he who is beyond all deviation, change, modification, and distraction. Only God, the Lord, the soul, is *achyuta*.

Arjuna's answer is, "My delusion is destroyed; I have recovered my memory; I am well established; I am free from all doubts; I am ready to follow all Your commands.

"O Achyuta! Krishna! Due to delusion and attachment, I was always tempted and attracted to the body and the senses. I thought they were my relatives. I wondered what would I gain if I went beyond the body, mind, and senses? That was my illusion. You told me to remove the charming sensory temptations because temptation is the greatest enemy.

"In the beginning my body was trembling and my hair stood on end. My throat was dry. I was bewildered and dizzy. I didn't know what to do. Extreme attachment made me depressed and dejected, afraid of destroying the evil qualities and enemies in the body. I thought they were my dear relatives.

"Through Your teachings, I understood that the world is full of temptation and apparent pleasure. But I also realized that what is pleasing in the beginning is extremely painful in the end. My weak heart and narrow understanding disappeared through Your love, guidance, and grace. You constantly consoled me. Placing Your hand on me, You utterly convinced me. Now, I am free from delusion born of ignorance. My vision and understanding are clear. The truth of life is clear to me.

"I am the imperishable soul. I forgot it, thinking I was the body. When I recovered my memory I realized that You and I are one. We are both in one body chariot. Firmly established in truth, I see no deviation. Your presence is in me and everywhere. Now, I am free from all doubts. I have no questions. I have advanced—back into Your presence. I am free. Therefore, I am Your instrument. I will follow You, my guide. I will fight, I will work, and I will follow Your commands. You are my real friend."

Verse 74

Samjaya uvāca
ity aham vāsudevasya
pārthasya ca mahātmanaḥ
samvādam imam aśrauṣam
adbhutam romaharṣaṇam

Translation

Samjaya said: Thus I have heard from Vāsudeva and the great soul Partha (Arjuna), this mysterious and thrilling conversation, which caused my hair to stand on end.

Metaphorical Interpretation

The Bhagavad Gita starts with blind king Dhritarashtra's question to his minister, Sanjaya. These final verses are Sanjaya's reply, his concluding remarks, which are the real essence of this scripture.

Sanjaya has completely conquered all his negative and evil qualities in the battle of life. Thus, he has achieved divine sight. He recited the Bhagavad Gita, the conversation between Vāsudeva and

Partha. Vāsudeva, another name for Krishna, has deep spiritual meaning. While it is true that the son of Vasudeva is called Vāsudeva, the real meaning of this name is "worldwide illumination, which is formless, Purushottama".

Sanjaya says, "I am extremely happy to have heard the whole dialogue between Shri Krishna and Arjuna. It was so thrilling and touching—I cannot express the feeling with words." Hearing the divine discourse of Vāsudeva, Arjuna enjoyed complete transformation. He remained near the pituitary, near the soul, Krishna. The chariot is not on the ground.

A seeker becomes Partha when, by his deepest desire, he leaves his attraction and attachment to the lower centers and comes up into the cranium where he is absorbed in formless perception, Vāsudeva. In this state, the essence of the scriptures is automatically revealed, all spiritual experiences are possible. Even by remembering this state, the devotee experiences extreme joy, love, and divinity.

Verse 75

vyāsaprasādāc chrutavān
etad guhyam aham param
yogam yogeśvarāt kṛṣṇāt
sākṣāt kathayataḥ svayam

Translation

By the grace of Vyasa, I have heard this supreme and most secret yoga, which Krishna has directly imparted to Arjuna before my eyes.

Metaphorical Interpretation

In the beginning of the battle that is central to the Mahabharata, Vyasa blessed Sanjaya with the yogic power of seeing and hearing what was happening on the battlefield, some hundred miles away.

Sanjaya, minister to the blind king Dhritarashtra, was thereby able to describe the battle to his king.

The breath maintains life. That breath is Vyasa. By the help or grace of Vyasa a human being can ascend from the lower centers to the upper center and to the pituitary where he will forget the mundane world entirely. Every human being is blind and unable to see and realize the truth, but by the grace of Vyasa, the divine master, any person can change his life and become *sanjay,* thoroughly controlled. Everyone can be blessed like Sanjaya with the divine power to see and hear the conversation on the battlefield between Shri Krishna and Arjuna, which is the subject of the entire Bhagavad Gita.

As Shri Krishna says in Chapter 4, Verse 1, and Arjuna says in Chapter 6, Verse 33, and Sanjaya reaffirms here, the subject matter of this divine conversation is yoga. The secret science of yoga helps the aspirant realize God through breath control. Every single breath goes in and out from *paramakrishna*, the supreme father in the fontanel.

Shri Krishna is not an ordinary person. Although He incarnates in human form, he is superhuman, not born like ordinary people. Devaki, the wife of Vasudeva, meditated deeply in the sixth center and thereby became Shri Krishna's mother. Shri Krishna is the Lord of yoga, the sacred science that enables one to perceive the unity of body and soul, the unity of oneself with the one, the supreme self. Shri Krishna is always near the pituitary, where the breath goes in and out.

Sanjaya expresses his inner gratefulness to the great guru Vyasa and to the Lord of yoga, Shri Krishna. This reflects the quality of a true disciple, who is always grateful and thankful in thought, speech, and action to the divine master.

Verse 76

rājan samsmṛtya samsmṛtya
samvādam imam adbhutam
keśavārjunayoḥ puṇyam
hṛṣyāmi ca muhur muhuḥ

Translation

O king! Remembering again and again this dialogue between Keshava (Krishna) and Arjuna, which is marvelous and holy, I rejoice again and again.

Metaphorical Interpretation

Sanjaya describes the beauty of the dialogue between Keshava and Arjuna. King Dhritarashtra is the king of the body world and represents the blindness of the mind, filled with delusion, illusion, and error. Keshava is the name of Shri Krishna that means the Lord of creation, preservation, and dissolution. Sanjaya says, "O king! Shri Krishna taught the marvelous technique of yoga. I heard every detail with love. Arjuna is extremely charmed and I am overwhelmed with joy to hear the technique."

Dhritarashtra is the king of *maya*. Sanjaya, although full of divine power, is not free from association with *maya*. To be free from it, one must meditate deeply and become realized. In the Brihadaryanaka Upanishad, it says, *Atma va are drastavyam, śrotavyam, mantavyam, nididhyasitabyam*: "One must perceive, hear, recollect, and meditate to realize the Self." The previous verse explained the power of hearing about soul (*shrotavyam*). Sanjaya described listening to this divine dialogue about the science of yoga. Now he recollects and remembers (*mantavyam*) it. People cannot remember the presence of God. They constantly forget due to delusion; this is the cause of human suffering.

Remembering God and the soul creates romance and divine love in human life. Life is transformed. Sanjaya is so full of joy while remembering the divine gospel of the Bhagavad Gita that he moves toward a deep state of God consciousness. Ordinary people cannot understand it.

"O king! The more I think about this divine conversation that I heard, the more I experience continuous divine pleasure. It is marvelous." This dialogue is *punyam,* meaning "giver of liberation."

Verse 77

tac ca samsmṛtya samsmṛtya
rūpam atyadbhutam hareḥ
vismayo me mahān rājan
hṛṣyāmi ca punaḥ punaḥ

Translation

Remembering also, again and again, this most wonderful form of Hari (Krishna), even greater is my wonder and I rejoice again and again.

Metaphorical Interpretation

In the Bhagavad Gita, Hari is used two times: once in Chapter 11, Verse 9, and the second time, here. Hari is a name of God and Shri Krishna is referred to by this name. Hari is formless, the universal form of God.

In this verse Sanjaya is explaining *drashtavyam*, which is seeing, visualizing, and perceiving. In the Bhagavad Gita, the Lord revealed His divine all-pervading formless form (Hari's *vishvarupa*) to Arjuna, which Sanjaya also could see by the grace of the guru Vyasadeva. So Sanjaya says, "O king! I am fortunate to have this marvelous and wonderful vision."

This vision is *adbhuta,* which cannot be seen in the *pancha bhutas* (five elements) present in the five lower centers (chakras). When by the power of meditation and grace of the *sat guru*, the devotee rises above the five lower centers to the pituitary, pineal, and fontanel, he enters into the formless state.

The body land must be properly cultivated and the seeker must be physically, mentally, and spiritually ready to reap the divine harvest. Sanjaya has achieved this state by the grace of Vyasa: First he sees and hears, then with self-effort he remembers, recollects, and meditates.

"O king! When I hear, recollect, and remember the teaching as told by Shri Krishna to Arjuna, the worthy disciple, I am full of awe, wonder, love, and divinity because of this divine perception.

Verse 78

yatra yogeśvaraḥ kṛṣṇo
yatra pārtho dhanurdharaḥ
tatra śrīr vijayo bhūtir
dhruvā nītir matir mama

Translation

Wherever there is Krishna, the Lord of yoga, and Partha (Arjuna, the archer—holding the bow), there is glory, victory, prosperity, and morality. This is my conviction.

Metaphorical Interpretation

Rama and Krishna are one. God is Rama–Krishna. In the *treta yuga*, He was Rama, and in the *dvapara yuga*, Krishna. In this body, the soul is 'atma–Rama', the indwelling self, and 'prana–Krishna', the life force of each living being. Formless, He breathes from the top from birth until death.

This wonderful statement by Sanjaya is his concluding remark to king Dhritarashtra in answer to the blind king's question in the first verse of the Bhagavad Gita.

Human life is most blessed and rare, but it is very short and difficult. Human life is filled with delusion, illusion, and error, but at the same time, the soul is present and free from limitation. Arjuna has the desire to destroy his negative qualities. Like Arjuna, everyone should kill their negative qualities so they can perceive that they are God in a human being and a human being in God.

To succeed, one needs the company of the realized master. Arjuna took refuge in Shri Krishna, the divine master. Sanjaya calls Shri Krishna the Lord of yoga—Yogeshwara. Although people wish to practice yoga by reading books and seeking out people whose knowledge of yoga is scanty, yoga can only be learned directly from the mouth of a divine master who teaches how to practice yoga constantly and continuously so the supreme power can be perceived. Every disciple must be Partha, who is Arjuna, the disciple filled with divine inquisitiveness, intelligence, and devotion to the master. Sanjaya calls Partha *dhanurdharah. Dhanu* means the bow. *Dhanurdhara* means one who holds the bow in the hand.

What is the bow? The spine is the bow. The spine is used to fight the battle of life. With the help of the spine you can rise to the state of God consciousness. You magnetize your spine by bowing in the sitting posture, so your spine becomes a perfect bow. But to fight, you must also have arrows. Every breath is an arrow. As a successful archer shoots arrows at the target, similarly, every breath must be targeted to reach the fontanel. *Dhanurdhara* signifies someone who has thorough control over the spine and chakras. Every spiritual seeker must hold the bow of the spine by the scientific technique of Kriya Yoga.

When the divine master and the worthy disciple live together and the disciple follows the master sincerely, the disciple is sure to succeed and perfect his life. In this verse, Sanjaya lists the four achievements:

1. *Shri* (glory, splendor): Through breath control, one can remain in the cranium and find constant peace, bliss, and joy. One will also attain material prosperity, glory, and grace.

2. *Vijaya* (victory): Every human being is a battlefield, where the negative propensities of life must be slain. By the grace of the guru and the disciple's efforts, the disciple is able to overcome the negative qualities of human life.

3. *Bhuti* (prosperity, wealth): By the power of meditation, life becomes enriched with divine qualities, the real wealth. From meditation one also receives material well-being.

4. *Dhruvaniti* (established in morality): A moral, God-conscious life is the real beauty in each human being. Through spiritual practice and constant God awareness, one can become well established in truth, purity, and morality.

"O spiritual seeker! Travel on the path of yoga with love. Please understand and practice Sanjaya's last statement. The soul, Krishna, is with you. Seek His guidance. Follow Him in every breath. Then, surely, you will find *moksha,* emancipation, and God-realization.

In the Guru Gita (5) and also in Shvetashvatara Upanishad, it states, *yasya deve parābhakti yathā deve tathā gurau tasyai 'te kathitā hyarthāḥ prakaśante mahātmanaḥ:* "For he who has supreme love for God and guru, God-realization is at hand."

Summary

The concluding chapter of the holy Bhagavad Gita is called *moksha yoga*—"The Yoga of Liberation through Renunciation." What is *moksha?* Different commentators define it in different ways:

1. *Moksha* is liberation. Many think that it means to be free from the cycle of birth and death (*janma-marana-chakra*).

2. According to some, *moksha* means to enter the kingdom of God, heaven. But also according to some, heaven is not the place of eternal life. In the Bhagavad Gita (9:21), it says, *kṣīṇe puṇye martyalokam viśanti:* "When the merits accrued to a person through the performance of virtuous deeds are exhausted, he is bound to return back to the world of mortals."

3. *Moksha* is from *moha* and *kshayam*. In Sanskrit, *moksha* (liberation) is formed of two parts, *mo* and *ksha*. *Mo* means *moha*, which is delusion, dejection, and infatuation. *Ksha* means *kshayam*, complete elimination or destruction. So *moksha* is the complete cessation of the delusive play of *maya,* the cosmic delusive force, so truth can be experienced in every breath.

4. *Moksha* also means *duhkha nivritti,* the elimination of suffering, and *paramananda prapti*, the attainment of supreme bliss. *Moksha* is the state of attaining bliss, by which one is no longer in the grip of suffering, where one enjoys eternal peace, bliss, and joy.

Moksha is the state of perfection. This state of perfection is achieved through the practice of right action. In this chapter, the blessed Lord uses the word *moksha* twice. In the last confession of Arjuna (*see the Bhagavad Gita 18:73*), Arjuna says, "*nashto mohah,*" meaning, "All my ignorance is removed." Many people try to be free from suffering using a negative approach. But by shouting "darkness, darkness," darkness does not disappear. The darkness of delusion only disappears with the dawn of light.

This chapter may be summarized as follows:

Verse 1: Arjuna's quest to know in detail about renunciation and detachment.

Verses 2–6: Renunciation (*sannyasa*) and detachment (*tyaga*) are explained.

Verses 7–9: The sattvic (pure), rajasic (materialistic), and tamasic (idle) types of detachment are described.

Verses 10–12: The qualities of a detached person are described.

Verses 13–15: The five factors or instruments of action are described.

Verses 16–18: The principles of action are explained.

Verses 19–28: Knowledge, action, and the three types of doers are described.

Verses 29–39: There is an elaborate discussion about the three types of intellect and the three categories of happiness.

Verse 40: Nature's play has three qualities.

Verse 41: The four categories (*varnas*) of people are introduced.

Verse 42: The natural quality of a spiritual person (*brahmin*) is described.

Verse 43: The natural quality of the warrior class (*kshatriya*) is described.

Verse 44: The natural quality of the other two categories of people are discussed.

Verses 45-49: How to get perfection through actions as prescribed in the scriptures.

Verse 50: The qualifications of a yogi.

Verses 51–53: The helpful virtues for those who seek spiritual evolution are explained.

Verses 54–55: How to achieve supreme devotion.

Verses 56–57: The commandment to be dedicated to the Lord.

Verses 58–59: When one does not lead a divine life, there is gain and loss.

Verse 60: The blessed Lord describes the strength of one's natural habit.

Verses 61–63: The grace of the Lord is described.

Verse 64: The Lord directs mankind to listen to the supreme commandment.

Verses 65–66: One must surrender to the Lord.

Verse 67: The worthy person must listen to the holy words of the Lord.

Verse 68–69: The glory of disseminating the divine knowledge is described.

Verse 70: The merit of reading the holy Bhagavad Gita is narrated.

Verse 71: The benefits of listening to the Bhagavad Gita.

Verse 72: The Lord questions Arjuna about his state of mind.

Verse 73: Arjuna makes his last declaration at the feet of the Lord.

Verses 74–77: The blissful state of Sanjaya is expressed in his own words.

Verse 78: Sanjaya predicts the outcome of the battle to the king, Dhritarashtra—his concluding remark.

This concluding teaching of the holy Bhagavad Gita is really the beginning of spiritual practice. In this chapter, the Lord gives a beautiful commandment, "O Arjuna! You have heard in detail the different aspects of life. You have listened to Me carefully about the goal of life. Now, do as you wish" (*yathe 'chhasi tathā kuru*—Verse 63).

Everyone knows what is good and what is bad, right and wrong, but one who is not free from negatives is like an animal. One who overcomes is rational and spiritual.

Shri Krishna is the most beautiful teacher. Having taught everything, he looks at his student and observes what he is going to do with his life—whether or not he will eliminate *jivattva* (individuality) and merge in *brahma tattva* (divinity).

The eighteen chapters of the Bhagavad Gita, divided into three books of six chapters each, can be categorized as:

1. *Jiva tattva*: the principle of the individual self
2. *Brahma tattva:* the principle of divinity
3. *Jiva-brahma-ekatva*: the unity of the individual with the supreme.

Through sincere and loving practice, and by following the instruction of the guru preceptor, one can reach the realm of realization.

Where the guru and the disciple live together and work together with the goal of realization, success is at hand. The guru is the source of encouragement and enlightenment. In the concluding verse, Sanjaya, the minister and communicator to the blind king Dhritarashtra, declares the future of the battle of life: When one is ready to fight the evils and emotions under the guidance of the guru preceptor, there is success. Sanjaya predicted the outcome eight days before the end of the battle. The eight days symbolize the time required to overcome the eightfold nature of man—the five elements, mind, intellect, and ego.

Try sincerely, without rest, to reach the height of perfection. Arise, awake, keep the inner awareness in the fontanel until you are crowned with the glory of realization. Remove the ego. Merge with divinity in the ocean of cosmic consciousness and wisdom.

Om tat sat

brahmarpanamastu

This is an offering at the feet of the God and gurus and in the hands of true seekers on the spiritual path.

Om

Glossary

abhaya: absence (*a-)* of fear (*bhaya*); fearlessness.

Abhimanyu: he was one of the sons of Arjuna, cousin of Krishna, one of the most heroic warriors of the Pandava side. His name comes from *abhi*, to destroy, and *manyu*, which means all evil qualities in mankind.

abhyasa yoga: the yoga of practice of self-discipline.

Achyuta: one of the names of Krishna. It is derived from *a* "not" and *chyuta* "deviation"—i.e. "One who is not separated from the body."

adharma: absence (*a-)* of righteousness (*dharma*); irreligion.

adhyaya: to read and study; part of a book, viz. a chapter.

advaita vedanta: the philosophy of non-dual realization of the One.

Agni (the deity): the fire-god from ancient Vedic times.

agni (the elemental energy): the fire present in all the seven centers. Its special elemental presence is in the navel (food) center.

ahamkara: this word is made of *aham* (I) and *kara* (maker), i.e. the ego, one's sense of doership.

ahara ("food"): eating, drinking, and sense perception.

ahavaniya agni: the name of the fire in the dorsal (heart) center.

ahimsa: non (*a-)* violence (*himsa*), non-injury to others in thought, word or deed.

ajña chakra ("command wheel"): the place of concentration inside the pituitary, i.e. the soul center.

akarya: unwanted work by which the life or *prana* is not in harmony or peace.

akasha ("ether"): the sky or space; ether.

akrodha: absence (*a-)* of anger (*krodha*).

akshara-brahma ("immobile God"): the imperishable indwelling Self.

akuler: helper of the helpless.

alasya: dullness; lacking vitality, and strength. One of the obstacles of yoga.

aloluptva ("non-wavering"): freedom from greed and desire.

amla : acidic food and alcohol.

amrita ("immortal"): nectar which gives immortality; the deathless state.

anahata: non-stopping.

anahata chakra ("wheel of the unstruck [sound]"): the dorsal (heart) center

ananda: bliss

Anantavijaya ("Infinite victory"): the name of king Yudhisthira's conch.

andaja: creatures born (*ja*) of eggs (*anda*).

anganyasa ("placing (*nyasa*) the limbs (*anga*)"): practicing God perception in the different limbs of the body.

apaishunam: aversion to fault-finding; freedom from jealousy.

apana ("down breath"): one of the five main *pranas* (vital energies), responsible for elimination; metaphorically, *apana* means "not yet taken or drunk", i.e. the fresh air for inhalation.

apara vidya: knowledge of the phenomenal world or material knowledge.

ardana: to crush or destroy.

arjava ("rectitude"): straightforwardness or simplicity; literally, this is uprightness of the body, mind, senses, and behavior.

Arjuna: one of the five Pandava brothers; he was the third son of Kunti, born mystically through union with the god Indra. His name comes from *a* (not) *rajju* (rope) *na* (not), "One who is not bound by the rope of the world, although he thinks he is at first". His power resides in the food center.

arogyam: a healthy, disease-free body.

artha: material prosperity; to earn wealth in a righteous way; one of the four vital accomplishments in human life.

asad: falsehood.

asamshakti: a stage of *samadhi* in which a yogi experiences a divine nectar coming down from the fontanel. Yogis perceive tremendous bliss from tasting it, which gives them transcendental joy.

asana ("seat"): sitting; posture; a place to sit for prayer and meditation; the third limb of Patañjali's *ashtanga yoga* system.

ashtanga yoga ("eight-limbs yoga"): the path of complete spiritual development propounded by sage Patañjali.

Ashvatthama: The son of Dronacharya, guru to both the Pandavas and the Kauravas. His name comes from *a* (no) *sva* (up to tomorrow) *tha* (existence), "That which has no existence tomorrow".

astikya ("it-is-ness"): perceiving the power of God in every breath ; literal belief in the Vedas and the doctrine of rebirth.

atma or *atman* ("Self"): the soul.

atmakasha: cosmic-conscious stage at the fontanel; one of the five levels of the subtle vacuum located between the *ajña* (soul center) and *sahasrara* (fontanel) chakras.

atom-point: a point of no breadth, no length and no depth, which contains the whole power of creation, maintenance and dissolution of the universe; the fontanel.

atyusna: food that is very hot in temperature.

AUM: the primordial, eternal divine sound heard in deep meditation; it represents the three bodies of every human being or the triple divine qualities: *A* is the causal body (sound), *U* is the astral body (vibration), and *M* is the physical body (light).

avabodhasya: wakefulness—the true seekers of soul always remain alert on God in every mental and emotional state.

avankvak: the talk of the formless.

avyakta ("unmanifest"): beyond the perception of the senses.

ayamatma brahma: "This soul is Brahman"—one of the four great pronouncements of the Vedas.

Ayodhya: a capital city where Lord Rama reigned after his 14 years of exile.

ayuh: life; life span; health.

ayukta: one who is not (*a*) disciplined (*yukta*), i.e. not on the path of yoga.

ayurveda: ("life science"): medicine of mind, body and soul; one of the *upavedas*, divinely revealed sciences in India.

Babaji Maharaj: the great incarnation (*mahavatar*) of God who re-introduced the lost spiritual science of Kriya Yoga in 1861.

bahu ("that which enables to carry"): arms (upper extremities).

bala: power, strength, vitality, vigor.

bandha ("bond"): one who is in bondage; obstacle.

Bhagavan (or Bhagawan, Bhagwan): God; a title given to a great realized saint, such as Ramana Maharshi, Ramakrishna Paramahamsa, etc.

bhakti kanda: pertaining to the yoga of divine love.

bhakti yoga: the yoga of divine love.

Bharata: India; one of the first kings of India; an epithet for Arjuna (sometimes also for Yudhisthira). *Bha* means divine illumination and *rata* means engrossed—the state of expansion attained by the life force (*prana*), in which brilliant divine light is perceived.

bhargah: the almighty father, the real sun of the universe.

bhava: mood; being; feeling.

bhavan: the pronoun 'You'; the creator.

bhaya: fear. The greatest fears are death and losing happiness.

Bhima: one of the five Pandava brothers; he was the second son of Kunti, born mystically through union with the god Vayu (air). His power resides in the heart and lungs.

Bhishma: the commander-in-chief of the Kauravas. His name means firm determination of mind, but he also has a false sense of prestige and strong will power; he cannot make correct decisions due to his occasional wrong associations.

bhoja: enjoying divine bliss. In this material world, there are many persons who are born for God-realization, but if they remain attached to their ego and whims, their life is not complete and they do not attain the supreme goal.

bhokta, bhoktri: the experiencer.

bhuh-loka: the first of the seven upper spheres of existence (*loka*). Corresponds to the money (earth) center.

Bhurishrava: one of the warriors on the side of the Kauravas. *Bhuri* means many, and *shrava* means to hear. So Bhurishrava means one who is hearing many things about someone or something, so his mind becomes bewildered and indecisive.

bhuta yajña: oblation or offerings to animals, spirits, and the elements.

bhuti: prosperity, wealth, glory.

bhuvah-loka: the second of the seven upper spheres of existence (*loka*). Corresponds to the procreation (water) center.

bija: seed.

bija mantra ("seed word"): seed-syllable (most basic mantra).

Brahma: soul, Krishna; God in His aspect of Creator; the first of the Vedic trinity.

brahmachari: one who observes the vow of *brahmacharya*.

brahmacharya: literally means celibacy and sense-control; esoterically *brahmacharya* means "to roam (*char*) in God (Brahma)", i.e. to live in constant God-consciousness.

Brahman: God the formless. Derived from the root *brih*, "to grow" or "to expand".

brahmananda: divine bliss; the perennial joy of God.

brahmanirvana: to be absorbed in soul and to feel that in every action, the soul is doing everything from within.

Brahma Sutras: one of the three fundamental scriptures (known collectively as *prasthana trayi*) for God-realization, written by Veda Vyasa.

brahmavadi: those who are always after God, truth, and the soul in every thought, word, and deed.

brahma vidya: the knowledge of the Absolute.

brahmin: the first caste in the ancient Vedic social system of priests and teachers; metaphorically those who are on the spiritual path; to be in God (Brahman).

buddhi: the intellect; faculty of decision.

Chaitanya Mahaprabhu: a realized master and God-intoxicated monk of fifteenth-century India.

chakra ("wheel"): a spiritual center-plexus in the spinal column and brain. Derived from the root verb *char*, "to move".

charvya: food which is chewed. One of the four types of food described in the Bhagavad Gita.

chaturanga ("four limbs"): refers to the last four limbs of the *ashtanga yoga* system.

chaturveda: the four Vedas.

Chekitana: a spiritual warrior on the side of Pandava. Chekitana comes from *chekit*, which means within a short time, and *tana*, which means the divine sound and the various melodies which are the inaudible talk of God.

chidakasha: "life force" of human beings in the pituitatry; one of the five levels of the subtle vacuum located between the *ajña* (soul center) and *sahasrara* (fontanel) chakras.

chitra: a nerve channel inside the spinal canal which gives extreme attachment and delusion at the navel and heart centers.

chitta: memory. Derived from the root *chit*, "to be conscious".

choshya: food which is eaten by sucking. One of the four types of food described in the Bhagavad Gita.

coccygeal center: the *muladhara* chakra located in the bottom center, corresponding to the earth element.

cosmic consciousness: a state in which one is merged in God–free from all bonds. In this state one feels the vacuum, hears divine sound from the high heaven down to the ground, and sees light pervading the universe.

daharakasha: "inner fire" born of meditation above the pituitary; one of the five levels of the subtle vacuum located between the *ajña* (soul center) and *sahasrara* (fontanel) chakras.

daiva: destiny or providence; God.

dakshina agni ("fire of the south"): fire of the money center.

dama: self-restraint.

Damodara: the name given to Shri Krishna by His adoptive mother Yashoda, meaning "very big belly."

dana: generosity; donation; charity.

darshana ("vision"): holy vision or experience; the path of knowledge; philosophy.

dasha: the ten stages of life in which ego, desires, and attachments gradually develop, from birth to death.

Dasharatha: Lord Rama's father. Metaphorically, each human body is *dasha* (ten doors) and *ratha* (chariot), the chariot of the ten doors of the sense organs, out of which nine doors are open and the tenth door, the fontanel, is closed.

daya ("sympathy"): compassion; *da* means to give or donate, and *ya* means motion or the power of God.

deha: the body. Derived from the root *dih*, "to anoint", "to smear".

dehin ("embodied one"): the indwelling Self.

deva ("shining one"): a god or deity; divine quality.

Devadatta ("God-given"): name of Arjuna's conch.

Devaki: the wife of Vasudeva, father of Krishna.

devil's kingdom: when the consciousness remains in the five lower centers below the pituitary.

dhairya: patience and perseverance, calmness.

dhanam: ordinarily means "wealth", but it also represents the six human qualities of birth, death, sorrow, happiness, appetite, and thirst.

Dhanamjaya: derived from *dhanam jayati iti*—he who conquers the six human qualities (*dhanam*) of birth, death, sorrow, happiness, appetite, and thirst.

dhanurdharah: one who holds the bow—a metaphor for self-control.

dharana: concentration; the sixth limb of Patañjali's *ashtanga yoga* system.

dharma: ordinarily translated as "religion" or "righteousness", *dharma* comes from *dhri*, which means the power of receptivity, and *man*, which means life. Thus *dharma* means "that which upholds", i.e. the breath. Breath is the true religion.

Dharmakshetra: name of the battlefield where the great Mahabharata war took place. *Dharma* means the power of breath, and *kshetra* means place. *Dharmakshetra* means where our living soul remains.

dhatu ("constituent"): the power that is remaining inside the pituitary; metal; vital energy; semen.

dhri: root; firmness.

Dhrishtadyumna: a great warrior on the side of the Pandavas; the brother of Draupadi and son of Drupada, born fully grown to kill Dronacharya. *Dhrishta* means obstinacy and restlessness, and *dyumna* means the power to control the obstinacy which comes from the external world.

Dhrishtaketu: a great warrior on the side of Pandava. His name comes from *dhrishtan ketava yakshah*. *Dhrishtan* means without head, having only a body, while *ketu* is a dragon's tail. So Dhrishtaketu is always seeking his head. The true seekers of God will always keep their attention focused between the neck cervical junction and the fontanel.

Dhritarashtra: the blind king, representing the mind. He was the eldest brother of king Pandu, and the father of Duryodhana and the 100 evil Kaurava bothers.

dhriti: fortitude; steadiness.

dhruvaniti: established in morality.

dhwani ("sound"): inner sound perceived during and after meditation.

dhyana: meditation; the seventh limb of Patañjali's *ashtanga yoga* system.

dirghasutri: a procrastinating person.

divine Kingdom: the fontanel; the cave of the cranium; the abode of the Almighty.

divine Mother: the ever-compassionate God, who teaches the supreme secret with extreme love to the able disciple and obedient child.

divya: light; divine; sky, heaven.

dorsal center: the heart center or *anahata* chakra.

drashta: a seer.

drashtavyam: object worth of seeing and perceiving.

Draupadeya: the five sons of Draupadi, who is the common wife of the five Pandava brothers. Her sons are the essence, or the atom power, of the five Pandavas.

Draupadi: the wife of the five Pandavas. "Wife" means *shakti*, or power. Here, Draupadi is the *shakti* of the five gross elements. *Shakti* means the life of the plants which comes from the five gross elements (earth, water, light, air, and vacuum), or the five Pandavas.

Dronacharya: the guru of both the Kauravas and the Pandavas. The word Dronacharya comes from the word *druban dhatu*, which means something that melts quickly. Dronacharya is a person of vacillating temperament who cannot judge right from wrong.

Drupada: the greatest warrior on the side of the Pandavas. Drupada is short for *druta pada*, which means you are to walk quickly and to finish your duty—to realize the superconsciousness within you.

duhkha ("sorrow"): deviation from one's real state; to be engrossed in the lower centers, which breeds pain. . Derived from *duh* "difficult" and *kha* "space".

duhkhanta: the end (*anta*) of suffering (*duhkha*).

Duhshasana: the second oldest son of Dhritarashtra, the blind king. Having disrobed the virtuous queen Draupadi, he symbolizes lust.

Duryodhana: the eldest son of Dhritarashtra the blind king; he is evil-minded, malicious, and always misguided by evil ministers and bad company.

dvesha: hatred, aversion; one of the five causes of afflictions (*klesha*).

dvija: twice born. The first birth is from the parents, for our physical existence; the second birth is from the spiritual master, for our liberation.

dwapara yuga: the "bronze" age in the Vedic cosmological system of cyclical time.

Dwaraka: the impregnable city founded by Krishna in the middle of the sea. It comes from *dwara* "door" and *ka* "where". It symbolizes the fontanel, about which all seekers are asking "Where is the door?"

fire ceremony: when one feels that every breath is an oblation to the fire in the fontanel for the love of God.

food-center: *manipura* chakra; also called the navel center, where the fire of digestion takes place.

formless stage: the state of vacuum and nothingness, where there is no feeling of body or worldly sense.

Ganesha: the elephant-faced deity, remover of obstacles and incarnation of wisdom. It corresponds to the money (earth) center.

gayatri mantra: the 24-syllable Vedic mantra for spiritual evolution and liberation.

ghee: clarified butter.

Gheranda Samhita: a classical treatise on yoga as taught by sage Gheranda.

Girish Ghose: a householder devotee of Ramakrishna Paramahamsa, who was completely transformed from extreme negativity to deepest spirituality.

Gita ("song"): usually refers to the Bhagavad Gita, "The song of the Lord".

God-consciousness: every thought, word, and action are God-oriented; there are no other thoughts.

God-realization: a state of constant peace, bliss, and joy.

goraksha: consists of two parts: *go* and *raksha. Go* means the world, i.e. the body land; *raksha* means its maintenance. Thus when the senses and the mind are well regulated and trained, the body is maintained and protected. Another meaning of *go* is tongue, so *goraksha* also refers to the control of the tongue that a student of Kriya Yoga practices. Goraksha is also another name of Gorakhnath, the great hatha yogi.

Govinda: one of the names of Krishna. It is derived from *go, vin* and *da*. *Go* means the whole world, *vin* means energy and pleasure, and *da* means to give to the entire universe. Govinda is the one who gives energy and pleasure to the entire universe.

granthi: knot; attachment.

grihapati agni ("fire of the householder"): the fire in the sacral (second) center used in household activities.

Gudakesha: another name of Arjuna; derived from *gudaka* and *Isha*. *Gudaka* means sloth, idleness and sleep, *Isha* means conqueror. Arjuna is the conqueror of sleep–always wakeful to the presence of Krishna, the soul.

guhya: the secret in each human being, hidden in the cranium.

guhyavidya ("secret science"): Kriya Yoga, which is personally from the teacher to the qualified disciple.

gunas ("strand" or "quality"): the three qualities of nature known as: *tamas* (idleness and sloth), *rajas* (extreme activity and restlessness) and *sattvas* (spirituality).

gunatita ("transcending the qualities"): beyond the play of the three qualities of nature (*gunas*).

gunatraya: the triple qualities (*gunas*) of nature.

guru ("weighty one"), *gurudev(a)*: spiritual preceptor. It is made of two syllables: *gu* is the invisible soul body, and *ru* is the luster of the physical body. This luster is remaining because the indwelling Self is inhaling from within. This is *guru* consciousness. See also *hamsa.*

ham: the gross body or instrument of the soul. The soul is the doer and the gross body is the instrument. *Ham* also refers to the ego.

ham-ksha: the last two letters of the Sanskrit alphabet, representing the individual self and the supreme Self in the pituitary.

hamsa: the material perishable body is *ham*. The power by which you inhale through your nose is *sa*, which means your own soul. In the *hamsa* stage you forget your existence and only feels that *sa*, inhalation, is the life of the gross body.

hamsa sadhana: *ham* denotes the physical which cannot survive without *sa* the soul. *Ham*, which is absorbed in the biological body gradually comes up into the pituitary where *sa* abides.

Hanuman: the son of air and faithful servant of Lord Rama, in the form of a mighty monkey. According to mythology, he was a half-brother to Bhima.

hatha yoga ("union (*yoga*) of the sun (*ha*) and moon (*tha*) [principles]"): a branch of yogic discipline, designed to regulate the energy in the body and mind.

heart-center: see dorsal center.

himsa ("harm"): maliciousness, injury.

homa ("offering"): a fire ceremony to achieve a specific aim.

hridaya: the heart. Derived from *hri*, "to receive", *da*, "to give", and *ya*, "Godl".

Hrishikesha: derived from *hrishika*, which means each body part and the five senses, and *isha*, which means soul. So Hrishikesha means the one who is the conductor of our five sense telephones and of each of our body parts.

ida: a nerve channel on the left side of the *sushumna* in which the vital air passes through. The *ida* corresponds to the tamasic quality of nature.

Ikshwaku: a king of the solar dynasty. Solar means 'from the sun', but the soul is the real sun.

ikshwaku nadi: a small cord (*nadi*) in the spinal canal near the neck center which gives extreme attachment and delusion in the heart center.

indriyas ("difficult to control"): the sense organs.

Isha ("ruler"): the Lord.

Ishana ("ruler"): one of the names of Lord Shiva.

Isha Upanishad: one of the principal Upanishads.

Ishvara ("foremost ruler"): the ruler of the universe.

ishvarabhava: lordliness; metaphorically this describes your relationship with God and the soul—to love God and accept His sovereignty in every aspect of life.

Jagadisha Gita: A commentary of the Bhagavad Gita by Jagadisha Chandra Ghosh.

Jamuna river: see Yamuna.

janah-loka: the fifth of the seven upper spheres of existence (*loka*). Corresponds to the neck (ether) center.

Janaka: a sage and great king, father of Sita, the wife of Lord Rama.

Janardana: a name of Krishna. It is derived from *jananan* and *ardana*. *Jananan* means a demonic power that is always in every human being; *ardana* means to crush or to destroy.

janman: birth or life. Every inhalation brings birth or life.

japa ("recitation"): chanting and remembering the holy name of God, as in a mantra.

jarayuja: mammals born of wombs.

Jayadratha: derived from *jaya*, which means to win, and *drath*, which means to bluff with eloquent words. Jayadratha was an uncultured person. He was always bluffing, and people were convinced by his exaggerations.

jayati: victory, success.

-ji: a suffix attached to a person's name or title, connoting love and respect. Example: Swamiji.

jijñasu: a true spiritual seeker who has constant desire for God-realization.

jit: to conquer, to win.

jivanmukta ("living liberated"): one who is liberated while still abiding in the physical body.

jiva tattva: the principle of the individual Self. *Jiva* means "life" or "alive", and *tattva* "thatness".

jñana: knowledge of the essence, secret, and significance of all the holy books. Spiritual knowledge is also obtained from personally listening to the words of a realized master.

Jñana Sankalini Tantra: a classical treatise on the knowledge of the Self.

jñana yajña: one who closes all the doors of the body, who comes up from the lower centers and sits in the fontanel and offers the whole mind, thought, intellect, ego, body sense, and worldly sense to the fire of knowledge, is practicing *jñana yajña*; the discussion of scriptural truth by the teacher and the student.

jñana yoga: the path of reasoning and discrimination; yoga of knowledge.

jñanayogavyavashitis: one who is established in the knowledge of the Self.

jñanendriyas ("cognitive senses"): the five instruments of perception: eyes, ears, mouth, skin, and nose.

jñata: someone who is truly willing to know God.

jñeya: perceiving only God, perceiving God in everything at all times and in all places.

jyotis ("light"): illumination; see also: *navadwara-ruddha mudra*.

jyoti mudra: the process of regulating, controlling, and channeling the energy of the nine doors.

Kaitabha: the destroyer.

kaivalya ("aloneness"): the highest state of God-consciousness; the Supreme.

kala: time; death.

Kali: the divine Mother.

Kaliya: a pond in Vrindavan that contained a venomous snake, which was tamed by Krishna.

kali yuga: the dark or "iron" age in the Vedic cosmological system of cyclical time.

Kamadhenu: the divine wish-fulfilling cow, a metaphor for the soul which is in the body or the power of God that has entered into all the creation. Anything that you ask from her will be given to you immediately.

Kamsa: the evil maternal uncle of Krishna who tried to kill him.

kanda ("bulb"): a branch.

kapidhwaja: derived from *kapi*, "son of air" (i.e. Hanuman), and *dhwaja*, "banner". On Krishna and Arjuna's chariot was a banner bearing the emblem of Hanuman. The principal meaning is that Krishna (soul) is the life of every human being, constantly pulling the air through our nose (inhalation).

Kapila: *kapila* means copper color; in meditation, one perceives this copper color. Kapila was a perfect being, realized from the moment of his birth.

karana: the twelve instruments or organs—five organs of action (vocal chords, hands, feet, rectum, and sex organ), five organs of perception (touch, taste, smell, sight, and hearing), and the mind and intellect.

Karar Ashram: founded by Swami Shriyukteshwarji in the holy city of Puri, on the east coast of India.

karishye: the promise to do or accomplish something.

karma(n): action; duty; the law of cause and effect.

karma-phala: fruition of actions.

karma sannyasa: to renounce attachment to action—to remain calmly in the fontanel and compassionately detached while doing any kind of work and perceiving that the soul is the real doer in your body.

karma yoga: the yoga of action—to offer every action as worship to God.

karmendriyas ("action organs"): the five organs of action: vocal chords, feet, hands, rectum, and genitals.

Karna: eldest son of Queen Kunti, the most powerful warrior among all the armies of both the Kauravas and the Pandavas. Karna, in Sanskrit, means ears. Our ears want to hear melodious song, sweet words, praise, flattery, and soothing talk.

karna rasayana: holy word, mantra, divine sound, pleasing to the ears.

karta: the agent of action—the cause by which the body is activated.

karya: duty, real activity. The work that should be undertaken, in other words, the practice of Kriya—*pranakarma* is the real work to be done.

Kashiraja: literally, the king (*raja*) of Kashi (another name for Benares, or Varanasi). Metaphorically, it comes from *kashyate* which means "to illuminate" and *rajyam,* "kingdom". This is the kingdom of brilliant illumination, i.e. the human body.

katu: a pungent, disagreeable taste.

Kaunteya: "son of Kunti", i.e. Arjuna. Kunti means sharp intelligence. Arjuna is the son of sharp intelligence because he is always seeking the truth and striving to fix his attention in the pituitary and above.

Kaurava: the evil warriors opposed to the Pandavas in battle. Kaurava comes from *kuru*, or *kur*, and *rava*. *Kur* means to do work, and *rava* means disposition given by the soul from above for the delusion of human beings. So the Kaurava party represents the millions of cells, tissues, and atoms in our gross body which are forcing us to commit evils, giving us delusion and illusion.

keshi: the delusive power or negative qualities.

kevali kumbhaka ("absolute retention"): a special breathing technique.

Kena Upanishad: one of the principal Upanishads.

Keshava: another name of Krishna that means the Lord of creation, preservation, and dissolution, but this word has a special significance. *Keshava* is made of *ka* (in the head)+ *isha* (lord) + *va* (abode).

khechari: a special *mudra* practiced in yoga. It is derived from *kha* ("space") and *char* ("to roam")—to roam in the vacuum of meditation.

kri: any work, activity or action.

Kripa ("grace"): name of the guru of the Kauravas and Pandavas.

Krishna: made of *krishi*, "cultivation" (of the body land) and *na*, the power of God. Lord Krishna, the divine incarnation, represents the indwelling Self who is conductor of the body.

kriya: action.

Kriya Yoga: the science of self-control and Self-realization through meditation.

krodha: anger, one of the "gates to hell".

kshama ("patience"): forgiveness.

kshanti ("forbearance"): forgiveness, accommodation.

kshara ("mobile"): perishable.

kshatriya: the second caste of warriors in the ancient Vedic social system; metaphorically, those who constantly fight with lower qualities to reach the divine goal.

kshayam: complete elimination or destruction.

kshetra: the body land; a holy place of pilgrimage.

kshetrajña: the knower of the body field; the one who is the director, conductor, evolver, and protector of the body.

Kubja: a very ugly hunchback who decorated Krishna with sandal paste, thereby obtaining His grace.

kulakshaye: the word *kulakshaye* is composed of *kula* and *kshaye*. *Kula* means "dynasty" or "family" *(akuler kul* means helper of the helpless—so God is the only helper of every helpless person). *Kshaye* means destruction. *Kulakshaye* means that one who is not seeking God will find spiritual destruction and will be deprived of joy, peace, and bliss.

kumbhaka ("potlike"): retention of breath.

kundalini: serpent power; tremendous life-force energy centered at the base of the spine.

Kunti: mother of the five Pandava brothers and of Karna. The power that is remaining inside the pituitary is called *kun (dhatu) ti*; *kun* means atom–the finest atom point in the soul.

Kuntibhoja: one of the warriors on the Pandavas' side. His name is derived from *kunti* (pinpointed attention in the soul) and *bhoj* (enjoying divine bliss)—one who is constantly absorbed in God and in divine bliss. Kuntibhoja also means one who holds his attention, like the needle of a compass, in the pituitary.

Kuru: the ancestor to both the Kauravas and the Pandavas. *Kuru* means "to do"—to do work.

kurukshetra: contains the words *kuru* and *kshetra*. *Kuru* means "to do", and *kshetra* means "field". Every human life is a work field. But the doer of the body field is soul, Krishna. Kurukshetra is also a holy place where the Mahabharata war took place. The battle also occurs in the body of each human being.

Kurunandana: a descendant from the line of Kuru; a name of Arjuna; metaphorically, one who is very active in selfless soul culture.

kutastha ("anvil"): changeless; metaphorically, designates the soul center, the unchanging 'anvil' on which the different life experiences are molded.

Lahiri Mahasaya: the beloved disciple of Babaji Maharaj, who brought back the ancient forgotten science of Kriya Yoga to the modern world.

lam, long: the seed sound in the first center (four-petaled lotus) which means earth.

lavana: salty.

laya ("dissolution", "absorption"): dissolution; the experience of the formless state.

lehya: food which is licked with the tongue. One of the four types of food described in the Bhagavad Gita.

lobha: greed, possessiveness.

loka ("realm"): plane of existence.

lumbar center: the spinal center in the abdomen known as the *manipura* (food) chakra.

madbhakta ("My devotee"): a devotee of God; one who constantly inquires about God and searches for Him.

Madhava ("Lakshmi's husband"): one of the name of Vishnu, Krishna.

Madhusudana: another name for Krishna. *Madhu* was a demon symbolizing delusion and error, and *sudana* means "destroyer"; Krishna as the destroyer of delusion.

madhyama: the middle.

Madri: second wife of King Pandu, and mother of Nakula and Sahadeva.

maha: great.

maha bahu ("mighty-armed"): the person who can perceive soul through each action is called *maha bahu*, which means the best seeker of God.

Mahabharata ("great [epic of] the Bharatas"): the great Indian epic which includes the Bhagavad Gita.

mahabhuta ("great elements"): the gross elements.

mahad-brahma: refers to the great Brahma, the *prakriti* in every human being.

Mahadeva ("Great Lord"): a name of Lord Shiva.

mahah-loka: the fourth of the seven upper spheres of existence (*loka*). Corresponds to the emotion (air) center.

Mahakala: the supreme time; destiny; a name of Lord Shiva.

mahakasha: "great emptiness", the wisdom stage of *nirvikalpa samadhi*; one of the five levels of the subtle vacuum located between the *ajña* (soul center) and *sahasrara* (fontanel) chakras.

mahamudra ("great seal"): the yogic technique of physical, astral and causal purification.

Mahaprabhu: see Chaitanya.

mahaprana: the supreme spirit hiding in each human being.

maharshi ("great seer"): a person of right vision.

mahavakyas ("great sayings"): the four great pronouncements which make up the essence of the Upanishads: 1) "Wisdom is Brahman (the Absolute God)." 2) "I am Brahman." 3) "That thou art." 4) "This soul is Brahman."

Maheshvara: another name of Lord Shiva.

mala ("garland"): a rosary, made of beads stringed together.

manas ("mind"): the faculty of discursive thinking.

manasa tapasya: inner purity of thought and mind, a gentle and divine mood, silence and self-control; silent meditation with the tongue pointing to God.

mandali: a group; association.

manipura chakra ("wheel of the jeweled city"): the lumbar (stomach) center.

manipushpaka: the name of Sahadeva's conch. Its name refers to the divine sound of the bee heard in meditation at the bottom center.

manisha: knowledge; conviction; understanding.

mantavyam: to recollect and remember.

mantra: a holy syllable or prayer; formula of mystic power. Derived from *man* "to think" and *tra* "instrument".

Manu: the father of mankind; the Noah of Indian mythology.

manyu: sin, evil, malice and all other evil qualities which keep human beings from God-realization.

mardava: gentleness.

Mathura: a holy city in India where Lord Krishna was born.

matrikanyasa ("placing (*nyasa)* the little mothers (*matrikas*)": placing the 50 letters of the Sanskrit alphabet (*matrikas*) in the whole body; to experience calm and God perception throughout the whole body.

maya ("she who measures"): the cosmic delusive force.

moha: delusion, dejection, and infatuation.

moksha: liberation; the state of complete soul-awareness, emancipation, and *samadhi;* freedom from the bondage and attachment that arise from delusion.

money-center: see coccygeal center.

muddha: a dull state of mind.

mudra ("seal"): a Kriya Yoga technique or posture.

mukti ("release"): liberation; freedom.

muladhara chakra ("wheel of the root (*mula*) foundation (*dhara*)"): the coccygeal (money) center.

mulam: root; base; cause.

muni ("sage"): one who seeks truth; man of meditation.

na: not; no.

nada brahma, shadba brahma: the continuous, non-stopping *aum* or *amen* sound; manifestation of the Absolute in the form of sound.

nadi ("conduit" or "artery")): pranic channel.

naiskritika: someone insulting and torturing others.

Nakula: one of the five Pandava brothers; he was the first son of Madri, born mystically through union with the twin gods Ashwins. His power resides in the sexual center.

Narayana ("He Who is man's (*nara*) abode"): the Lord who is the cause of all life; a name of Lord Vishnu.

nari: woman; the female element representing the gross body which unites with the male element (the soul).

natimanita: freedom from pride, humility.

navadwara-ruddha mudra: the process of regulating, controlling, and channeling the energy of the nine doors. See also: *jyoti mudra*.

navel-center: *manipura* chakra (Arjuna's abode); also known as the food center.

neck-center: vacuum center; cervical center.

neti: composed of *na* "not" and *iti* "thus"; *neti neti* ("not this, not that") is a vedantic process of arriving at the ultimate Reality by denying the accuracy of any description of the Real.

nihsangata ("non-contact"): complete cessation of all activities; the pulseless, breathless stage.

nimitta karana: instrumental cause.

nirguna ("without (*nir*) attributes (*guna*)"): the formless Reality or God, beyond the triple qualities of *maya*.

nirvikalpa samadhi ("without (*nir*) conceptualization (*vikalpa*) ecstasy"): the state of no pulse and no breath, the state of cessation of all activities of the body, mind, thought, intellect, and ego—merged and absorbed in God.

nispriha: desirelessness.

nisudana: the complete destroyer.

nitya karmani: daily duties of oblation and prayer.

nivritti ("cessation"): the path of renunciation and detachment; a state of dispassion, which is the cause of liberation.

niyama ("restraint"): principles of self-restraint; the second limb of Patañjali's *ashtanga yoga* system.

niyata: always.

nriyajña: serving mankind.

nyasa ("casting"): renunciation; elimination; metaphorically, watching the power of God in every activity.

ojas: power; derived from the root verb *vaj*, "to be strong".

om: also written as *AUM*—this represents the three bodies of every human being or the triple divine qualities. *A* is the causal body (sound), *U* is the astral body (vibration), and *M* is the physical body (light).

omkara: the syllable "*om*"

pada: the feet; the world.

padartha bhavini samadhi: a state of *samadhi*.

padma: lotus; chakra.

paksha: side; fortnight.

pancha: five.

pancha bhutas: the five basic elements or constituents.

Panchajanya: the name of Krishna's conch. He obtained it by killing a demon named Panchajanya. Metaphorically, *pancha* means five and *janya* means being born of. *Panchjanya* means the divine sound that is due to the combined effect of five elements of the five chakras.

pancha klesha: the five afflictions as described in sage Patañjali's Yoga Sutras.

pancha mahabhuta: the five gross elements: *bhumi* (earth), *apa* (water), *anala* (fire), *vayu* (air), *kham* (ether).

pancha pandava: the five Pandava brothers.

panda: all the qualities born of knowledge.

Pandavas: those who remain in knowledge, consciousness, superconsciousness, and cosmic-consciousness are the Pandavas. The Pandavas are the friends of Krishna and the soul. They are always at war with the Kauravas or negative qualities.

para, param: supreme.

paradharma: literally, the duty or religion of others; metaphorically, attachment to the sense organs and the external world. No matter what someone is doing, if proper attention is not given to the breath and the soul, it is *paradharma.*

parakasha: "nothingness", superconsciousness state below the fontanel; one of the five levels of the subtle vacuum located between the *ajña* (soul center) and *sahasrara* (fontanel) chakras.

paramahamsa, paramhansa ("supreme swan"): the swan is the only creature that is capable of separating milk from water once they have been mixed together. Similarly, a *paramahamsa* is the realized master who, having attained the supreme yogic state, or *nirvikalpa samadhi*, can always distinguish between the Real (*sa*) from the unreal (*ham*).

Paramahamsa Hariharananda: the greatest living realized master in Kriya Yoga, is a legend among the spiritual seekers and has attained *nirvikalpa samadhi*.

Paramahamsa Yogananda: the foremost disciple of Swami Shriyukteshwarji, who brought the message of Kriya Yoga from India to the West in 1920. Author of the *Autobiography of a Yogi*.

paramatmakasha: the wisdom above the fontanel, where the soul is merged with God in the pulseless state of *nirvikalpa samadhi*.

parabrahman ("supreme absolute"): the Absolute—indestructible, imperishable, and supreme.

paramtapa: composed of *param shatrun tapati*. *Param* means supreme, *shatrun* means enemy, and *tapati* means one who can burn. The real meaning of *paramtapa* is one who can easily burn the supreme enemy, the delusion and error hidden within us.

Parashara: a great sage, father of Veda Vyasa.

paravastha ("supreme (*para*) stage (*avastha*)"): super-conscious state above the perishable body; the state of extreme tranquillity.

Partha ("son of Prithi", Prithi being the former name of Queen Kunti): a name of Arjuna. Its name comes from the root verb *prath* which means to be renowned through one's own effort.

parushyam: harshness (cruelty, stiffness, insolence).

paryusitam: stale, contaminated food.

Pashupati ("Lord (*pati*) of animals (*pashu*)"): a name of Shiva; he who has mastered his animal qualities.

Patañjali: the author of the Yoga-Sutras, a classical text dealing with concentration and its methods in Raja Yoga.

paundra: the name of the conch blown by Bhima, who is remaining in the heart center. Its name refers to the long and continuous sound of the bell.

peya: the type of food which is taken by drinking. One of the four types of food described in the Bhagavad Gita.

pingala: a nerve channel on the right side of the *sushumna* in which the vital air passes through. It corresponds to the rajasic quality of nature.

pitri yajña: praying for the liberation of diseased and departed souls, especially the parents.

prajña: wisdom.

prajñanam brahmam: one of the four great pronouncements of the Vedas which summarized the essence of the Upanishads, meaning: "Wisdom is Brahman (the absolute God)".

prakriti ("creative force"): the veil of nature, or the material substratum of creation, consisting of the three *gunas*.

prana ("life"): life-force or breath; one of the five main *pranas* (vital energies), responsible for absorption; metaphorically, *prana* refers to exhalation.

prana karma: with every breath, if one perceives the presence of God, the creator of life in the body, then every breath will be an oblation to God with love. This is *prana karma*, "action" of *prana*, the real worship of God.

Pranava Gita: an interpretation of the Bhagavad Gita by Swami Pranavananda, disciple of Lahiri Mahasaya.

pranayajña: offering oblation of breath to the soul fire in the pituitary and to the God fire in the fontanel.

pranayama ("restraint of *prana*"): regulation of breath through control of the life force (*prana*); the fourth limb of Patañjali's *ashtanga yoga* system.

pranic: that which relates to the life force or breath (*prana*).

Prapti ("attainment"): wife of Kamsa; her name means one who has immense desire for worldly things.

prasada ("grace", "clarity" or "tranquility"): that which comes from God as His grace, gift, and greetings; consecrated food.

Prashna Upanishad: one of the principal Upanishads. *Prashna* means "question".

prasthana ("exit"): sacred books for liberation.

prasthana trayi: the three sacred books for liberation, viz. the Upanishads, the Brahma Sutras and the Bhagavad Gita.

pratyahara ("withdrawal"): principles of self-control; the fifth limb of Patañjali's *ashtanga yoga* system.

pravritti ("activity"): involvement; attractive delusive desires.

prema: love for God.

puja: ritualistic worship.

punya: auspicious; good; merit.

pura: city; house; metaphorically, the body.

Puranas ("ancient"): scriptures of India.

purnima: full moon day or *holi.*

Puru: a royal dynasty in India; metaphorically, the body (from *pauran*).

Purujit: a great king, the maternal uncle of Bhima and the brother of Kunti. The inner meaning of Purujit is derived from *puran* and *jayati. Puran* means whole body sense and intellectual sense, and *jayati* means one who can conquer everything. Thus, Purujit is a powerful and spiritual man who has gone above his body, mind, intellect and senses and who has merged in God.

purusha: the indwelling Self; the conductor of the life-force of every human being.

purushottama ("the supreme (*uttama*) Self (*purusha*)"): the supreme almighty father.

Putana: an impure woman, a devil who tried to poison Krishna. The metaphorical meaning of her name comes from *puta*, which means purity, and *na*, which means no—"One who has no purity".

Radha: a great devotee of Krishna. Krishna and Radha are often pictured together, clasping each other, side by side. Radha symbolizes the gross body of every human being and Krishna represents the soul.

raja: king; royal.

rajarshi: comes from the word *raja ca rishi ca. Raja* means king, and *rishi* means a person of right vision. Right vision comes from the spiritual force, which remains in the cranium. Through the practice of Kriya yoga, if you come up near the soul, then you will be a *rajarshi*, a person of right vision.

rajas: one of the three qualities of nature (*guna*), expressing extreme activity and restlessness. Derived from the root *raj/ranj*, "to be colored" or "to be excited, charmed".

rajavidya: the royal science.

raja yoga: the royal science of self-control.

rakshasas: demonic personalities; those who hoard out of greed, and for sense pleasure.

ram (rong): the seed sound in the third center (10-petaled lotus) which represents fire.

Rama, Ramachandra: an incarnation (*avatara*) of Lord Vishnu, like Krishna.

rasa ("essence"): juice; taste; a play.

rasapurnima: a special spiritual celebration in India which occurs on the full-moon day in the month of August to celebrate the events in Shri Krishna's childhood in Vrindavan. *Rasa* means transformation of the inhabitants of Vrindavan into Krishna, and *purnima* means the full-moon day.

rasya: juicy.

rata: to be engrossed and attached.

ratha: a chariot.

Ratnakara: a murderer and extremely sinful person who, through good company, became highly realized and later became known as Valmiki, the author of the Ramayana.

Ravana: the 10-headed demon king, symbolizing the ego, as described in the Ramayana.

rishi ("seer"): man of right vision and action, also known as a sage.

ruksha: fried and roasted food with butter, oil, or *ghee*.

rupa: form; beauty.

sa: the real doer, the soul.

sacral center: the *svadhisthana* chakra (sexual center) representing the water element.

sadhaka ("practitioner"): a meditator who treads the path of spirituality.

sadhana ("means of realization"): sincere spiritual endeavor.

sadhubhava ("virtuous mood"): the attitude of a real monk or spiritual person. It is freedom from ego and any negative qualities. This is the divine mood.

sadhu ("virtuous"): literally, a saintly person. The real *sadhu* is he who keeps his attention on the breath and through every breath loves God.

sadhu mandali: a kind of yogic association.

sahaja ("innate"): easy, natural—and that is the breath. It comes from means *saha jayate iti*—with birth comes the breath.

Sahadeva: one of the five Pandava brothers; he was the second son of Madri, born mystically through union with the twin gods Ashwins. His power resides in the money (bottom) center.

sahasrara chakra ("thousand-spoked wheel"): the fontanel (God center).

sahasrara padma: the thousand (*sahasrara*) petalled lotus (*padma*), i.e. the fontanel.

Saibya: a great spiritual warrior on the side of Pandava. He is very calm and divine. Saibya means one who is just like Shiva, the formless god of ether, air, and sound. Saibya had attained that stage.

sakshin ("witness"): the witnessing consciousness.

sam (song): seed-syllable in the money center.

sama ("same", "equal"): harmony, equality.

samadhi: unity with the almighty father; merged and engrossed in God consciousness; complete freedom from nature's three *gunas*; the eighth and last limb of Patañjali's *ashtanga yoga* system.

samana: equality; name of one of the five main *pranas*, responsible for bringing nourishment and balance to all parts of the body.

samidbhavanama agni: the fire of religious ceremony, symbolically remaining in the neck center.

Samjaya: a *brahmin* minister, and messenger of the blind king Dhritarashtra (the mind). Although the mind takes little interest in spiritual awakening, the inner intelligence, Samjaya, speaks to Dhritarashtra. When one practices meditation and lives a spiritual life, the mind and thoughts become silent. This is the state of *samjaya,* the power to hear and see inwardly.

samkhya yoga (school of philosophy): the path of knowledge.

samlina: dissolved.

sampad: wealth; prosperity.

samprajñata ("with conscience"): a state of conscious *samadhi*, corresponding to Vedanta's *savikalpa samadhi*.

samskaras: impressions of previous thoughts and actions; latent tendencies.

samuchaya: of equal height.

sannyasa: renunciation; *sannyasa* is not merely a renunciation of the physical world, it is inner detachment.

sapta loka: the seven higher planes of existence.

sarvam: all; everything.

sat: truth; reality; the soul; the real; the essential; the best; the learned; the excellent; the good; the virtuous man. *Sat* is the supreme Self, the conductor of everything.

satbhava: harmony; goodwill; good wish.

satguru: a title attributed to a loving spiritual preceptor.

satha: hypocrite; fraud.

satsanga ("association with the real"): good company; spiritual communion; to be established in the Self.

satta: existence.

sattapatti: a stage of *samadhi* where some superhuman power is obtained—divine sound, divine light, divine vibration are felt.

sattva: one of the three qualities of nature (*guna*), expressing calmness and spirituality.

sattvika tyaga: spiritual renunciation; in every activity, one perceives the living presence of God, remembers Him, and loves Him constantly.

Satyaki: Krishna's chariot driver.

satya loka: the seventh of the seven upper spheres of existence (*loka*). Corresponds to the fontanel (God center).

satyam: truth.

satya yuga: an era where people only practiced *ashtanga* yoga and *chaturanga* yoga, which is Kriya Yoga. Through practice of this yoga, all people were divine and powerful.

Saubhadra: the son of Arjuna and nephew of Krishna, also known as Abhimanyu. Saubhadra entered a tunnel of the Kauravas and killed innumerable soldiers.

Saumadatti: the seventh great warrior of the Kauravas. Saumadatti is the son of Somadatta; his name is also Bhurishrava. (See Bhurishrava)

savikalpa ("with (*sa*) form (*vikalpa*)"): a state of *samadhi* in which the state of duality remains.

sayujya mukti: to merge in God.

seed-syllables: all fifty letters of the Sanskrit alphabet have mystical power (see *mantra*).

sex(ual) center: the *svadhisthana chakra*.

shakti (power): energy or power.

Shakti (the deity): the divine Mother.

Shakuni: Queen Gandhari's brother, and maternal uncle of the Kauravas.

shama: to have control over the heart, making one serene and divine.

shambhavi mudra: an open-eye meditation technique to perceive the divine light.

Shankaracharya: a great 6th century spiritual master, incarnation of Lord Shiva, who revived the monastic tradition in India.

shanti: serenity, peace.

shantipatha: invocation of peace.

sharira: body; the perishable. From the root *shri*, "to fall apart".

shastras: the holy scriptures.

shatrun: enemy.

shaucha: purity.

shaurya: heroism; the hero is not someone who fights enemies without, but he who is able to maintain his inner strength so he can destroy the enemies within, the weaknesses experienced in human life.

shava: corpse.

Shikhandin: a warrior on the side of the Pandavas, instrumental in bringing the downfall of Bhishma.

shivashraddha: love for Shiva.

shraddhatraya: threefold love or faith—sattvic, rajasic, tamasic.

shravana: attentive listening to sacred teachings.

shri: a name of goddess Lakshmi; as a prefix, a title of respect, like the English "Sir".

Shriyukteshwarji: the great spiritual master, disciple of Lahiri Mahasaya, and preceptor of Paramahamsa Yoganandaji and Paramahamsa Hariharanandaji.

shrotavyam: hearing about soul.

shruti ("heard"): to hear without any utterance; Vedas.

shudra: the lowest caste of servants in the ancient Vedic social system; metaphorically, those who keep their attention below the pituitary.

Shvetashvatara Upanishad: one of the principal Upanishads.

siddhi ("accomplishment"): perfection, namely, attaining the state of *nirvikalpa samadhi*, becoming merged in God and God-consciousness.

smritis ("remembered"): scriptures of moral rights.

snigdha: fat, creme, soothing, soft. As *snigdha jyoti*, it means soothing light, like the moon light.

so'ham ("I am He"): the perception of oneness of body and soul; to feel the human being in God and God in the human being.

Somadatta: a great warrior on the side of the Kauravas, father of Saumadatti.

soul: that which maintains the life and does the work; Krishna.

stabdha: rigid, obstinate.

sthira: still; tranquil; protein.

sthita: established; attained.

sthita prajña ("established in wisdom"): one who feels that whatever he sees, thinks, or experiences is the power of God.

sthitih: being completely and firmly established; steadfastness.

sthitosmi ("I am well established"): calm and quiet.

Subhadra: Krishna's sister who married Arjuna and bore him their son Abhimanyu; a name of the blissful mother nature.

subhechha samadhi: a state of *samadhi*.

sudana: destroyer.

Suddhambodhi: name of an Indian scripture.

sughosa ("good sound"); name of Nakula's conch.

sukha: happiness; real happiness is keeping your consciousness in the pituitary and above, in the state of vacuum and nothingness. Derived from *su* "beautiful" and *kha* "space".

sundara: beautiful.

Suradhuni Gita: a deep mystical interpretation of the Bhagavad Gita by Suradhuni Devi, wife of Panchanan Bhattacharya, one of Lahiri Mahasaya most prominent disciples.

sushumna nadi: the pranic channel between the *ida* and *pingala* which goes up from the bottom of the spine.

sutra: thread or link; aphorisms, as in Patañjali's Yoga Sutras.

svabhava: innate nature; *sva* means one's self, and *bhava* is one's perception, expression, and manifestation. Destiny, the aggregated balance sheet of all activities, is this innate nature. It predisposes a person to be either religious, full of activity, or idle.

svadharma: one's own duty. In the light of Kriya, *svadharma* means that it is every person's duty to watch one's own breath—to become aware of the indwelling Self.

svadhishthana chakra ("wheel of the self (*sva*) base (*adhishthana*)"): the lumbar (procreation) center.

svadhyaya: comes from *sva* (soul) plus *adhyaya* (culture or study); to study one's own self is soul culture.

svah-loka: the third of the seven upper spheres of existence (*loka*). Corresponds to the food (fire) center.

svarodaya: a yogic science based on the principle of the alternating of breath dominance from one nostril to the other.

svedaja: that which is born (*ja*) of moisture (*sveda*), such as fungus.

Taittiriya Upanishad: one of the principal Upanishads.

Takshavill: a murderer who, after coming to the touch of Chaitanya Mahaprabhu, became highly realized.

tamas: one of the three qualities of nature (*guna*), expressing sloth, restlessness, and idleness.

tana: the body.

tandra ("sloth"): sleep; drowsiness.

tantra: techniques for acquiring supernatural powers.

tapah loka: the sixth of the seven upper spheres of existence (*loka*). Corresponds to the pituitary (soul center).

tapas: ordinarily this means doing penance and austerities, but the metaphorical meaning is to watch the breath as an oblation in the holy fire that maintains the heat in the body. *Tapas* means that in every breath one loves God and remains alert.

tapasvin: those who offer oblations to the fire.

tapati: one who can burn.

tapo yajña: to offer *ghee* in the fire for a long period and to chant some mantra with every oblation. But the metaphorical meaning of *tapo yajña* is to offer the breath to the soul, which is the divine fire in the cranium.

tat: that.

tava: yours.

tejas: fearlessness, valor—through the power of regular meditation the advanced student develops mental strength and can easily remain in the upper center for a longer periods of time. This powerful quality is called *tejas.*

third eye: the divine eye, the spiritual eye, also known as the eye of wisdom.

tikta: bitter.

tistha: to stay.

tonumanasa samadhi: a state of *samadhi.*

treta yuga: the "silver" age in the Vedic cosmological system of cyclical time.

tri: three, triple.

triveda, trayi veda: the three Vedas (Rik, Sama, Yajur).

Tulsidas: a 15th century seeker who became realized through good company, and later author of the famous Hindi spiritual treatise *Ramacharita Manasa.*

turiya samadhi ("fourth stage of ecstasy"): another name for *nirvikalpa samadhi.*

tyaga ("abandonment"): it refers to renunciation of all action, but not outwardly. Inner detachment is possible only when one is meditating sincerely and surrendering completely to the will of God.

ucchista: food that has been taken, touched, or leftover on a person's plate.

udana ("up-breath"): a special breath taken with an extremely calm, short, and slow respiration; name of one of the five main *pranas*, responsible for digestion.

udhbija: vegetables and plants.

upadana karana: material cause.

upadrashta: the witness who remains in the north of the body (i.e. the fontanel).

Upanishad: the conclusion portion of the Vedas, also known as *vedanta.*

uttama: the supreme, the highest, the best.

Uttamauja: a powerful warrior for the Pandavas. *Uttama* means extremely powerful, and *ojas* means strength.

uttistha: comes from *urdhe*, the north of the body (i.e. the fontanel), and *tistha*, to stay.

vacuum (or space, ether) center: *vishuddha* chakra (neck, religious center).

vaishvanara agni: the fire in the lumbar center.

vaishya: the third caste of merchants and farmers in the ancient Vedic social system; metaphorically, those who cultivate the body land and think carefully how to use precious time for making the most spiritual profit.

vajra ("thunder" or "diamond"): strong determination and willpower.

Valmiki: see Ratnakar.

vam (vong): the seed sound in the second center (6-petaled lotus), which means water.

vanamaya tapasya: worshiping the formless by words and speech, and giving oblation to the ears and hearts of the people—sweet, truthful, beneficial, and pleasant talk.

vanijya: to do business, to work with expectation of profit or reward. Each person, in the beginning of the spiritual life prays or meditates with the expectation of good health, prosperity, or other gain. To undertake any activity with expectation of reward is to work with desire, and thus is *vanijya*.

varna: color; caste.

varnashankara: the mixture of biological and spiritual force; amalgamation; mix of races; illegitimate child.

Varuna: the deity of water residing in the second center.

Vasishtha: a great sage, guru of Lord Rama.

Vasudeva: Krishna's father.

vedanta ("the end or last portion (*anta*) of the Vedas"): the essence or culmination of all the knowledge within the Vedas; a system of philosophy and the science of spirituality, based mainly on the teachings of the Upanishads, the Bhagavad Gita, and the Brahma Sutras.

Vedas: the most ancient recorded scriptures of knowledge of the Self.

vedavid: man of wisdom, a state achieved by deep meditation.

vibhaga: division.

vibhuti ("manifestation"): divine powers or experiences which one gets through spiritual practice: divine glory, *siddhis* (yogic powers), material prosperity, superhuman power, strength, and holy ash. In many cases, the *vibhuti*, which are lower spiritual attainments of superhuman qualities, become a spiritual hindrance—all sincere seekers should beware of their allurements.

vicharani samadhi: a state of *samadhi*.

vid: to know.

vidahina: food that creates a burning sensation, such as mustard, asafoetida, and so on.

vidya: knowledge.

vijñana ("applied knowledge"): the way to reach or realize the truth, which is the application of knowledge, the states of super consciousness and cosmic consciousness.

Vikarna: a soldier of the Kaurava army. He is a dangerous warrior. His name means one who is a strong believer, is malicious, and is addicted to improper works.

vimudhah: the extremely dull, foolish, deluded, ignorant, materialist, and spiritually blind.

Virata: a great warrior and king on the side of Pandava. The metaphorical meaning is derived from *vigata*, that which is completely free from all body sense, and *rat*, kingdom (body). Virata means that you are completely free from your mind, intellect, thought and body sense.

virya: strength, vitality, vigor, and valor.

vishada: sorrow; dejection; depression. The state of Arjuna at the beginning of the Mahabharata War.

Vishnu ("pervader"): the preserving or sustaining aspect of God.

vishnu granthi: the knot of the heart.

vishuddha chakra ("pure wheel"): the religion or throat center.

Vishvamitra: a great sage, guru of lord Rama.

vishvarupa: the universal form, the extraordinary glory and beauty of the Lord.

vishvarupa maha agni: the fire present in the crown of the head.

Vivasvan: the first king of the solar dynasty.

vividha chesta: manifold endeavor.

Vrajadham: the place where Krishna spent His childhood, a.k.a. Vrindavan; metaphorically, to perceive Krishna in the whole body and to merge with the divine.

vrata ("vow"): a vow to abide by a moral and spiritual discipline in thought, word, and deed.

Vrindavan: see Vrajadham.

vyaghra: explained in the Sanskrit scriptures as *vyajighrati ity vyaghra*: "One who has strong smelling power." This is the tiger, a most powerful animal whose power of nose (breath) is very strong. Arjuna, through the power of meditation, has thorough control over his animal qualities, and he devours all his ambitions. He also has a powerful ability to regulate his nose (he has breath control).

vyana: one of the five main *pranas* (vital energies), supporting the function of inhalation and exhalation.

Vyasa: the divine teacher of spirituality. Author of the Mahabharata and author/compiler of numerous scriptures.

ya: the soul.

yah sah: "he who".

yajña ("sacrifice"): oblation in fire; sacrifice. The breath is constantly offered as an oblation to the soul fire in the cave of the cranium. In a broader sense, every activity of every living being that is in the form of enjoying sense objects, is sacrifice *(yajña).*

yakshas: deities in charge of protecting wealth.

yam ("to him"): the seed sound in the heart center (12-petaled lotus) which means air.

yama ("restraint"): self-discipline, restraint; the first limb of Patañjali's *ashtanga yoga* system.

Yama: the god of death.

Yamuna (or Jamuna) river: one of the three holy rivers of India.

Yashoda: the mother of Krishna.

yoga ("yoking"): to perceive the constant union, unity, or copulation with the divine self in every breath, in every moment, in every activity, and in every achievement. Yoga is the way one can perceive divinity manifested in the whole universe as well as in the entire body.

yoga maya: mother nature.

yoga nidra: *yoga* means oneness of body and soul, and *nidra* means sleep. But *yoga nidra* does not mean sleep; it is constant awareness of the inner Self or conscious *samadhi.*

Yoga Sutras: the classical treatise on yoga by sage Patañjali.

yoga yajña: using the power of the yoga of action and knowledge to withdraw all power from the lower centers to the upper center and remain beyond the mind, thought, intellect, ego, and body sense in the formless stage.

yogi: one who is constantly united with the supreme Self.

yoni ("holder"): the place of origin, of procreation; womb; progeny.

yoni mudra: see *jyoti mudra.*

yudha: war; battle; fight.

Yudhamanyu: a spiritual and powerful warrior on the side of Pandava. The actual meaning of Yudhamanyu is derived from *yudha*, which means to fight constantly and to subdue; and *manyu*, which means sin, evil, malice and all other evil qualities which keep human beings far from God-realization.

Yudhisthira: one of the five Pandava brothers; he was the first son of Kunti, born mystically through union with the god Dharma (truth). His name comes from *yudha* (to fight) and *sthira* (steady, calm), "One who is calm in the battle of life". His power resides in the neck center.

yuga: the ordinary meaning of this word is "age" or "era", but the real meaning is "dual" or "two". Every breath consists of an inhalation and an exhalation; this is the dual state or *yuga.*

Yuyudhana: a warrior on the side of Pandava. *Yuyudhana* means one who has the greatest desire for soul culture and deepest regard for God.

Sanskrit Pronunciation Guide

The Sanskrit language numbers 50 letters: 15 *vowels*, 25 *consonants*, 4 *semi-vowels*, 3 *sibilants*, 1 *aspirate*, and 2 *compounds*.

Vowels

Note: a long vowel (e.g. *ā*) is held twice as long as its corresponding short vowel (e.g. *a*)

a - as in m*a*m*a*	Example: yog*a*
ā - long form of a, like the *a* in f*a*ther.	Example: Sw*ā*mi
i - as in f*i*t.	Example: G*i*r*i*
ī - long form of i, like the *ee* in s*ee*n	Example: *Ī*śa
u - as in f*u*ll	Example: g*u*r*u*
ū - long form of u, like the *oo* in r*oo*t	Example: m*ū*ladhara
ṛ - rolled *r* followed by a very short *i*	Example: K*ṛ*ṣṇa
ṝ - rolled *r* followed by a long *i* (rare)	Example: k*ṝ*t
ḷ - short *l* followed by a rolled *r* (rare)	Example: k*ḷ*p
e - as in *pray*	Example: V*e*da
ai - as in r*i*ce	Example: Bh*ai*
o - as in *o*blation	Example: G*o*vinda
au - as in c*ow*	Example: Dr*au*padi
ṅ or *ṃ* - a nasal *n* or *m*	Example: aha*ṅ*kara ; o*ṃ*

ḥ - a final unvoiced aspirated *h* sound. However, if it comes after a short vowel, this vowel is repeated after the *h* sound, i.e *aḥ* is pronounced like *aha*, *iḥ* like *ihi*, etc. Example: śanti*ḥ* is prononced shant*ihi*.

Consonants

k - regular *k* as in *k*aya*k*.	Example: *k*riyā
kh - like the *t_h* in tea*k_h*ouse	Example: su*kh*a
g - regular *g* as in *G*od	Example: *g*uṇa
gh - like the *g_h* in bi*g_h*ouse	Example: *gh*at
ṅ - as in ri*ng*	Example: pi*ṅ*gala
c - regular *ch* as in *ch*ant	Example: *c*akra
ch - like the *ch_h* in ran*ch_h*ouse	Example: gac*ch*ati
j - regular *j* as in *J*esus	Example: *j*īva

jh - like the *geh* in hed*geh*og Example: *jh*alā
ñ - as in ca*ñ*yon Example: Pata*ñ*jali
ṭ - pronounce the letter *t* with the tongue rolled up Example: ku*ṭ*astha
ṭh - same as above, followed by an aspirated *h*. Example: ha*ṭh*a
ḍ - pronounce the letter *d* with tongue rolled up Example: kuṇ*ḍ*alinī
ḍh - same as above, followed by an aspirated *h* (rare)
ṇ - pronounce the letter *n* with tongue rolled up. Example: prā*ṇ*a
t - regular *t* as in *t*alk Example: sa*t*
th - like the *t_h* in ligh*t_h*ouse Example: ta*th*ā
d - regular *d* as in *d*isciple Example: *d*eva
dh - like the *d_h* in re*d_h*ouse Example: samā*dh*i
n - regular *n* as in *n*ectar Example: *n*irvikalpa
p - regular *p* as in *p*rayer Example: *P*aramahamsa
ph - like the *ph* in u*ph*eaval (not *f* sound) Example: *ph*alam
b - regular *b* as in *b*lessing Example: *B*ā*b*ā
bh - like the *bh* in ru*bh*arb Example: *bh*akti
m - regular *m* as in *m*aster Example: *M*ahāraj

Semivowels

y - as in *y*ellow Example: *y*uga
r - rolled *r* Example: *r*āja
l - regular *l* as in *l*ife Example: *l*ī*l*ā
v - regular *v* as in *v*acuum, Example: *v*yāna

Sibilants

ś - *sh* sound pronounced at the back of the palate Example: *ś*rī
ṣ - as in *sh*arp Example: Upani*ṣ*ad
s - regular *s* as in *s*pirit Example: *s*ādhana

Aspirate

h - aspirated *h* as in *h*eaven Example: *H*ari*h*arananda

Compounds

kṣ - like the *ksh* in bac*ksh*ift Example: mo*kṣ*a
jñ - like the *g_y* in eg*g_y*olk Example: *jñ*āna

Kriya Yoga Contacts

For more information please contact the following centers:

U.S.A.

Kriya Yoga Institute
P.O. Box 924615
Homestead, FL 33092-4615
Tel: +1 305-247-1960
Fax: +1 305-248-1951
Email: institute@kriya.org
Web Site: http://www.kriya.org

INDIA

Prajnana Mission
Nimpur, P.O. Jagatpur
Cuttack 754021, Orissa
Tel/Fax: +91 671-682724

EUROPE

Kriya Yoga Centrum
Heezerweg 7
PP Sterksel 6029
THE NETHERLANDS
Tel: +31 40-2265576
Fax: +31 40-2265612

Kriya Yoga Zentrum
Pottendorferstrasse 69
2523 Tattendorf
AUSTRIA
Tel: +43 2253-81491
Fax: +43 2253-80462
Email: kriya.yoga.centre@aon.at

Kriya Yoga

Kriya Yoga is a direct gift from God. The modern revival of Kriya Yoga began in 1861 by Mahavatar Babaji and has been handed down to this day through the master-disciple method of teaching.

Most of us live with a conception of God as almighty, omnipotent, and omnipresent, but few are searching for God within ourselves. More so, we do not feel the living presence of God within us through our daily chores and duties. Kriya Yoga can make us feel the living presence of God through breath control and meditation. Any work, *kri* is done by *ya*, the indwelling soul.

This mission has brought ancient secret teachings within the reach of householders and families who are searching for eternal peace and happiness, and who are hungry to know God. It will provide information about initiation into the original Kriya techniques and explain how this meditation can be added to enhance one's religious and spiritual practice.

About the Author and Editor

PARAMAHAMSA HARIHARANANDA, the greatest living master in Kriya Yoga, was the head of Karar Ashram, Puri, India, founded by Swami Shriyukteshwar Giri. He is the founder of the international organization, Kriya Yoga Ashram. He began as a devoted disciple of Shriyukteshwar and learned other higher techniques of Kriya Yoga from Paramahamsa Yogananda, Swami Satyananda Giri and Shrimat Bhupendranath Sanyal.

He is widely known as a self-realized Kriya yogi in the lineage of Shri Shyama Charan Lahiri Mahasaya and Swami Shriyukteshwar Giri. He received divine instructions to come to the Western countries and teach the original Kriya Yoga.

The master saint of the scientific technique of Kriya Yoga, Swamiji occupies a very high rank among the Indian yogis of this century. He has attained the supreme yogic state of *nirvikalpa samadhi*, and has demonstrated his pulseless, breathless state many times. It is extremely rare for a saint to attain this *yogic* state.

SWAMI PRAJÑANANANDA GIRI is an accomplished orator, philosopher, scholar of scriptures, author and editor of many books, proficient in many languages, highly advanced in Kriya Yoga practice, and a truly young reflection of his master, Swami Prajñanananda is currently teaching and propagating the authentic and original Kriya Yoga in the East and West.

His brain power is remarkable, and he is deeply versed in all of the world's scriptures—Vedas, Upanishads, Patanjali Sutras, Brahmasutras, Bible, Koran, and so forth. He is Paramahamsa Hariharananda's designated spiritual successor.

On August 10 1998, his 38th birthday, he was conferred the title of *Paramahamsa*, the highest honor given to a monk. He is therefore also known as Paramahamsa Prajñanananda.

Current Books on Kriya Yoga:

Kriya Yoga: The Scientific Process of Soul Culture and Essence of All Religions, 5th revised edition, by Paramahamsa Hariharananda.

Isha Upanishad: The Ever New Metaphorical Interpretation for Soul Culture, by Paramahamsa Hariharananda.

Bhagavad Gita in the Light of Kriya Yoga—Book One (Chapters 1–6), and *Book Two* (Chapters 7-12) by Paramahamsa Hariharananda.

The Bible, The Torah and Kriya Yoga: Metaphorical Explanation of the Torah and the New Testament in the Light of Kriya Yoga, by Swami Prajñanananda Giri in consultation with Paramahamsa Hariharananda.

Words of Wisdom: Stories and Parables of Paramahamsa Hariharananda, compiled by Swami Prajñanananda Giri.

Nectar Drops: Sayings of Paramahamsa Hariharananda, compiled by Swami Prajñanananda Giri.

Babaji: The Eternal Light of God, by Swami Prajñanananda Giri.

Lahiri Mahasaya: Fountainhead of Kriya Yoga, by Paramahamsa Prajñanananda.

Swami Shriyukteshwar Giri: Incarnation of Wisdom, by Paramahamsa Prajñanananda.

Paramahamsa Hariharananda: River of Compassion, by Paramahamsa Prajñanananda.

Yoga: Pathway to the Divine, by Paramahamsa Prajñanananda.

To be Released at a Later Date:

Jñana Shankalini Tantra in the Light of Kriya Yoga (working title), by Paramahamsa Prajñanananda.

The Yoga Sutras of Patanjali in the Light of Kriya Yoga (working title), by Paramahamsa Prajñanananda.